The Liberated Woman
and Other Americans

The Liberated Woman and Other Americans

Midge Decter

Coward, McCann & Geoghegan, Inc.
New York

ACKNOWLEDGMENTS

Coward, McCann & Geoghegan, Inc., wishes to acknowledge with thanks the courtesy of the following:

The Gay Divorcee, Sex, My Daughters, and Me, Anti-Americanism in America, St. Paul and the American Condition, and *The Stevenson We Lost* appeared originally in *Harper's* magazine;

A Good Man Is Hard to Find and *Riesman in the Sixties* appeared originally in *The New York Review*;

A Visit to Dachau appeared originally in *The Atlantic Monthly*;

Novelist of South Africa, A Good Piece of Goods, Stanley Kramer's On The Beach, Marriage As a Way of Life, Women at Work, Popular Jews, Growing Old in America, Norman Mailer's Campaign, The Strangely Polite Dr. Strangelove, Kennedyism, Highbrowland, and *The Liberated Woman* appeared originally in *Commentary*;

Secrets appeared originally in *Book Week*; and

Fitzgerald at the End appeared originally in *Partisan Review*.

For Norman

Contents

Introduction

This book is a collection of incidental essays and reviews with only a few exceptions published in the course of the past ten years. It can, then, I suppose, be understood to be a book about the 1960's. Moreover, since all the pieces brought together here address themselves to some aspect of the public life—books, films, movements, ideas in currency—no doubt collectively they can be seen to provide a measure of reflection on certain of the main currents and, as I would hope, undercurrents of that troubled decade.

Yet looking over these essays and reviews now, it seems to me that what they have all really attempted to deal with is something whose relation to the 1960's—or, for that matter, to the 1950's and very likely to the 1970's as well—is only a coincidental one. For I can see that in one sense every one of them, no matter the particular subject, has been framed within the setting of the same general problem. This problem need not be given a name; it expresses itself best in the form of a question: How is it that Americans have such a difficult time thinking and talking naturally about themselves?

No people, after all, can have been more given than we to

habitual enactments of national self-consciousness. Not a day goes by, for example, when we cannot find in the press at least one assessment of a significant shift of mood taking place somewhere; or the announcement of a newly discovered condition—social, political, economic—whose existence must sooner or later touch the lives of everyone; or an appeal to us to redirect our attention, reorganize our thinking about ourselves, or reconstruct our national behavior. Nor does a week go by without bringing us in some form, through some medium, a raft of messages from honored spokesmen and thinkers telling us who and what we are, who and what we ought to be. Privately, too, there is hardly one of us who has not learned an extra vocabulary for describing his own life so as to make it accessible to one or another general theory of American society. On the other hand, despite this almost obsessive recourse to self-examination, no people can also be more given than we to the kind of sudden and ever-renewing fits of astonishment with which we greet the findings. We are in this combination of preoccupation and ignorance at a point very closely akin to hypochondria. For the victim of that perhaps most dread of all diseases is someone who devotes an overwhelming amount of his time and spirit to measuring the potential malperformance of each of the functions of his body and yet simultaneously intones his outraged wonder at any new discovery of imperfection. He thinks to be intimate with his physical nature and yet must in panic call upon the doctor to name for him every sensation, every twinge, it produces. In just this way, we seem to find it equally impossible either to take any aspect of our collective existence for granted or to examine it without deeming ourselves uniquely afflicted. And we, too, have called upon doctors, in our case doctors of social theory, who have been ready with diagnoses no less impressive to us for the fact that they are rarely borne out by the symptoms we actually experience and so bring us no ease.

But whatever the complicity of those who provide formulations for our perpetual process of distancing ourselves, abstracting ourselves, from the conditions of life we officially seek to understand, it is this process itself that lies at the source of our difficulty. Take the example of one of the major public issues thrown up within the years covered by this book, namely, America's attempt to improve the lot of her poor people. Consider the sense of awed revelation with which educated people greeted the evidence, first, that there *were* poor people; second, that poverty left them discouraged and passive ("alienated," it was called, thereby creating the first distance); third, that they conducted their lives by a different order of relative valuation from that of people who made a decent living (the "culture" of poverty, it was called, thereby adding to the distance); fourth, that some of the poor were responsible for their own condition and others were not, but even if they were victims, they tended to be frightened and defensive in the face of new possibilities ("social pathology," this was called, thereby virtually placing the problem beyond the reach of ordinary human intervention); and fifth, that withal, they continued to live their lives and seek the pleasures available, that they loved their children and coveted the worldly goods of their neighbors and had no special plans to wipe themselves off the face of the earth—in short, that they were people like all others (and here, for some among us, began a dastardly celebration of the poor for their humanity that promises to bring the issue full circle to nothing, thus leaving it to yet another generation's wondering consideration). I do not mean by this example to claim any special wisdom of my own about how to lead the poor out of poverty; I mean rather simply to illustrate the way in which each new attainment of public "knowledge" and enlightenment bespeaks only more pronouncedly our plain refusal to have seen or imagined a particular reality in the first place.

Even more stirring examples come to us in the realm of what might, if we were in any natural relation to it, be considered everyday life: marriage, divorce, raising children, working for a living, getting old, and, lately above all, sex. Americans, it seems, will endure any amount of theorizing on these matters and suffer at least very large amounts of political and social manipulation without offering resistance from, or even making reference to, the stuff of their own lives.

Husbands and wives who have grown up together and are perhaps the most intimate of friends will, when a notion circulating through the culture asks it of them, accede to participation in a discussion of their respective "roles," quite as if they were strangers analyzing the structure of some organization they both happened to join. Parents will, when asked, speak of the children whose entire lives have been led under their very noses in categories of psycho-politics whose terminology only dimly makes sense to them. The divorced will agree to recognize themselves in studies and general assertions whose terms could not possibly refer to any known human behavior. Men and women the bulk of whose waking lives have been spent at one or another kind of regularized work will submit to being advertised—if such, as it does these days, happens to be the command of the culture—as ciphers, the wiped-out, dehumanized cogs of an oppressive machine called the system.

That so many people have been ready to relinquish a lifetime's earnings in the currency of self-knowledge and knowledge of the world is one kind of problem—perhaps even an eternal one. That the culture in which they currently see themselves reflected asks, nay encourages, them to do so is another. There have been cultures, there have been periods and pockets of this one, which have done honor to the limited, compromised terms in which men live out their lives by taking the existence of such terms for granted. They have done honor to human nature by acknowledging in advance that it is composed in not so differing proportions of such qualities as affection, greed, cowardice, vanity, the capacities for murder, sympathy, and disinterestedness. To dishonor these terms and these qualities as they are so much presently dishonored among us is to imagine that one (defined here as an individual, a class, or adherent to a social idea) is exempt from them. To discuss, say, some issue of private or social life without reference to the concrete material and spiritual conditions in which it operates is to imply that one is not bound as others—other men, other societies—are bound. It seems nowadays more acceptable to characterize oneself as the victim of a monstrosity, or even as a monster oneself, than as simply human. Apart from its terrifying arrogance, this attitude leaves us as a people gasping every five years for an understanding of what has happened since the last set of formulas captured our collective mind, and, in our breath-lessness, empty and waiting for the next set to replace it.

This, then, has turned out to be my main preoccupation as a writer: to account for the distance between what is, or must be, the experience of something and the way that experience has come to be talked about, in political life no less than private. "Between the desire and the spasm," T. S. Eliot said, ". . . Falls the shadow." Between the spasm and the "poem" lurks an even more threatening possibility: that both desire and spasm will become negligible, mere material for the arbitrary manipulations of some not very gifted or not very honest observer of our common existence.

M. D.

ONE:

Being a Woman

1

Marriage as a Way of Life

The appearance of a volume like *American Marriage* by Ruth Shonle Cavan acts to remind one that there are colleges in the United States offering courses in how to have a happy marriage. The book is a textbook, complete with discussion questions and suggested readings at the end of each chapter —designed, as the author states in her preface, "primarily for young people with middle-class backgrounds, since experience has shown that these young people are very numerous in college courses and discussion groups on preparation for marriage." All the possible problems arising for someone of marriageable age are examined here: dating, premarital sexual intimacies, love, picking the right mate, engagement, wedding arrangements, marital adjustments, budgeting, birth control—and, interestingly enough, mixed marriages (both religious and racial).

It seems to be a characteristic of our civilization that only its most precious artifacts can be taken for granted, while elementary biological functions and social institutions so universal as to be almost a condition of nature must now become objects of full consciousness. The same young people of middle-class backgrounds who are so "numerous" in marriage classes will drive automobiles, live in the newest style of housing replete with the very latest in electrical comforts, and engage in revolutionary forms of work and recreation without giving it a second thought—certainly without imagining that they have any other choice. But it is only with the aid of innumerable guides, texts, discussions, and classes that these young people approach marriage and sex. And they may even devote years of study to the matter of conceiving and giving birth to a baby and to the question of how most effectively to love their children. (Nothing, I think, indicates more clearly the lengths to which self-consciousness has driven us than the recent popularity of the movement to reinstate "natural" childbirth.)

Nor need it be regarded as ironic that within ten or fifteen years probably one out of five of the marriages and families so carefully considered will break down. Marriage has in fact become something of a mystery; and like all mysteries, the power of its image is only strengthened by a measure of internal contradiction. One can very easily imagine, then, that the dean or professor who decides to include family living in a college curriculum does so not out of any simple progressive belief in his obligation to "fit the students for life," but rather in response to a popular need for some non-technical specialization in a knotty subject.

In any case, the student who takes up *American Marriage* will find that he has enrolled in a hard and elusive course— one that involves the flexing of every last bit of his will and personality and yet whose conditions he can do nothing about. "You may place yourself in the sequence ['step by step from early dating to the early stage of family build-ing']," Professor Cavan tells him, "review your past experi-ences, and look forward to the logical future steps." The end of his studies—his final examination, as it were—is to be his own happy marriage, and this in turn (he will learn from the discussion of "Enduring Love") depends on his successful adaptation to a "we-group." Moreover, while Professor Cavan assures him that his preparation for marriage consists of "all [his] experience from birth on," he will not be able to earn an A in the course except precisely by doing violence to what must have been his experience had he ever been permitted to have any. For the happy marriage he must achieve is no longer that institution founded on solid rock which creates a rational economic organization for the fam-ily; nor even that shakier institution whose function is to thrust him into adulthood and responsibility. In fact, it is no institution at all but a "relationship"—the expression of his capacity for "we-feelings": on the basis of which he is to create a family and a home; to the furthering of which he entirely gives over his choice of friends, recreation, habits, hobbies, his professional aspirations, standards of conduct, and his values; in which he must find his "deepest sexual expression" and otherwise bear witness to a constant and unfailing love. Perhaps most important of all, marriage is the mirror in which he must see the only reflection of himself as a valuable, decent, mature, and happy person. And all of this—at least according to the unrevised official rules—with one mate.

(If, in addition, our student is a male, he will quickly learn that the whole enterprise—like the games of potsy and the skipping ropes of his childhood—has been set up to disadvantage his natural talents. In parked cars, and later in the marriage bed, his virtues as a lover will be found in his ability to submit to female terms and desires; and those as a father will be measured by his capacity for participating in his wife's pregnancy, delivery, and physical care of the children. His success in the world of affairs will be credited to him insofar as it contributes to the welfare of his family, and in that event, will be credited equally to his wife. He will be working hard, as he has been taught, to support his household and then will happily and considerately cast his one vote in its democratic process of making decisions.)

The young good-marriage seekers, however, are apt not to cavil at the unreality of these teachings, just as Professor Cavan finds little occasion to take note of the phenomenal divorce rate in this country—and for the same reason. Most likely teacher and class will be engaged in a peculiar conspiracy of silence on the matter. That the kind of marriage so precisely delineated here is more and more leading to divorce—or at the least to a restlessness and discontent and dislocation staggering in their dimensions—is beside the point: which is, that it will certainly lead to *something*. This book, for all the sociological studies it cites, makes no attempt to contend with the real problems that have been afflicting marriages in the last generation; what it does succeed in doing is to project the terms by which everyone can convince himself that the abstraction "marriage" is something worth contending with, deserving of the greatest effort and highest aspiration. Professor Cavan's course is after all a form of training for citizenship; what she and her students really discuss together is a *Way of Life* (the subtitle of the book) that will bring them willingly into the neat little houses and neat little destinies society has prepared for them. By making that way of life marriage, particularly marriage at its most problematical, thousands of young Americans may be persuaded that living in the organization and in front of the television screen is not the void it seems: it wants only a little more digging into the self, a little more intensification of personal preoccupation, to take on meaning. Who would not—in exchange for having *some* sense of purpose— be willing to occupy himself with marital bliss? It seems a small price to pay.

1960

2

Secrets

Tolstoy is once supposed to have said that the real truth about women was a truth he had never dared to tell. I have often, since reading the reminiscence by Gorky in which it is recorded, pondered that remark. What was it that the old wizard of the human heart, who surely came closer to knowing everything than any man who ever lived, could not bring himself to say?

The most obviously appealing answer is that Tolstoy had instinctively divined those discoveries about female sexuality later brought to light by another, perhaps more courageous, wizard named Sigmund Freud. I like to think, however, that what made him timid about his truth was not how deep and dark and shocking it was—that in fact he understood women well enough to realize they could only be delighted, finally, to find themselves "shocking." After all, even Freud ended his days with the despairing cry that his researches had failed to answer the one enduring question: *"Was Will Das Weib?"* No, I like to think that what Tolstoy dared not venture was precisely something all too simple—perhaps even something for which men and society could not be held responsible.

In any case, it is fortunate for publishers and readers and students and the countless experts who have made the problems of women their special field of expertise that he did remain silent. How many books would have been lost to us, how many studies, how many hours of vague or not so vague titillation, if even a few people had come to believe that the subject of women in the bedroom was not really a matter of the utmost secrecy.

Take these two new books, one (*Sex and the College Girl* by Gael Greene) about college girls and one (*The Grapevine* by Jess Stearn) about lesbians: both written by serious reporters in an honest spirit of investigation, both based on extensive and sympathetic interviewing, both making a modest and sensible claim to be bringing some current information about what goes on in the sex lives of a certain category of women. Gael Greene, the author of *Sex and the College Girl*, is even more than serious, honest, modest and sensible; she is intelligent. She has an understanding, rare among American reporters, of what is a relevant detail and how that detail might relate to things in the culture outside the particular subject at hand. And Jess Stearn, if he is more traditionally newsy and solemn than she, manages, nevertheless, to avoid several of the pitfalls of writing informatively about homosexuality—most notable among them being the temptation to assembly-line psychology.

Yet both Gael Greene and Jess Stearn, and their books, operate from the same unspoken assumption made by writers who deal only in sexual sensationalism: there is something ultimately mysterious and unmanageable in the relation of women to sex.

Now what *Sex and the College Girl* really tells us, and in very convincing detail, is that educated middle-class American girls no longer worry about the necessity for being chaste or virtuous before marriage. Their worries about sex and marriage have shifted to a new ground. It is themselves as individual personalities and not themselves as objects of erotic conquest that they must nowadays make use of in the unceasing struggle to domesticate men. This shift, coming

though it has with an enormous increase in premarital sexual activity, has not at all been a liberating one. For one
thing, a girl's personality is a much more delicate and treacherous thing for her to trade on than her female honor; and for
another, pregnancy, abortion, the fear of desertion have
easily outstripped restlessness and shame as hazards of the
unmarried young woman.

Read as a companion piece to *Sex and the College Girl*,
then, *The Grapevine* seems to be describing a possible response to the modern difficulties of womanhood. Lesbianism
comes to be seen as a growingly popular new form of female
chastity. Lesbian chastity differs from the old-fashioned feminine kind in that it is not a weapon to be used in the war
between the sexes but a means of opting out of the battle
altogether. But this difference is merely one of degree. Many
of the women interviewed by Stearn were of course not even
technically chaste, having drifted gratefully into lesbianism
after abortive heterosexual affairs or marriages; several had
children. The one thing that all of them reveal, however, is
that lesbians, far from being sexual deviates, are merely retreating to a point of girlishness from which grown-up life in
the world cannot really make its full and painful demands on
them. As one of them, an active leader in a national lesbian
association, succinctly put it, ". . . I wasn't ready for the
female responsibilities of marriage. I didn't like to do housework."

In some ways, such a woman takes sex more seriously than
other women. It is not the male himself so much as the larger
and sterner consequences of heterosexuality—like being a
dependable and responsible mate—that she escapes in the
embraces of her butch or femme, as the case may be.

These are simple and, if somewhat threatening, not in the
least fearsome observations. Yet the very books from which
they emerge most vividly refuse to make them explicit. The
funny thing is that there *is* a secret about women, and the
most closely guarded part of it is just how uncomplicated it
is. Both Gael Greene and, inadvertently, Jess Stearn come
right up to it—and turn quickly away. Partly they turn away

because, despite their sobriety, in the end these books are exposés, and the exposé must pretend that it cannot quite tell all. More important, though, is the way modern notions of sexual enlightenment—and both Miss Greene and Mr. Stearn wish above all else to be enlightened—demand that one be as complicated as possible about everything.

The plain truth of the matter is that for women the *act* of sex has very little significance—it neither traumatizes nor liberates nor fulfills. It is, to be sure, as *necessary* for them as for men. Nor does its being necessary have anything to do with the individual woman's capacity for sexual response; a frigid woman would be as much disposed to suffer over an impotent husband as any other. Nevertheless, spiritually as well as physiologically, making love is something women always lend themselves to: it requires no effort on their part beyond a split second of acceding and is therefore something they can undertake with any amount of indifference and, unlike men, even quite successfully pretend about. The lesbians in Stearn's book, for instance, prefer women to men but have not the slightest difficulty going to bed with men if and when it suits them. And why should they? (This is what makes female homosexuality an essentially different phenomenon from male homosexuality.) In some sense, then, lesbianism is not "real."

Nor, however, is the new fashion of equality in heterosexuality. Time and again the girls interviewed by Gael Greene stand at the point of revealing that the only things they are really preoccupied with are what comes before and what can possibly follow from a sexual engagement. In-between is as easy as falling off a log. It is staggering to think how much male bewilderment and how much unhappy female chicanery might be avoided if they were ever simply permitted to come out and say so.

1964

3

Women at Work

If you find yourselves troubled with too strong a competition from female workers, just prove yourselves worthy to be their husbands, marry them, provide good homes, and thus remove them from competition with you.—HORACE GREELEY to the New York Typographical Union No. 6.

According to the United States Department of Labor, by 1970 there will be 30,000,000 women in the American labor force. This number (predicated, of course, on a "normally" expanding economy) would represent an increase over the present of 25 percent, that is, 6,000,000, as against a predicted increase of only 15 percent for men in the same period. Now, such figures stated flatly tend to conjure up an image as misleading as it is frightening to the popular imagination, an image of men and women coming to be less and less differentiated, elbowing one another for room in some kind of sexual and occupational jungle. Whereas the fact is that as yet women do not—nor does it seem likely that in the foreseeable future they will—have the same relation to salaried employment as do men: they do not upon leaving school enter the labor force and remain there permanently to support themselves and others, or as a general rule define themselves by what they do, or try to be as successful as possible. As it has become more common (to the point, now, of near universality), and as it has begun to assume a rather uniform, predictable pattern, female employment outside the home has become all the more casual and voluntary—and, what seems at first glance paradoxical, more than ever before dependent on the role of women as homemakers and mothers.

What the current statistics on the whole question of womanpower (a somewhat ambiguous though useful term for which we are indebted to studies by the National Manpower Council*) reveal about the crisis in the inner life of the American woman is not so certain as some psychiatrists and social workers would have us believe; for to judge by the literature in popular magazines and professional journals, American society is about to be confronted by nothing less than the eventual castration of its entire male population. The statistics do, however, tell us a good deal about critical changes in many of the American woman's practical plans and expectations. More than one-third of all women over fourteen years of age can be found at work either full or part time in any month; during a whole year the number is as high as two-fifths. A young girl in school will probably have had some kind of part-time working experience—summers or Saturdays or afternoons—by the time she has completed her studies, whether this means at the end of college or only high school. (And since research findings do not even include the ever-widening occupation of baby-sitting, the figures above are undoubtedly far too modest.) Once out of school, the same young girl will as a matter of course have a job until she marries. There is no longer any social prestige to be gained for the family making its way into the middle class, and certainly none for the family already entrenched there, by keeping its unmarried daughters at home: a society whose paragons are not the idle but the active rich liberates its aspiring members from this costly and uncongenial necessity. Nor by the present system of household economy is the adolescent girl of much use to her mother; there are not apt to be any real tasks, such as the care of several younger chil-

* *Womanpower*, by Ell Ginsberg *et al.*, 1957; *Work in the Lives of Married Women*, Proceedings of a Conference on Womanpower, 1958; and *Women and Work in America*, by Robert W. Smuts (Columbia University Press, 1959).

dren, for her. So she will work, in a factory or an office or, if she is one of a small minority, in some profession, at least until she is married and often after that. It is becoming more and more likely that she will work until her first child is born.

All this will not take much time, though—probably only a little more than two years—for if she is anywhere near that compelling abstraction, "the average," she will be married by the age of twenty or twenty-one and will have had her last child by the age of twenty-six or so. The economists tell us that in the most prosperous period of the American woman's early married life, when she and her husband are jointly bringing in the family income, her patterns of consumption get set. She is well dressed and well entertained. All or part of her income may be used for the purpose of furnishing the house or buying such luxuries as television sets; some of it may be saved for the purchase of heavy household appliances at such time as she assumes the full role of housekeeper. Her husband's income will not reach its highest level until he is forty-five. Therefore just at the point when the family's minimum financial requirements suffer a sharp rise, that is, when there are little children to be housed, fed, dressed, and given medical care, a fair part of the family's income is cut off.

Somewhere in her early or middle thirties our average woman sends her youngest child to school. This is generally the point when she will go back to work or busy herself with voluntary civic activities or both. One-third—more than 7,500,000—of the working women in America are mothers with children under eighteen (though it is important to keep in mind that this figure includes all women working, whether full or part time) .

The picture just presented is naturally oversimplified. Among the working mothers of minor children is a notable number of widows, divorcees, and women separated from their husbands. These women are obliged to support themselves and in many cases, at least in part, their children. In

1946 one-fifth of all women workers in nonfarm families were found to be either the sole support of their families or the major wage earners.

But the trend in womanpower that seems most startling and is therefore in some way necessarily the most significant, regardless of its momentary ratio to an overall statistic, is the one now bringing a number of married women with young children, though under no absolute economic pressure, to leave their homes and find jobs. The widow who suddenly finds herself with no means of support and sets about to insure her survival and that of her children, often with nothing but the crudest and poorest paid skills, has always existed and has continued to elicit the feeling of compassion and even admiration. The working spinster, too—and if she passes the age of thirty-five in America she will belong to only 7 percent of the entire female population—is an age-old figure. The divorcee, subject to a certain lingering, vestigial disapproval, has again always been expected to work. Also, the existence of the driving career woman is a thing now generally taken for granted—far more generally, in fact, thanks to the ceaseless public discussion of women's rights and to such glamorizing image makers as the movies, than her numbers would warrant.

Even if no more than their present number are ever caught in the trend, however, the fact that a certain percentage of young married mothers in America have come to seek employment, as part of a matter-of-course development of their lives, speaks of something irrevocably taking place in our society. However much this process may or may not be truly cause for alarm, it is being viewed with at least some measure of alarm by spokesmen for the public interest (except by economists like the members of the National Manpower Council, whose concern with the question is one of finding ways to tap all of America's available manpower resources). But the working wife is not, it seems safe to say, unless through some unimaginable social reversal, going to disappear; one might as profitably continue to be alarmed about the automobile.

I

What is it that women *do* when they go to work? The answer to this question, if laid out in lists of occupational categories, would be: everything. Women, though not as physically strong as men, seem to be strong enough to manage most jobs in our technologically improved industry. The things that men alone, or that women alone, are considered fit to do, as anthropologists have long taught us in connection with primitive societies, is a matter determined quite simply by prejudice. World War II, in addition suddenly to setting millions of badly needed female hands to new tasks, created an enormous shift in American sexual-occupational prejudices. The huge accession of women into heavy industry during the manpower crisis of that period found and left them competent operators of assembly-line machinery and most of the tools and equipment pertaining thereto. After the war, many women left the factories, but the adjustment in personnel practices had been permanently effected. There were new jobs and new kinds of jobs for the returning veterans to take, or if they insisted on having back their old jobs, for the women they displaced.

Shifts in prejudice can work both ways. For instance, women can now be waitresses in all but the most elegant restaurants, while men, with the rapid decline in the number of domestic servants, can under the right selected conditions be housecleaners. Retail selling of everything but men's haberdashery and automobiles has within the last four or five decades come to be taken over almost completely by women, as have such things as employment agencies, bank cashiering, bookkeeping. Being involved in the canning and packaging of food, on the other hand, is now acceptable employment for men. Certain once exclusively feminine precincts of the textile mills have, as a result of the introduction of much heavier machinery, been invaded by men. And the examples multiply. One interesting handicap men seem to suffer in the competition between the sexes for jobs is that women are willing to regard anything open to them as proper, while men will often avoid work once classified as women's, no matter how good the pay. The case comes to mind of certain sewing operations in the men's shirtmaking industry, the machinery for which would be better operated by men but will not be touched by them.

But although there are some women doing nearly every kind of work in existence, and although the going prejudice has turned in their favor in certain formerly hostile industries, it is not yet correct to imagine that they roam freely over male territory. "Rosie the Riveter" may no longer be the heroine she was in the comic song in 1941; she is still no more likely than before to be advanced to foreman. Just as the girl behind the bank teller's cage will not be moved to the loan department, or the girl joining the ranks of a large corporation be eligible for executive training. There are sound reasons for this, and therefore the situation will not easily change: employers hesitate to invest the time, and the money, required for training women to assume responsibilities which they will chuck for marriage, or to have a baby, or to answer the urgency of some other family need.

The work women can do may be redefined here and there, then, but in the main it will continue to be what it has always been. More jobs for women still largely mean either the expansion of their peculiar areas of operation or the elevation to professional status of work that has been theirs all along. We have the simple evidence of our senses for this. Nurses, schoolteachers, librarians, laundry workers, sewing-machine operators, social caseworkers will doubtless always be women; such jobs are merely translations either of basic household functions no longer performed in the home or of the American woman's idealized historic role as the tamer of rough men. (Men do of course teach school but usually in high schools; male librarians are almost always to be found in the upstairs offices.)

Probably the single largest source of new employment for women is the filing cabinet. Offices in our vastly bureaucratized society pile on top of one another and spread from one end of the land to the other; and offices are places filled with "girls," often four or five to a man, typing, filing, keeping books—setting up records in a system unprecedentedly intent on recording itself. Strictly speaking, office work can be counted as something taken over from men. However, the sheer volume of inter- and intra-office communication by which today's corporations and institutions operate makes clerical work an industry totally different in kind from that of the days of the clerk and scrivener. Historians of the subject claim that the advent of the typewriter was responsible for the creation of the female secretary, one of the common notions about women as employees being that they have a much higher degree of manual dexterity than men and a good deal more patience with monotonous detail work. The typewriter may perhaps be a more naturally feminine tool, but certainly a no less reasonable explanation for the presence of women in offices is that the file has become a sort of combination closet and dustbin, and filling it a form of national housekeeping.

In factories the situation seems to be more complicated. There the work of men and women may be parts of the same process. But one has only to watch the HELP WANTED sections of the newspapers to see that, at least within a given geographic region, men and women will not be performing the same task together or even any particular task interchangeably.

II

It naturally makes an enormous difference to the fortunes of a female job aspirant whether she is white or Negro, how much education she has, or how old she is—in this she obviously differs very little from a man. However, the very rhythm of her life as a woman will itself play a peculiar part in determining her age and the state of her education when she goes out to seek work. The relative weights of the three factors mentioned have changed very rapidly in the past few decades, so rapidly they are by now rather difficult to sort out in any fixed order of importance. As we are forever being told, age in this time of penicillin and lighter work loads no longer means what it once meant, for good *and* ill. The question of color and employment, certain to be with us and significant for decades and decades to come, is happily at best getting to be a tangled one, admitting to many more variables. Education therefore remains the most manageable factor in calling the turns of women's employment (even granting the dour prediction that soon virtually every adolescent in America will be going to college).

The education of young girls has certain essential characteristics. More girls than before attend and are graduated from high school and they are also better students there. Girls generally conform more closely to the school's demands on them, and they get, on the whole, better grades. There are powerful cultural influences which make it possible for them with honor to be nicer, quieter, better behaved in school than boys and inevitably to achieve a superior grade average. Nevertheless, while girls are disproportionately represented in the top 50 percent of any graduating class, boys predominate in the top 5 percent. Again, when it comes to the so-called hard subjects—mathematics and the physical sciences —girls generally display a lesser gift or a weaker mastery or perhaps both. Following from this, their showing in college entrance examinations and scholarship competitions is significantly poorer than that of the boys they have been besting academically for years. Without entering any theoretical dispute about whether male intellectual superiority is divinely ordained or merely culturally determined, it is easy to see that the girls' expectations play a crucial part here. For one thing, many fewer girls are enrolled in academic or college preparatory courses (probably their number will increase considerably in the next few years); the majority still take commercial courses, planning to work and largely unambitious about it, until they marry.

Nor is there any reason to suppose that of the girls who do go off to college more than a handful are powerfully motivated by the idea of a professional future or, in any case, a career outside the traditional feminine professions. Attention to studies like physics and mathematics presupposes, in addition to what might be called a talent for them, ambitions in the direction of medicine, engineering, or science. Going to college for girls, far more than for boys, is still an assertion of economic privilege; it is, after all, a more interesting and more carefree way of whiling away the time before marriage than being shut away in the filing rooms and typing pools of large corporations. And the young men one meets there are in the long run more eligible. A college degree does entitle a girl to a better job: she can, if she wishes or needs, be a schoolteacher or social worker or nurse (though it comes as something of a shock to be reminded how recent, and for many regions of the United States how vaguely enforced, is the requirement of a college education for the pursuit of these professions). The most telling importance of a degree for girls, even today, however, is that it attaches its possessors to a higher and wider standard of living.

If one considers that the lengthening of years of education in this country has been accompanied not by a commensurate delay in, but rather by a hastening of, marriage, the bald statistics of female education take on a rather different meaning than might have been attributed to them. Spiritually they mean that girls take their intellectual achievements and broadened perspectives back into the home, there to ferment some new kind of family existence. While practically, by a somewhat ironic twist, the statistics mean that a majority of the women who will be entering the labor force will be doing so with very little specialized training, few skills, and a considerable lapse of time since even these skills have been used.

Educators are beginning to show a good deal of concern about such problems. The National Manpower Council, for instance, at its conference on womanpower in October, 1957, devoted a session to the question of secondary education. The entire discussion concerned itself with suggestions about how better to prepare American girls for the work they will almost inevitably be doing someday. A new form of vocational guidance in high school was suggested, as was the setting up of special courses to keep nonworking young married women in training. On the level of suggestions like these, it is hard to believe that any plan or series of plans can aid in overcoming the situation. Perhaps some or even a large number of girls can be effectively encouraged to allow ahead for the new pattern of their lives, which may or may not involve simply more education for them—for some kinds of training, *e.g.*, stenography and nursing, can be laid away for a time and with a little brushing up be put to use again, and some cannot. Certainly for a woman in her thirties with growing children to *begin* training for something would involve a psychological wrench, really a form of humiliation, that only the most pressing will to make something of herself could justify. The real difficulty in organizing their training for work seems to be that, in the very teeth of their emancipation and hard-won freedom, girls go on dreaming of being married and loved and happy, in fact, more than girls have ever done before.

A woman must still live where her husband's job takes her and live largely in the style that his work imposes. These things have nothing to do with the "inequality" of women or with prejudices against them, and they have almost everything to do with the kind of opportunities a woman will find for work. If, for instance, she lives in a mining town in Pennsylvania or a steel town in Indiana, chances are she will not be able to find a job. If her family is settled in a suburb some distance from the city, her choice will be limited to what is available without sacrificing too much precious household time to travel.

It does not promise to be the case, either, that wherever and whenever possible the women who have careers will pursue them straight through, stopping to have children for only as long as is medically required. Though the number of working women with children under eighteen is growing, the number with children under six is getting proportionately smaller. A mother's care for her infants, precisely to the extent that it is being threatened by other possibilities, has been elevated from an unconscious process to an overwhelming national piety. There are of course some women, those with a profound commitment to the nature of the work they do and the success it brings them, who make arrangements for their childbearing years that permit them to continue working; but they are too few and too special to be considered here. It is enough to note that among the rest of the group who make up the figure for working mothers of preschool infants—and because of higher rates of poverty, desertion, or nonsupport by husbands, its majority is black—any improvement in economic condition brings with it a decline in their number.

For employers of women, their pattern of work poses two related problems. First, as the number of women in their employ increases so does the average age. As of 1960, according to the Federation of Business and Professional Women's Clubs, the average age of the working woman was forty. Although because of Social Security benefits the number of working women over sixty-five (these, again, are largely blacks) has sharply declined from, say, 1890, the percentage of those between the ages of forty-five and sixty-five has risen during the same period from a little over 10 percent to nearly 40 percent. Second, the proportion of women who do not absolutely need to earn their living but are merely trying to supplement the family income is also on the increase.

Most employers would seem to have mixed feelings about these problems. Mature women in many ways make better employees. They tend to be more responsible, less skittish, and less disproportionately ambitious. On the other hand, they are also a good deal harder to handle. Unaccustomed as most of them have been for so many years of their lives, or perhaps for all, to conditions in the world of work, they are both touchy and rigid about necessary changes of pace or all the countless minor emergencies that can occur on the job. And while women who are neither totally dependent on their jobs nor vitally concerned about advancing themselves make a useful manpower cushion—a labor supply that can be taken on and let off rather casually—they are by the same token given to a troublesome amount of absenteeism and various other forms of unreliability.

Perhaps the radically shortened work week promised for America's future will shift the entire question of women's employment into another realm. But for the present the situation seems to hinge on the following proposition: more women marry, and marry younger, in the United States than in any other Western country; and since a married woman's first obligation is to her family, she is unable and unwilling to make a man's commitment to work. If she must stay off the job when her children are born or leave it altogether when, for instance, her husband is transferred to another place, the terms of her employment are bound to be not so much "unequal" to a man's as different in kind. Assuming that some of the economists are right, and America can indefinitely expand its exploitation of manpower resources, the American economy must make its adjustment to a new quality, as well as a new source, of labor.

III

When the individual mother in her middle thirties waves her youngest child off down the road on the school bus and decides that it is time to look for a job, she will offer various explanations for her decision. She will say that there are accumulated debts to be paid or that she wants to find better housing in a better neighborhood; or she will cite all the extras—orthodontia, music lessons, summer camping—that she means her children to have and that her husband's present income cannot provide; or she will simply announce that time now lies heavy on her hands, which is to say, she wants to get out of the house. If she is like most people, one crucial explanation for her behavior will probably not even occur to her: namely, that she is part of a national trend, that she is going to work because her culture now enables her to take for granted the possibility of doing so.

In any case, when and if she finds an acceptable job, she will be putting herself and her family under a great deal of new physical and moral pressure. She may work only part time, during the morning or a couple of days a week, in which case her life and the life of those around her must become a carefully timed affair, with household chores, marketing, laundry, meals, etc., on a close and fixed schedule. A good part of her daily existence will be governed by the clock, and run-of-the-mill difficulties, like sniffles or bad temper or an automobile that needs repairing, will become major problems requiring immediate solutions. If she gets a full-time job, she will have to find someone to help her with all or part of her housekeeping, which is expensive and means the family's adjustment to a new personality in its midst. She will be apt to demand more help from her husband and more responsible cooperation from her children. She will come home tired and in moods imposed by events outside her home to which her family will be asked to be sensitive.

The money she can make under such circumstances may or may not seem worth the trouble. As we have seen, she will not, except in a rare case, find particularly lucrative work. And in addition to the strain and inconvenience, her expenses will increase enormously. Quick shopping for easy-to-prepare or packaged or frozen foods can add as much as 10–15 percent to her food bills. She will need a larger and a better wardrobe. Lunches and transportation for her will now have to be included in the family budget. If she has a maid or baby-sitter to look after the children, even only part of the time, a sizable portion of her salary will be committed before she has taken it out of its envelope. And the family income taxes will go up, while most of her working expenses are not deductible.

Chances are, then, it is precisely those outlays required for her to be able to work that are the very extras and luxuries she is seeking with her new income: new clothes, meals in restaurants, certain labor-saving devices, help with the housekeeping, the possibility of giving her children over for at least part of the day to someone else's care. She will be paying her way, as it were, for a bit of freedom from a purely domestic existence.

The question of why it is that the American woman can find it preferable to do any amount of routine drudgery on some assembly line or behind some sales counter rather than involve herself in all the physical details of caring for her husband and children has become a matter of grave concern to observers of American society—and even to herself. For her new pattern of living is undoubtedly plunging this country into a domestic crisis of major proportions, from which it will emerge with a good number of traditional family arrangements no longer intact. One of the reasons offered for her feeling so impelled to get out of the house is that the terms of her culture no longer place sufficient value on what she does there; this is surely true, in part. The girl in school is being educated to believe herself a "person," someone with full responsibility for the affairs of her country, her world, the quality of her life, and someone fully obliged to prepare herself to meet it.

But though in some ways her functions as wife and mother are no longer given their proper weight, in others they are given too much. If her husband grumbles that she should be content to look after him, his home, and his children, and if on his behalf the social experts are inclined to regret the vanishing woman of yesteryear, they might both be reminded that our young mother is also forced to live up to entirely new demands. The number of hours she must devote to her children's welfare may be shortened, thanks to automatic washing machines, store clothes, canned foods, but she is to an extent undreamed-of by her own mother held accountable for every aspect of their psychological and emotional development. She has been made aware that, whether she stays at home with them or not, her children's habits, pleasures, and feelings are given over directly into her keeping. Similarly with her husband: she has been taught to believe in both his right to personal happiness and the dependence of such happiness on her own success or failure to provide it. Insofar as she is a "good" wife, whether she spends hours preparing her husband's meals or throws them together from the food freezer, she is his companion. She must be at least conversant with what interests him; she must be attractive to him; she must be his partner in sex. American families, falling apart though they be, are not nearly such natural and casual arrangements for women as they once were. And the houses in which they dwell have become peculiarly crowded, intimate places.

In addition, the young woman today is a creature plagued with choices—and it is choice, not the lack of it, that breeds restlessness. Much has already been said on the subject of choice and love in contemporary marriage. We know that such decisions on the part of young girls or boys as whom do I love, whom should I marry, are never altogether genuine, that is, never independent of the influence on their attitudes of the world all around them; nevertheless, the very illusion of having chosen freely lends its quality to their lives. In this connection, not nearly enough has been understood about the meaning of birth control for the new condition of women. That they now choose to be mothers, and when to do so, for all its very great physical benefit has created a disruption in the natural order of their lives that perhaps cannot yet be measured. When babies were inevitable—unasked for, un-looked for, and totally expected—so too was the way of life that followed from them. In their study of the use of contra-ception in the working class,* Lee Rainwater and Karol Kane Weinstein point out that most lower-class women cannot be interested in birth control because they regard sex as their husbands' business and therefore the making of babies as not their responsibility. Though these women dread the arrival of more children, and know very well that they will be the ones to suffer most concretely from it, they carefully keep themselves off the one hook that catches their middle-class sisters: life is decided for them. They do not have to be good mothers, good wives; they do not *have to be* anything. And they rarely go to work—though food and shelter often have to be provided by welfare agencies.

The middle-class woman, however, particularly if she has had any education (and by now all have), will feel she is choosing a job, a mate, a style of life, to have children, how many to have, whether or not to nurse them, how to bring them up. As soon as she reaches the first relaxation in pres-sure she often discovers she doesn't know what to do with herself, so she looks for some definite employment.

---

* *And the Poor Get Children*, by Lee Rainwater assisted by Karol Kane Weinstein. Quadrangle Books, Inc.

While the job she finds will be definite, thus telling her how her life must be organized, it will not be defining. Her husband is a steam fitter, a lathe turner, a lawyer, or an engineer; she, unless she is an exception of some kind, will be still a woman, a wife and a mother who happens to be doing *x*, *y*, or *z*.

Many working women complain of this, complain they are not taken seriously, are discriminated against. And a few of them have a right to such a complaint, for of course there is still a good deal of prejudice against women in the men's world. A woman who does the same work as a man for less pay—and there are some, though many fewer than there once were—is a victim of it. A professional woman with the same training and qualifications as a man, say an engineer or chemist, who must take an inferior job is being, to say the least, unfairly treated. But there is a good deal more involved in commitment to work than seriousness or talent or even educational qualification. It is easy to forget that the dedicated career woman is doing something much more than sloughing off the special responsibilities and burdens of her womanliness: she is also staking her pride, her vanity, her very ego on the great fortune wheel of success in America, just as a man does. She is, in short, risking failure. If women suffer the disadvantage of being deprived of opportunities to hold the best jobs on the highest echelons, this very circumstance grows out of their one irrevocable privilege: they always have a place of retreat when failure threatens—this is not what they really are, what they really do. The men who on their side complain that if women are to become a permanent part of the labor force they will soon become full competitors might remind themselves that regardless of what women think they think, their ultimate feminine advantage is one not easily given up in the dark jungle of work.

1961

4

The Gay Divorcee

A woman whose marriage breaks up nowadays has to give an account of herself. For precisely to the extent that divorce has become an everyday occurrence in America, it is no longer to be easily understood. Divorces used to be very concrete affairs, for there was no mistaking the meaning of those situations in which a husband beat his wife, abandoned her, fell in love with another woman, or was impotent, or in which a wife stayed out all night, drank too much, refused her husband her favors, or was sterile. There was no mistaking them, and the law itself provided for them. But with one out of every four marriages in this country scheduled for the courts, it is no longer possible to think of divorce as a dramatic last recourse for people suffering in such situations. It cannot be that so many millions of marriages have been "bad" in the ways that law and tradition have always understood—or perhaps in any way at all.

How, then, does a divorcee—and let us say that she is in her late twenties, fairly well educated, of moderate to decent means, with a couple of small children, formerly married to a male counterpart of herself—explain what drove her and her husband to such a drastic step? She will clearly not claim to have been mistreated or neglected. Nor will she admit to any significantly bad behavior on her own part. Chances are she and her husband have been unfaithful to each other but in a way that at the time did not seem relevant to their feelings for each other. She will not even say that she no longer cares about him.

A prominent New York lawyer once told me, "Once upon a time most of my divorce clients were sheepish middle-aged men who, against what they knew to be all reason, were leaving their devoted middle-aged wives and families for the young girls they had fallen in love with. Now I see only young women who tell me, 'He is a nice boy and a good husband. I like him. We have had a nice time in bed, and we have rarely ever quarreled. *I want out, that's all.*'"

Having no further explanation than this, our divorcee will be felt by everyone around her to be selfish and irresponsible, at the least seriously neurotic. And during that first gorgeous burst of guilt, toward children, parents—of course husband—she is apt to feel so, too. The guilt will persist for a long time, if not forever—possibly it will send her to the office of a psychological counselor—but she will nevertheless maintain a dumb certainty that the reasons for her decision are right and real.

But what, if she cannot even speak of them, can these reasons be? The commonest twentieth-century answer for anything that renders people imprecise or inarticulate is sex. Louis Nizer, a vastly experienced attorney, recently asserted that he had never handled a divorce whose real cause, when dug deeply enough for, was not sexual incompatibility. Sex *is* the most obvious answer—indeed it begins to seem that there can be no public discussion of divorce if we have not the "courage" to get straight to the problem of the orgasm— but nevertheless an unreal one. In any case, our about-to-be-divorced woman would not honestly offer it; she might even suggest that in her collapsing marriage sex was the last, not the first, thing to go.

For her divorce germinated in a particular moment, and

one that can only be described circularly. Her divorce began
in that moment when she first conceived divorce to be a
possibility for her. She can arrive at divorce because however
shocking the figure one in four may be, it is a respectable
one. Divorce is now openly offered as a solution to the
malaise of life by her time and her culture.

The divorcee's experience in marriage will not have been
much different from that of her friends who remain married.
She had in fact a good marriage by any reasonable, and by
some fairly unreasonable, standards. She and her husband
were a good wife and husband by altogether unreasonable
ones. When she married, she was very young and very high-
minded and more than a little pretentious. Her pretensions,
moreover—if one must have them—were of the best kind,
having mostly to do with being superior to all sorts of petti-
ness. If after her divorce she was open to the charges of
selfishness and irresponsibility, in the years before she would
have found very little in this regard to reproach herself for.
She and her husband had had a few ugly moments, over her
first pregnancy, over a flirtation, over anxiety about money,
but these are standard ugly moments and were recovered
from quickly and high-mindedly.

The major principle governing their conduct toward each
other—and there were many—was fairness. At the time of
their wedding her husband had been a student, say, or a very
junior member of his profession. She was pleased to work for
a while to help support the family. And her vanity was
tickled, though she was sometimes inclined to feel a little
overtender toward herself, by the thought of all she was
cheerfully doing without. Because she was working, then
unaidedly taking care of her babies, her husband on his side
became competent at several forms of housework, notably
cooking and dishwashing. (Domestically competent husbands have become a kind of obscene joke in the literature of
suburban life; but it was "not like that" with them. *They*
were only two busy people sharing unpleasant duties. As a
matter of fact, they firmly disapproved of suburban mar-

riage.) They were good friends, committed to supporting each other's demands, committed to understanding each other's point of view.

They were often intense lovers. They had become lovers, in the usual way of these things, a few months before marriage and were somewhat anxiously, though on the whole fruitfully, concerned about the quality of their lovemaking. Their sex life was "important," they knew; each of them took on the obligation to be ever more "satisfactory" to the other. If there was anything a little less than proper in their relation to life, it was a certain tendency they had to find their own relationship so deeply promising by comparison with other people's. (More than once they were known to be in a state of deep compassion for the difficulties of that wife or the other husband.)

And this is the marriage that broke down in its prime, after ten years: far from the adolescent's Hollywood dream of romance ever after, and farther even from the battle of neurotic projections and misplaced aggressions—to which social critics and mental healthers so confidently attribute broken marriages. Theirs was a relation rooted in the values of responsibility and maturity, acceptance and consideration. The divorcee, looking back, might find some of this description delusory; but if so, she also knows that her delusions felt real enough to her at the time.

In the weeks or months before the fatal series of "long talks" from which they both knew there was no returning, she might suddenly have found herself powerfully irritated by things in him she had never objected to before. But such irritation was a signal rather than a substance and provided her with the feeling of disgruntlement necessary for getting through the act of separation.

What had really happened was something she herself could only describe allegorically. She had "looked into the mirror one morning" and for the first time feeling truly young—in the sense that she saw years and years of life stretching before her—asked herself in horror, "Is this *all* there is going to be *forever*?" Now, this question is nothing new; it is probably asked with the same horror at least once

in every lifetime. In her case, however, it was inevitably to
have dire consequences for her marriage. People like our
young divorcee are taught to believe that marriage must be
the means for fulfilling all their personal needs. It is as wives
and husbands that they will be loved and lovable, admired
and admirable, excited and exciting. And since marriage is
that which stamps the quality of their being, rather than
simply assuring the physical arrangements for it, any dissatisfaction with self goes right to the heart of married life.

Divorce for such people is not an act of immaturity; they
ask nothing more from marriage than they have been willing
to put into it. They have been willing to put too much (but
only as much, be it noted, as the wise counselors of stability
have said was needed to water the gardens of the good life).
They have to extricate themselves completely in order to
effect any change at all.

So much did her divorce have to do with restlessness about
herself, and so little with all those carefully nourished resent-
ments against her husband, that he quickly seemed to fade
from the proceedings.

Be that as it may, in the lawyer's office neither she nor her
husband was important, but rather a whole host of things
about the relations between a married couple that they had
always kept carefully concealed. These are the things law-
yers and courts deem important: money, for one; real property; legal obligation; the respective functions of male and
female parents; ". . . in the event of death." She had gone to
see a lawyer because to do so marked the seriousness of her
intentions, and also because she knew, though she could not
really imagine, that she would one day have to appear in
court. But she could not have said why this should be so; she
regarded divorce law as a fiction of the official imagination.
She and her husband, of all people, needed no outsiders to
effect some arrangement between them.

Her lawyer was patient with her. He had seen her kind
before: it would be a matter of explaining that civilized and
honorable as she felt, the possibility of unpleasant contingencies and demeaning impulses must be provided for; that
his way of providing was best because it was impersonal.

What would she do, for instance, if her husband took it into his head to be spiteful, or if she found herself unexpectedly greedy about money, or if—after all, there were cases known —they began to fight over the children? The lawyer entered into their discussions with the kind of relish that people reserve for deflating foolishness. In his system of instruction money came first because it was the hardest—money being such an obvious thing for people to pretend they care nothing about. The property was not enough to bother the law with—some furniture, books, records, a car. Naturally there would be no alimony; alimony is the blood money that goes to women whose husbands are desperate to divorce them. But she was asked to consider how much money was needed to maintain the children each week. And slowly she began to reduce her life, past and future, into figures and claims and demands that could be put down on paper. Whose life ought to be insured? How often would her husband see the children? How would they settle questions about religion, education? By the time they had arrived at such contingencies as her death she had found her legs in the lawyer's world, where real and hard things might happen, even to her.

Finally she signed a document called a separation agreement. Only in deciding the terms of her divorce had she discovered what society means by marriage. At college she would not have taken a marriage course, nor would she have read marriage manuals; but even if she had, she would never have learned that getting married involves people in legal rights and obligations. The law, then, was not an arbitrary imposition on her private affairs. It was the last bastion wherein society holds out against the vagaries and self-deceptions of personal feeling. For her the discovery was enormous: not only because it forced her to talk about herself in a real way, but because it taught her for the first time that her womanly nastiness and her husband's manly nastiness were so clear to the world as to have been institutionally provided for. So, far from feeling cheapened by the law, she was exhilarated: life already had a new adventure in it.

They could not be divorced in the state where they lived because of the stringent grounds that state imposed. They found another state which offered her a not quite fraudulent residence and in which the courts were not so precise. Several months after he had moved out of their house, she stood before a judge and testified under oath that her husband had abused her in several ugly but vaguely described ways.

Even for those most unhappy about it, divorce sets off a wholesale round of self-indulgence. A woman is apt to buy a new wardrobe, for instance, and a man a new car; or perhaps it will be the other way around. The main thing is, they must signalize—and primarily in things that involve the expenditure of money—their new condition of not being implicated in each other's needs. It may even be essential to spend more money than one can afford. Certainly two together can live more cheaply than two apart, even allowing for the fact that there are now double earnings (naturally, the divorcee has gone back to work). For divorce does away with dependent priorities. It no longer affects the woman's plans that the man needs a new suit, or his, that she is longing for a silver coffeepot. Their needs and longings they have to themselves now.

Spending money is essential, but there are other indulgences as well. The divorcee finds that she likes to lie in the tub for hours every night without having to excuse herself; or to eat a peanut butter sandwich for dinner without having to explain herself; or to frown, sigh, giggle, without having to tell her thoughts. She feels released as she has never felt before in her life.

I make her sound too lighthearted, perhaps. Does she, then, pay *no* price at all for turning over what is after all still a sacred institution, for disrupting her family, for creating God knows what unhappiness for her children? The answer to this question cannot be a simple yes or no. If she is released, it is surely not from care. She has a lonely responsibility for her children six days a week; their problems and her involvement in them are now intensified a hundredfold by her sense of the children's deprivation. Very likely she has embarked on the career she had once been so pointedly careless about. And through all this she has lost the support of that ready sympathy having a husband had always provided her. She worries a great deal not only about her children but about her health (so much depends on her!), her job, the state of her household, the condition of her soul.

Still, it is her worry, she is answerable to no adult. She is paying her way and making her way; her behavior brings its own consequences and she asks no one to share them with her. She has a great sense of accomplishment because she now knows what she can do, however inadequately, however self-pityingly, alone. This knowledge is important just because her marriage had been primarily the condition of being bound to and bound up in another personality. All of this is to say that she feels strong. And strength breeds its own gaiety.

Her family and friends tend to be wary of the divorcee's insouciance, however grateful that she does not make a nuisance of herself. They could so much easier forgive her the trouble she is in if only she would appear more troubled by it—if only she would not so often parry their lugubrious expressions of sympathy with assurances that she is fine, thank you. But along with her new dresses she shamelessly persists in affording herself others of the world's goodies. She will not say her marriage was tragic, she will not say her divorce is tragic, she will not even say her children are tragic, she does not want forgiveness. She might even feel herself entitled to a bit of admiration.

If her high spirits continue, she finds that she is being treated less as a problem than as a threat. A threat to something as high-sounding as "the fabric of our society" or to something as simple and direct—if she cares to be explicit— as the marriages all around her. She can see in the eyes of even her closest female friend a momentary flicker of anxiety as she addresses herself to the friend's husband: not that she is fatally attractive, but, after all, her moment of possibility can breed others just as others once bred hers. And smiling and managing, she makes the whole thing look too easy.

But she does not want a husband—not yet—not even someone else's. She is against not only marriage but any form of entanglement. She wants, she says, to move into that new special underground of toughness and truth (for how let her pleasure in the lawyer's office slip away so quickly?) .

And curious things have begun to happen to her social life. For one thing, despite their many protestations, most of the friends of her married life have disappeared from view. Some of them have chosen to see her husband, some probably to see neither. It is not so much a matter of their disapproving of her or taking sides against her—"civilized" divorces leave very little occasion for that—but of the great strain in maintaining social contact with two people who must be kept apart. There are certain dutiful invitations to a quiet dinner, and then silence. Anyway it is more natural and convenient for people to spend time with others in their own situation. Just as she was once pulled into the orbit of young families, she now finds herself easier with those who are footloose in some way.

She is dating again, like a young girl, and involved in a young girl's delicate problems—only this time without the advantages of innocence. If her having been married now makes impossible a certain dreamy anticipation, by the same token it makes her much more sensitive to the real game of men and women. She can be coy if she needs to, but no longer without feeling foolish.

Men had begun to call her up almost as soon as her husband left the house. Again, not because she is fatally attractive but because she is available. Somewhere in the club of divorced men and no-longer-young bachelors there hangs a great bulletin board on which are posted the day's new crop of divorced or widowed women. Old acquaintances, sometimes strangers call her up: will she have lunch, dinner, cocktails? These men are vast consumers of female companionship, being as they are inhabitants of a world that makes it somehow unpleasant for people to do such things as eat in restaurants, attend the theater, or even arrive at parties, alone. And they seem to consume women—either by not being pleased with them or by marrying them—at a rate much faster than women of suitable age and circumstance can be produced.

She has, then, every opportunity to be consoled for her loss of a steady escort. Moreover, there is for her (as there is *not* for her would-be beaux, condemned by their singleness to be caught in the toils of female vanity and female sexual narcissism) the excitement of being sought and of the curiosity it is now in her power to satisfy. She has no intention of being alone and virtuous—there is nothing left in her values to uphold such an intention. But with each invitation comes the question: What is this appointment *for*? Even though, or perhaps because, she knows the answer—that the matter is entirely up to her—the question makes her gauche. For can she be so indelicate as to indicate to a man who does not really interest her that, no, she will not have cocktails with him because she does not want to go to bed with him? On the other hand, if she simply went to have cocktails, could she endure that moment when by word or deed her position was put to the question and she had to find a kind way of turning him down? The divorcee is a woman whose unanswerable question, "Why should you expect me to sleep with you?" can be met with the equally unanswerable one, "Why should you not?" Has she not learned from marriage above all that too much fuss is made over the sex thing? She has, but the lesson is one that goes both ways and therefore nowhere. She can ask herself one night, "What difference does it make?" but then as easily ask the following morning, "Was it for this I gave up hearth and husband?" Young girls don't have to be kind in refusal, indeed are expected not to be. But she, no virgin, no child, asking so hard for kindness herself, must find a graceful out if it is an out she wants. Her problem is no less real for being utterly ridiculous.

It is no less real, either, for being so incongruous with the rest of her daily life. She is no scarlet woman but a responsible mother of two children. Her days describe not a madcap round of high life and sexy adventure but a rather sobering routine of work, household management, and motherhood. She has a housekeeper looking after the children, to be sure, but the time she scrupulously, even compulsively, reserves for them is time filled with the notion that they come first. How her children are really responding to the divorce she does not know and probably will not know for years, if ever. Contrary to current theory, children do not act out their sufferings but carefully reserve them to some future retribution. They do let her know, however, that they will never again be able to regard the universe as quite a safe place. She prides herself on being truthful with them, and she will not assure them that it is a safe place. But she does fix little daily patterns, new family customs, for them. If she knows there is something forced and a little pitiful in their festive dinners together, their two stories and a song before bedtime, she still takes some comfort in "doing the right thing." All children today no less than hers are being brought up by a system of canned inspiration—and what other is better? She tells them the truth about their daddy, that he is a fine, wonderful daddy. She tells them the truth about themselves, that they do not understand now but one day will. She brings them, so far as is possible, into her outside life. They visit her office and meet the men with whom she goes to dinner.

Her children will not be actually responsible for the serious new love affair on which she embarks in a year or two, but they will be one of its contributing conditions. For children set her life onto what is, with or without a man, a settled domestic plateau, and to some extent define her aspirations for the future. Family life cannot be maintained beyond a certain limit of irregularity—at least not without a great deal of money it can't. Anyway, the divorcee has long since found that her restlessness was not a striving toward freedom but simply the will to change her life a little. Even so modest an ambition probably cannot be satisfied. And certainly it cannot long hold out against something so overriding as the way in which the entire adult world is set up for couples. Restaurants and theaters, we have said, drive men who have otherwise escaped them into the clutches of women. Many things more bring men and women, however reluctant, permanently together: from housing to hypocrisy, nearly everything involved in the delicate network of physical and social comforts. In the current discussion of society's powerlessness to prevent the dissolution of all those marriages, no one seems to mention society's fantastic efficiency in creating new ones. The demographers tell us that for every hundred men and women divorced by the age of thirty-nine, ninety-three of the former and eighty-five of the latter will remarry; such is the high rate of "belief" in marriage among the divorced—or, rather, the high rate of discovery that there is no viable alternative to it.

The divorcee now thinks she sees very clearly what is wrong with marriage, truths always known and only lately forgotten: that it requires a certain sacrifice of the very things "modern" marriage pretends to supply; that it is not a higher sexual fulfillment but a sexual limitation; not an achievement but a hindrance to achievement; not a challenge but the refusal of challenge. What is more important, marriage *need not be* any of the things her contemporaries—particularly American ones—pretend. Its proper justification is the one that her own future marriage will have: namely, it is the most sensible economic and physical arrangement available for most people's lives. If marriage provides this much, it fills the purpose for which mankind intended it.

Hardheaded as our divorcee has become, nevertheless for a while she will deceive herself and her new lover about the nature of their affair. She will feel too keenly the costliness of permanent commitment to admit that she is leading him into marriage. They will have fun together, she will say, and be friends, and she will demand very little of him and allow very little to be demanded in return. Her lover will know enough not to believe her—for he, too, will have been married once—but he will feel that if in the end he must have a woman, hers are not such bad terms. Of course she will make inordinate demands on him, and he on her; of course they will not be—never were—friends in the way she means. Soon the fun will go out of just being together, and she will tend to get querulous about the need to be discreet. She will want to create some definition of his relations with her children. She will grow afraid of losing him. One day she will place the ultimatum before him, and he will capitulate. Still, her early deception will bespeak a sort of ideal vision of their future together; her very rhetoric will impose certain standards of behavior which, if he cannot hold her to them, will yet help free them both a little from the necessity for being constantly adequate to each other.

And so, in two and a half years from her appearance in court, the divorcee will stand again before a judge and make her solemn vows, chastened, a little fearful, but with a whole new set of principles to keep her warm. Her new husband will try manfully, but not without complaint, to manage his sudden acquisition of an ongoing household with children. The children will set out on their lifelong game of familial musical chairs: to Daddy's on Sunday, while Stepdaddy's little boy takes their place at home; marching along somehow in the parade of four parents, siblings, half siblings, stepsiblings, new cousins, new aunts and uncles, and a few extra grandparents.

One can hope that her new pretensions—to the marriage of limited expectations—will serve her better than the old ones.

1962

5

Sex, My Daughters, and Me

My adolescent daughters are, as they have been brought up to be, my "friends." I have two, and they are very different people indeed; but what I have to say about them here applies equally to both. We discuss together the day's events in school and office. We gossip together, within understood limits, about our respective friends. We share a common pride in the accomplishments and a common irritation at the naughtinesses of the two youngest children in the family. We tell one another jokes—frequently off-color. We trade cosmetics and minor articles of clothing. I am as likely to seek out their advice in affairs of shopping and dress as they are mine.

In our talks, to be sure, we are never exactly equals: I know a good deal more than they about just those things they are most eager to know and have far freer access to that big world they are so eager to enter, while they on their side hold all the secrets to that which most disquiets me; still we all manage most of the time not to be too patronizing. I sometimes think them superior to me, as they sometimes think me to them. And to some extent I envy them, as they do me.

Of course, friendship does not truly define the relationship between us. What defines it—for, after all, we are mother and daughters—is a struggle for power. When the friendliness cracks, as it does with a fair, though not permanently disruptive, regularity, it is this struggle which stands nakedly revealed beneath. Now, no one of my age and circumstance—a member of what sociologists would call the professional or educated middle class in the second half of the twentieth century—can possibly conceal from himself the Freudian implications of this relationship. In fact, no one of my age and circumstance can even mention the subject without being conscious of the idea that a mother and her daughter constitute a primary sexual rivalry. Such indeed, then, must be the case between my daughters and me; how would I, even if I were inclined to, deny it? Nevertheless, that which two of us *experience* as the issue between us in any given hour of battle has far less to do with why we must, at bottom, be contenders than with a whole lot of questions nearer the surface of things. A dispute may arise over something so trivial as the condition of their room, or something so principled as the allocation of their time between work and play, or even something so stark as their choice of friends. These questions, too, boil down to one: the power we struggle for is power over their respective destinies. At least for now, and presumably for the next few years, what is at stake between us is quite simply the fact that they are dependent on me. And I wish them to be and not to be, and they wish to be and not to be.

The struggle is for them an unequal one. For at the moment, anyway, I have the big guns on my side. I have their past record of helplessness and error to use against them and shake their confidence; I have, at least when pushed to an extreme, the unshakable conviction of my right to exercise power; and above all, I have control over money. Their only weapons are to wound with the spectacle of their unhappiness or to hold themselves resisting and out of earshot. These can be very potent weapons—if they were not, all children would be helpless and all parents serene—but they are defensive ones.

Such disadvantages in a relation of power my daughters have in common with every dependent in every age, clime, and culture. They suffer from certain others, however, peculiar to such young girls as have been brought up in their kind of life. For my daughters are supremely children of their time. Whatever their individualities, they are also very much the products of those spiritual pretensions by which their enlightened parents, like all enlightened parents of this generation, chose to bring up their children. In short, they must suffer the great hindrance to growing up of being their mother's friends.

Apart from the emotional burden our casual intimacy places upon them—a burden about which the psychologists have now, too late, a great deal of wisdom to proffer—this intimacy acts as a practical and political handicap of very real dimensions. For it is not merely trite to say the young are trusting. And above all, they trust to the appearances of things. Thus in our condition of friendship, an attack of motherhood upon either of them is apt to come quite suddenly and unprepared for. A casual revelation on one of their parts might become the occasion for a far from casual response on mine. Or I might take them nine-tenths of the way through a discussion or story which is proving to be of the keenest interest and then refuse to go on, overcome by some squeamishness or fastidiousness I had not realized was working inside my nerves; within a single sentence, perhaps, they will have become "too young" to hear what their mother has not heart to utter.

Most of all, they are bereft of the defense of thinking me utterly stupid. They may think so now and then, on this point or that, but they have no really solid base in thought or feeling from which to resist me. Just as they have been brought up from earliest infancy on the assumption that they were being "understood"—this time with sympathy, that time with harshness, but with understanding always—so, too, it has been assumed that they "understand" me. Simple stupidity has never been one of the terms between us. Mothers like me do not believe their children to be incompetent. This may in fact be the prime axiom of our kind of parenthood. We take care to know at every moment of our children's development what the attainments of that moment ought properly to be and make our demands accordingly. (A good deal of fun has been poked at us for this, for we are the comic ladies who sit on park benches poring over our volumes of Spock and Gesell and Bettelheim. But the fun has usually been poked by people who are not entitled to it, by the people who think we ought to respect our children *more*, when what we are really doing is seeking out the widest range of possibilities to offer our children our respect.) And since we do not treat them as incompetents, they have no fund of experience from which to retaliate in later years.

Note, for example, the terms of the current adolescent rebellion against people like us. We are accused of being deficient in love, not simple enough, too adept at making our way, too successful. It is not that we know too little of the world—the major accusation of our own adolescence against our parents—but too much. They do not strive to alter our definition of reality, for no matter what they say, they acknowledge our competence to do the defining; they simply repudiate "reality" altogether, putting the word into inverted commas with, among other things, hallucinogens. As it happens, my own daughters' relation to the current intellectual and social fashions among their rebelling cohort is—so far— that of only fairly sympathetic onlookers. So far I have succeeded in spoiling the idea of direct participation for them. Which is to say, I have managed to talk them out of it.

And talk is of the essence. We happen to do a great deal of it in our house; for us as a family it is recreation, tool, and means of survival. But not only by the particular accident of birth are my daughters surrounded by talk. For all children like them, words constitute a kind of postnatal amniotic fluid in which they grow and are both sheltered from and introduced to their surroundings. On the most primitive level, for such children words have taken the place of physical violence as a means of instruction and discipline. They have also by and large replaced that network of instructions and disciplines called punishment. To be hampered from pursuing a noxious or harmful activity is to be "told no." Being the denizens of city or suburb, the children discover the world around them primarily by a process of giving names to things. Their hours of solitude are spent alone with the speech of others, in the form of books, television, radio.

The schools in which they spend such a large proportion of the waking hours of their childhood are, of course, veritable waterfalls, floods, volcanos of words, phrases, clauses, sentences, paragraphs. As you might expect, my daughters have gone only to "good" schools—that is to say, the most benign, most attentive, most enriching schools that were available. Thus they have not only been instructed by means of their teachers' use of language, they have also been taught through perfecting their own manipulation of language—in other words, to uncover what might be in their own minds by discussing it aloud. In such schools, the desire to fail can be fulfilled merely by keeping silent. As, indeed, can the desire to fail at home.

The society of the enlightened, then, does not beat or drive its children, does not drill them, but rather nags them, into growing up. And the measure of the children's progess along this path is their capacity to nag in turn.

The point about talk is not whether it is a good way or a bad way to bring up the young. As parents have gone—and as societies have gone—the attempt on the part of my contemporaries to give their children certain physical and social freedoms, to confront and harness for good some of their baser impulses, to help them reason their way toward being civilized, to befriend them, seems not so very malign. We are of course doomed by the absurdity of our pretensions—for naturally we are incapable of permitting our children all those things we pretend to permit them. And we are far from being so pure of motive as we imagined—for motives are never pure between adults and the young. Still, we are, I should think, no more pretentious or self-deceived than our own parents and very likely a good deal less. In any event, my daughters and their friends seem to me far more attractive, more open, and a good deal nicer than I remember myself and my friends in adolescence.

In some ways, however, they seem to me less fortunate than we were. For the point about talk is that it sets up a competition in which the children, particularly the children of the educated and enlightened, must lose.

Once upon a time, or so I imagine, children could manage their powerlessness by biding their time. They could, if they wanted to be comfortable, obey the rules and in the face of some unwanted imposition from the authorities or some supposed injustice, take to their closets. Their corporeal selves might be rendered up to Caesar, but their thoughts—undoubtedly of future vengeance—they could keep to themselves.

But my daughters have no means of retreat from the barrages of those bigger than they: not into the street and not into the closet. The wider world of school and playmates only confirms *me*, for what I have given them of speech is precisely that which best enables them to get along there. The books they read *I* have placed into their hands (even the dirty books with which they and their friends while away so many exciting, secretive hours they have taken from my shelves, where they stand in full view). Their imaginative life is one that I as a companionable mother once encouraged and helped them invent. Nor are their hiding places of any use, for I understand and even condone their behavior in taking to them. I am, as it were, huddled inside with them.

And if either of them stands and fights, she naturally loses. I know more words than she, and they are bigger words, more impressive. I can make them do such miraculous and unanswerable things as describe an irony, create an analogy, or cite an apposite witticism. I can dazzle her with words, amuse her against her will with them, distract her, frighten her, expose her motives, analyze her character, justify myself with words, and if need be, simply drown her in them. I can—one of the tricks of friendship—seduce her into answering and use what she says as a new supply of grist for my unending mill. Only pure rage can stop the flow. But my daughters, poor things, are not yet enough in command of themselves to produce that merciful condition in me without being already in the grip of it themselves.

So they have no recourse but to meet me on my own ground. It is a predicament from which only the distance and privacy of adulthood can rescue them.

But I, too, am caught in a predicament. Because when I speak to them, I often contradict myself. To the mothers who were trained as I was—by the Freudian precept that children's personalities are shaped not by what used to be called upbringing but by the quality of those family relationships into which they enter at birth—our children represent a total responsibility. We do not believe ourselves charged primarily with keeping them healthy and properly sheltered and teaching them the manners of the society into which we will one day send them. We believe ourselves rather to be the very creators of their psyches, their personalities, and above all, their capacities for success and happiness. What such a responsibility demands of us is something more than undying love, more even than wisdom—it demands that we know what is right and what is needed. This is a responsibility I am hardly able to undertake consistently or gracefully for myself, much less for these nearly grown female creatures who stand opposite me. They naturally do not ask it of me—at least not any longer. But this is the way of our relationship. Without it, I should have to turn away from them. It is too late to go back now.

Thus I contradict myself. I do not always feel what I think; I do not always think what I feel. Or rather, I belie myself—since it is my usual custom to tell them what I think (the words for thought come easier than those for feelings) and only indicate to them, so desperately unfairly, by my sudden passions what I feel.

Nowhere are my contradictions more evident, nor undoubtedly more painful to them, than in dealing with the problem of sex. This problem is about the last genuine one left to the transaction between us. Not that we do not struggle over other things, but we have nothing new to say to one another about these: they have learned what they have learned from me, I have failed them where I have failed them, the rest is for the most part now up to them and fate.

Sex, however, is another matter. As a real issue it is just now coming up in their lives—that is, becoming something they are required to *do* something about. And they are still young enough to ask me, sometimes—usually indirectly— what they should do. And I find myself wishing to the very bottom of my being that they would not.

They ask me, I think, for several reasons. First of all, because they are frightened. Such a to-do is made of sex in these days of the new, supposedly freer attitudes toward it that we are probably succeeding in making it as great a mystery to the young as it was in the era when "leg" was a dirty word: a mystery of a different kind, perhaps, now no longer shrouded in evil but partaking in some of those qualities of quest and conquest of the Holy Grail. In any case, it is partly their timidity that drives my daughters to seek the word of the Authorities, for the comfort, either way, of a denial or of permission.

They also ask me for the simple reason that they believe I know a good deal about the subject. They have not been permitted to assume about me—as the children of my generation, say, permitted ourselves to assume about our parents —that I live in ignorance (in both senses) of sex. I have not permitted it by the conversation, my own and that of my friends, which I have allowed to go on in their presence. I have not permitted it, either, by my style of dress, of behavior, of being. They ask me, too, because to do so is a way— and a very effective way, I might add—of announcing to me that they will one of these days be no longer my satellites but my equals.

But most of all, they ask me because they are too innocent of the danger I represent to them. Like all children raised in the advanced and liberal way, their sophistication and worldliness are streaked with an almost incredible naïveté. This naïveté does not have to do with facts, and certainly not with any of the actual facts of sex, about which they and their friends have a fund of knowledge more complete and accurate than that of many adults I know. Nor have they, since the years of fairly early childhood, acquired any of these facts from me; though once learned, they have often taken pleasure in discussing them with me (out of the desire to show off rather than for information). In fact, had they, as the textbooks recommend, come to me for all this information, they might have found out many of my reluctances in the matter a whole lot sooner. Nor is their naïveté psychological exactly—though its effects on me are clearly psychological—for as I said earlier, they understand me rather well. I suppose their innocence would have to be called spiritual.

Anyway, it has to do with the trust that my seeming openness as a mother has bred in them—so early and so thoroughly that all the disappointments they must have suffered have not served to make them appropriately wary. Our children, so wise to the world in other ways, have very little left of the child's genius for duplicity. They are bad liars and ineffective sneaks. We have deprived them of their natural and indispensable talent for keeping their secrets secret, and with it, of a certain insight into the nature of the dangerous or forbidden.

When I was my daughters' age, I knew exactly how much, for both our sakes, it was necessary for my mother to know about my own personal confrontation with sex: namely, nothing. My daughters have considerably more leeway than that; there, perhaps, is the rub. Sex as a subject is profoundly interesting to people like me. We think about it a great deal, wonder at it a great deal, and discuss it only somewhat less. We are amused by it as a phenomenon, find it comical, take it immensely seriously. We would, if we could, like to know how everyone we see around us conducts himself with respect to sex. And, if it would not entail a psychic monstrosity that no amount of self-deception could keep hidden, we would even like to know precisely how our own daughters and their friends conduct themselves. In short, like the highly emancipated persons we are, our minds are totally the creatures of the most fashionable currents of the culture that surround them.

Yet my daughters, too, are restricted, if not in what they may ask, then in what they may expect to receive an answer to. They are restricted by the intensity with which I wish they wouldn't ask me. All their questions, regardless of how they are put or whether the girls know it or not, can only be directed to one end: ought they, now or in the near future, to engage in sexual relations with one or another young man? And the truth of the matter is, I do not know how to answer.

My uncertainty, to be sure, does not take the form of a simple expression of uncertainty. It takes the form, rather, of a series of confident statements which contradict, supersede, or override one another—or which sometimes simply evade the point. I may, for instance, deride some display of sexual priggishness on the part of a relative, a teacher, or their headmaster—on this occasion planting myself foursquare on the side of the legitimate erotic expression of the children. I may at some other time, and not apparently apropos of them at all, find myself delivering a rather brutal lecture on the horrors of premarital pregnancy—attacking first the criminal immorality of the official posture by which proper contraception and legal abortion are kept out of the reach of young girls and, in the next breath, the criminal irresponsibility of the same young girls in surrendering themselves to something they have not first learned to manage. Or I may, in the name of civilization and decency, take up the cudgels for the boys, attempting to make my daughters aware of the acute suffering inflicted on their male contemporaries by the self-involved experimentation with their powers, *i.e.*, the teasing, of the girls. One of the things I say to them—and naturally it is the one I have the strongest sensation of conviction about —is simply mean: that the adolescent love affairs I have seen do not seem to me to be emotional and sexual adventures at all but, on the contrary, a series of enormous cop-outs. That is, I say, they seem to me to entail nearly all the commitments of marriage, dulling in people so young, and far from providing a wider range of experience, they are actually protecting their participants from having to undergo too much experience. How this must translate to my daughters' discerning and simplifying ears, of course, is: Even if you have sex, it won't be any good.

This particular piece of cruelty to them is not mine alone.

In somewhat different (and as I fancy, in far less subtle and clever) form, it represents the defense of an entire generation against the implications underlying its own sexual liberation. If you begin as we all did with the proposition that lust is not only natural but life-giving and good, and if you travel the path from there straight and true, you arrive at complete sexual promiscuity. Lust as an independent value divorces itself from institutions, personal relations, and travels with utter unconcern from creature contact to creature contact. This is, as a matter of fact, exactly how the Puritans understood the matter, and they were right. We understand it, too, in the pits of our stomachs if not in our minds and scurry about to improvise our excuses. We do not want to be promiscuous, for if lust is simple, the other major human passions—vanity, pride, acquisitiveness—are not. Our marriages barely survive so much of frankness about our desires as we already allow ourselves, and being unmarried is for us an agony of rushing about to stake our claims. And if we do not want promiscuity for ourselves, we will certainly never be able to bear it in our children.

What we want for ourselves and them is to hold onto our imaginings of complete sexual abandon and at the same time maintain the kind of emotional requirements which make such abandon impossible for us. The most notable of our excuses for this is one derived at two removes from a vulgarization of Freud. To wit: a mentally healthy and mature person seeks in sex the deepening and enrichment of an already and otherwise satisfying connection. Sexual conquest as an end in itself is "unhealthy"; in girls it is a mark of self-devaluation, and in boys, of "Don Juanism." On the other hand, an affair with one person undertaken out of curiosity or in a spirit of fun is emotionally irresponsible and therefore "immature." Thus while we promise our children a satisfaction that we had to wrest for ourselves, we nevertheless do our best to block their easy passage to it.

To be sure, we make no point of their having to be married. All of us, I believe, have settled, whether we admit it or not, with the idea that our children will have at least some sex experience before marriage. But we have only retreated to a nearer line of defense. The sex experience they have, in order for them not to earn our opprobrium, must be to some purpose. It must be good in itself, it must improve their lives, it must make them better people. And naturally, it must not end in pregnancy. As for myself, I might wish for the further condition that it take place without either my knowledge or complicity.

I ask too much, I know that. We all do. We always have. But, then, too much was asked of us and of our parents and will be of our grandchildren.

This whole problem is in the end really not my daughters', but mine. They will suffer the cruelties of this alternating titillation and denial that has been their introduction to sex, and, like the rest of us, if they are tough enough or brave enough or lucky enough, they will prevail. But what will be for them their experience and their life will be for me always the record of my inability as a parent to stand behind that person whose face I had so long ago chosen to show to the world. Not that having such a record is necessarily bad, but the chastening seems to have seeped into every corner of my life. My daughters' education at my hands has turned out to be a far profounder one of me at theirs.

1967

6

The Liberated Woman

Though she was born into a very real world, and not a princess, it may be only a little fanciful to imagine that her birth was attended by a visitation of good fairies. Of these, one wished upon her kindly and indulgent parents. One, good health. One wished that she be surrounded by wealth sufficient to provide her with comfortable shelter, rich foods, costly adornments and entertainments, and a protracted time of growth free from the foreclosures of necessity. One wished that her mind not be restricted to the disciplines and techniques of everyday survival; another that her imagination not be locked away from the gorgeous variety of recorded human experience; still another that no hint of talent on her part, no childish display of capacity or inclination, be left to wither from neglect. And last but not least, there was one to wish that she be comely, perhaps even beautiful, so that she might know herself beyond doubt to be desired. If in this visitation was included no benign spirit expressly to wish upon her a sweet and sunny nature, certainly among all the others the conditions for such a nature had been fully anticipated.

This truly blessed event took place, let us say, just at the close of World War II. Those first years of postwar adjustment—her father a student or resuming the long-interrupted practice of his profession, her mother in a fever of taking hold of an orderly domestic existence—were spent by her in the material unconsciousness of infancy. By the time society intruded upon her self-centered world, when she entered school, she was safely settled within a community of the economically secure. She was to want for no necessity and to be denied very little, actually, in the way of luxury—and of this latter such denials as she would suffer would be grounded not in the idea of superfluity but in the definition of her own best welfare. Of fundamental luxuries—learned doctors to straighten her teeth or ease her melancholy, instructors of all sorts to enlarge her accomplishment and enrich her leisure, travels, holidays spent at seaside or lakeside or mountain, and, above all, the best and most attractive schooling available—the limit would be set only at her own need and capacity. Moreover, nothing in the surrounding atmosphere would even offer the suggestion that such privilege was hers by any but divine right.

For in addition to being economically secure, the community in which she was to grow up had organized itself around one central principle: namely, what would be most pleasing and in the broadest sense of the term most beneficial to her. Unlike that of most of the world's children, past or present, her existence was not a thing taken for granted and hence left to piece itself in somehow with the general flow of life. From the moment of her conception, she had become the precise and elaborately defined responsibility of both her parents and of the society they were making. The house in which she lived would be architected to the centrality of her presence in it. The schools she attended would come under the sway of the idea that she must not be made to suffer in any way, physically, emotionally, mentally; that undue discomfort or anxiety would impede her fulfillment as both individual and pupil and thus constitute pedagogical failure. And perhaps most important, the mores of that community were adjusted to free her as much as possible from the sense of guilt that had been found so crippling by its adults. As a little child, she was not to be compelled to be clean or orderly or even formally well mannered beyond some minimal point of tolerability to those around her. She was to be allowed as much expression—certainly, in particular, verbal expression—of her aggressions as could be consonant with domestic survival. Finally, when the time came for it, she was not to be denied her proper and expected and healthy experience of sex. The notion of what was proper or expected in sex might have been left somewhat vaguely defined but at the very least included the idea that she must not, even if considerations of prudence had still to deter her, be made to feel *guilty* about it. For guilt was the mother of frigidity, and frigidity was the leading society-created crime against her humanity.

She, on her part, responded to these new expectations of home and community by appearing to fulfill most of them. That is to say, she tended to be somewhat disorderly and unmannerly but not intolerably so—compensating those around her for the chaos she created with a certain charm and generosity of spirit that might otherwise have been lacking. She was sometimes given to seizures of aggression that, once again, seemed compensated for by the intimacy and demonstrativeness that were their obverse. She went through school without any marked display of suffering and gave much evidence of the qualities deemed by everyone to be independence of mind and creativity. She was, in fact, to be accounted an educational success, having mastered her schoolwork easily, with time and spirit left over for the cultivation of special interests—which happened to be, in her case, literary—and in due course she and her school were repaid for their collaboration by her admittance to a prestigious Eastern college.

With her parents in particular, whatever difficulties she made were precisely the difficulties predicted, and so discounted in advance, by their ideology of parenthood. Thus while she often gave them great pain, particularly during her adolescence, in the very act of doing so she was also serving to vindicate them. If she showed them a certain disrespect, beneath that disrespect were felt to lie the kind of person-to-person relations made possible by their very refusal to take adult advantage. Hers, therefore, could never be the contempt in which they had once held their own parents, so basic, so full of plain snobbery, that it dared not be given casual utterance. If she tended to value at naught, though of course accepting without scruple, many of the comforts they had so mindfully provided her, this was no more than a tribute to the higher sensitivity such a life as hers had permitted to develop. If she tended to use her own still-unformed responses as the measure by which all things in the world were to be judged—instead of, as had generally been the case in her parents' generation, the other way around—this again was the result of an enviable refusal on her part to be spiritually bullied. Hers would never be that docility in the face of accepted piety which had once so damped and narrowed their own youths and which they had vowed not to impose on her. And if she seemed, despite all tendencies to disrespect and self-regard, somewhat overdependent on them —demanding their support in all her undertakings, their assent to all her decisions—this was seen to be the mark of an earned and merited faith in their devotion to her. So no matter what she did, the one thing she could not successfully do was storm the fortress of their anxious resignation to her will.

The years of her adolescence, then, were spent pretty much in accordance with the times—being in this case the late fifties and early sixties—and her specially privileged estate. She enjoyed, for one thing, virtually unprecedented mobility for someone of her age. By the time of her graduation from college she had owned a car in which she and friends had traveled twice across the United States and to Mexico; she had spent one year at school in, and two summers touring, Europe; she had spent several holidays with her family at an ocean resort, several others at camp or on bicycle trips, and served one stint as an *au pair* girl on an island in the Caribbean.

She also changed her style of presenting herself, which is

to say her wardrobe, with regular frequency: always in the name of a new freedom from convention, always expensively, and always in accordance with the new social message it was required to bring. Sometimes that message was, I am a naughty and rather rowdy child; sometimes, I am a sexless sprite. She was never quite conscious of what any given wardrobe signified; but of the possibility for adopting new personae and playing with each of them to a quickly reached point of boredom, she was never for one moment unconscious.

Being pretty and bright and usually high-spirited, she was a welcome presence among her peers. Boyfriends were never wanting, but these she took, after the going fashion, one at a time and on the basis of a steady, if temporary, commitment. Each of them in turn was understood by friends and family to be her momentary property, he was invited into her home as she was into his, and when she wished to, she was permitted by adults to speak in their presence of "love." This arrangement allowed her to exchange varying degrees of sexual bestowal for a large measure of personal security.

Somewhere in this process, say her senior year in high school or freshman year in college, the bestowal demanded of her was the final one: she entered into a full-blown affair. For this she was equipped by her family doctor with a diaphragm—later she would be given the Pill. She never discussed the exact nature of this affair with her parents, as some of her friends had done with theirs, but by their behavior they let her know that as long as she stayed out of trouble the terms of her sex life were naturally and rightly to be left to her own desires. They did not scruple to leave her at home alone if for any reason they were called away for a few days. Nor did they refuse her permission to travel off for a weekend on her own recognizance. With her girlfriends she discussed her sexual affairs in great detail—likely as not emotional rather than erotic detail. They judged her, as she judged them, merely to be engaged in the inevitable and taken for granted.

With her lover (s) there was also a good deal of discussion, also not erotic but emotional (sometimes psychoanalytic) in focus. Suffering no sense of sin within themselves and no undue pressure from the outside, they were not particularly venturesome either in their acts of love or in the conditions under which these acts were carried out. The whetting edge of danger for them, if and when it should be sought, was promised far more by the explorations and exposures of their minds under the influence of illegal chemical preparations. Out of bed, they became deeply dependent on each other for companionship. Any social activity sought by one which excluded the other was taken to be an intentional act of disloyalty. Between them they exchanged words of love but more often, and with more sincerity, competed for the right to expatiate on their respective hang-ups, fears, or new triumphs of emotional growth. He tended to flatter her for her powers of understanding or sometimes to revile her for her lack of them; and she tended, in the sense of power afforded by the secret, erotic knowledge of his unequal need for her, to baby him.

And out there in the daylight world were friends, parties, diversions both frivolous and serious, and all overlaid with promising and highly valued achievements. In short, a full and interesting life.

College, though it presented her at first with the shock of needing to establish herself as a uniquely identifiable person among strangers, was largely a continuation of what had gone before. To be sure, she now had to work harder at her studies and to manage relations with her peers and those in authority without the softening mediations of the familiar. Once the techniques for these were mastered, however, the charm, the openness to intimacy, the need for support, began to work their accustomed effect. Her school was a girls' school, traditionally famous for harboring creativity and for being the sexual preserve of certain neighboring men's colleges. Her classes, free of everyday male competition, were precisely on that account conducted in an easy spirit of flirtation between professor and student and vice versa. Self-expression was the highest demand of these classes and constituted their definition of attainment. "The thing I really feel about Emma Bovary is . . ."; "But I can't understand how Shakespeare, feeling as he obviously did about Cordelia, could have made her . . ."; "If, as you say, society and culture are not the same thing, how is someone like me to understand. . . ." In this atmosphere, no challenge of hers went unanswered, and no answer of her own was dismissed. She felt herself as each academic year went by to possess an ever greater grasp of the central ideas of her time and an ever keener sense of how to dispose of the errors and trivia of the past.

By the time of graduation she knew one thing for certain about her future: whether it immediately held marriage, a career, or some pleasant temporizing on the way to either or both, it was going to take place somewhere at the center of "the action." Her decision, naturally, had not come to such clarity solely or even mainly as a response to her studies. Certainly she had always had, though of late unadmitted, fantasies of chic; but all this provided no specific focus to her determination and by itself would only have sent her off passively down the track to meet whatever opportunity happened to come along first. Meanwhile, however, both on the campus and all around it, as far as her selective eye could see, she had found herself living in a turbulent and exciting —an *important*—world. First, of course, there had been the civil-rights movement, followed by the eerie titillations of black nationalist hostility. Then the war. Then the universities themselves, in their interesting new guise as the enemies and oppressors of people like her. She took no central part in these movements, preferring to remain a sympathizer, occasional demonstrator, but enthusiastic adopter of each new persona, replete with wardrobe, they engendered. Once again, her talent for personal demand, made palatable by the affectionate gentleness with which she pressed it, gave her easy entrée to the brotherhood she sought. It was this new persona, as vague but unmistakably virtuous radical, clad with the appropriately artful shabbiness, that was taking her straight to the heart of the big-city center of communications.

Beyond her education, academic and political, college had

meant for her the distillation of a way of life. This way of life, too, had been shaped by a movement, but a movement too amorphous to identify and one its adherents didn't join so much as were overtaken by. At one extreme end, the movement was called hippiedom and outspokenly advocated a life of quietistic bohemianism, a floating on the outer tides of a society too overpowering and too rigorous for the truly sensitive to manage. At the other extreme, it was a kind of training ground for the jet set, whose disciplines were created to promote the hard and unremitting pursuit of monied leisure. She and her friends located themselves somewhere in between, taking up the attitudes and behavior patterns of both of these extremes in some kind of mix that felt convenient to them. Those aspects of life they found unduly thorny or uncongenial they characterized with the adjective "establishment." "Establishment" could mean, in a leaning toward the hippie side, too rational and clear-cut, and it could mean, from the other side, simply too grubby. That massive though conspiratorial group from whose designation they derived their adjective—in addition to its broader responsibilities for the oppression of Negroes and the making of imperialist wars —was also, it seemed, concerned to see that they endure great boredom in the culture they were making for themselves. Thus their major forms of recreation, their music, their movies, their mystical readings and devotions, their pot and wine parties, constituted not only pleasure in themselves but the striking of a blow in behalf of a healthier society. Virtually nothing they did, and most particularly nothing they did with respect to sex, was devoid of this larger dimension.

Our heroine was never actually promiscuous as the learned doctors of the soul would have understood the word. That is to say, she had several affairs but continued, as before, to have them one at a time, each bearing, if briefly, the constraints of monogamy. Twice in her senior year she had spent afternoons in a motel with one of her youngest and most erotically inspiring professors. The actual experience was so alien to the fantasy that had overtaken her listening to the professor's lecture, however, that she found some delicate way of being unable to see him more than twice. Her secret sense of triumph in the classroom after that was not quite overborne by her disappointment. Once, for a weekend, she had submitted to the lesbian advances of a dorm mate. Something in the power of that experience both to repel her and to overwhelm her with longings for self-destruction spoke to her imagination of the decisively ruinous role of sex she'd read about in early works of pornography.

For the most part, though, she couldn't really understand what all the fuss was about. Either, as her culture told her and as she and her friends repeated ritualistically to one another, the lack of weight with which sexual activity floated among the other activities of her life was a sign that it had been put in its proper and natural place. Or, as in her secret heart she believed, there was something in the experience for others that she had been unable to attain to. The one lover who piqued her appetites—though, possibly by definition, he was the one who made the least observable effort to satisfy them—was a young lawyer she encountered her first year out of college. He talked very little, except about matters relating to the progress of his career; until one night at dinner he quite unaccountably began to revile her—characterizing her in certain forceful four-letter terms she had often heard used and had often used herself but never in connection with her —then left the table and walked out; nor did he call her to apologize. After a few days she pronounced him dull and boorish and came upon the insight that it had been precisely his unworthiness which had made him so attractive to her in the first place. She vowed she would never be so sick as to be publicly humiliated again, and she never was.

The deplorable experience with the lawyer had, in fact, been her first sexual encounter in New York City, where she had come, on being graduated from school, to seek her fortune. He was followed by a television documentary producer of some small but rather well-paid renown, a gentle and helpful but often gloomy man who had only recently separated from his wife and two young children. She and the producer took an apartment together, an arrangement which

was to last less than a year and to end in considerable bitterness (among the causes of which was her first and only, and
quite disagreeable, abortion) but in the meantime was to
provide them both with exciting times. She exaggerated, by
depending on, his strength and wordly wisdom, and he
helped by scolding her a lot to assure her of her talent.

She came to the city with a job already in hand. In her
senior year she had been first winner in an essay contest
sponsored by one of the fashion magazines—subject: "Is Sex
Freer on the Campus, and Why?"—and her prize was a
junior position on the magazine's staff. Once in the office, she
felt she had been a naïf to be pleased by the prospect before
her. For one thing, the magazine was staffed mainly by
women who were or were becoming technical experts in one
or another of the phases of fashion-and-food presentation the
publication specialized in. Mainly it was just not her kind
of place and had nothing to teach her. Under the goading of,
and enabled by the support of, her lover, she quit her job and
began to write. Through his contacts she acquired an agent;
and by the time they split up she had published two short
pieces of film criticism and a feature piece about the audience of the New York Film Festival in a new, expensively
produced magazine devoted to youth arts. Soon after this she
became a more or less regular contributor of pieces of special
reporting to an influential neighborhood weekly.

She made very little money but managed with it somehow.
Her parents gave her furniture for her one-room studio
apartment and sent her checks—not at exactly regular inter-
vals like an allowance but regularly enough so that she could
count on them and never needed to think of asking. In addition, her parents tried manfully to suppress all expression of
the anxiety that mingled, particularly after they learned of
her arrangement with the documentary producer, in their
pride and pleasure with her. And at certain of the parties she
attended, there were bound to be one or two strangers who
recognized her name.

Several of her former classmates had also come to New
York to live and work. They were all still close enough to
their school days to find social ease together. A couple of

these were secretaries or editorial assistants somewhere in the publishing industry; one worked in television, in what capacity she could or would never make clear; one taught school; one worked in the poverty program and lived communally with a couple of painters, a jewelry designer, a dancer, and a ragged young couple with no visible occupation other than the preparation of various interesting potations consumed daily by the entire household. Sometimes these girls would be visited for a weekend, over a holiday, or on the occasion of some especially important demonstration by a group of the young men they had known in the neighboring colleges and who had remained on in graduate school to avoid the draft. In accordance with the established custom in these matters, their guests would be farmed out among them to spend the night in sleeping bags on their floors or, if need be, in their beds—but not, as the rule had also been set down, there so casually to enjoy their favors.

She was always happy to see them, these boys (as she now took to calling them in her mind). But sometimes deep into the night, perhaps awakened by a certain discomfort in the sleeping arrangement, she could not evade the thought that were it not for the fury roused in her by society's wish to have them kill or be killed, they wouldn't be so very interesting to her anymore. They seemed so beclouded, so lacking in the sharp personal edge of definition, so . . . interchangeable. She feared she might not remember which of them she had once slept with and which merely exchanged deep confidences with. The curious thing she found was that one of these visits, should it occur while she was in the middle of an assignment, seriously disrupted her ability to work. Of all her group of college acquaintances, she was thus far the most successful. She supposed she felt guilty about that or at least inhibited about pulling rank. But her friends, particularly her male friends, made no trouble on that score. They were loyal, they praised the things she'd written, they suggested all sorts of hot, cool, or necessary subjects she ought to try her hand at next. They regarded her in fact as a sort of public-relations arm for their own particular concerns and causes.

Then—at some point in all this—came the most hopeful
love affair of all. She guessed, though she didn't want to push
things, that this affair would be the final one. How her feelings of attachment to this lover differed from those in the
past she would not have been able to say exactly. The two of
them just—got on better. Their life together seemed grown-
up and real. No man had been as sensitive to, or shown as
much respect for, her feelings. No man had expressed such
vulnerability to her erotic power. No man, in short, had been
so genuinely accepting of her. She felt free to be herself as
she had felt with no one except her parents and enthusiasti-
cally set up house with him. He, being a much employed
news and fashion photographer, was away from home a good
deal. She found his absences quite painful and his homecom-
ings eventful. About her work he was patient, sympathetic,
and totally permissive. He neither goaded nor inhibited her.
If she wanted to be a writer, fine. If she wanted to relax and
just be his girl, that was fine, too. For the first time she
bought a cookbook and began to think about planning a meal
now and then. He never demanded that either, being quite
heedless, though always appreciative, of what he ate. He did
make an absolute point of having certain of his comforts but
on the other hand insisted that she have hers as well. He
insisted, too, on making love a good deal more often than she
was accustomed to, but his demands were always expressed
in terms of her irresistibility to him and thus became themselves irresistible.

If the foregoing does not describe a situation to which
might be applied the traditional fairy tale ending, surely it
would be fair to say that the beneficent fairies who attended
her birth had not till then deserted her. She did receive the
tender nurture they had wished upon her. She did enjoy the
freedom of mind and spirit and at least a sufficient part of the
wealth they had invoked. She did always have reason to
know herself desirable. They did manage to bring her without undue pain to the opportunity to develop her talent and,
finally, even into the arms of, if not Prince Charming, then at
least the kind of man her great-grandmother might have mistaken for him.

The story does not end here, however. For where was that last ethereal spirit to bless her with contentment?

II

She could not have said exactly when she first became aware of Women's Liberation. As it does for most people with most movements, her consciousness of the new feminism developed and sharpened over time, following an accumulation of news items, incidents, conversations. Oddly enough, it was one of her old male college friends who supplied her with the first word of it to which she had a truly personal response. This took place over a dinner she had cooked for him—none too graciously, in fact, for he had not even bothered to tell her he was coming and she was afraid he would also expect to be put up for the night (a custom in whose innocence her lover absolutely refused to believe). As it happened, he was going uptown to stay with some Columbia friends, still engaged in assessing the victories of their "insurrection" of the previous spring and now planning their strategy for the coming school year. Thus Columbia was much on his mind and in the course of discussing it he mentioned in passing, for her amusement, the doings of some of the female radicals in an occupied building. The girls had deeply resented the expectation of their male co-revolutionists that they would fulfill such traditional feminine roles as that of providing food and doing the typewriting. They had posted a sign in a corridor of one of the occupied buildings which said something to the effect of: This is a liberated area; therefore do not make sandwiches or type unless these happen to be ways in which you genuinely fulfill yourselves. She joined with him, laughing and shaking her head, in the moment's insinuation of their common superiority, and then felt a sudden, overwhelming wash of resentment herself—at what she did not know, except that the dinner she had just cooked somehow came into it as well. To be sure, she did feel superior to those girls or, rather, ashamed of them: with the war in Vietnam, the oppression of blacks, the general decay of American society to feel passionately about, how could

they justify trying to get into the act as women? Yet why did
she, if she were the fully developed individual she claimed to
be, feel even so much of kinship with the female liberators as
to experience her disapproval of them as shame? And why
did she, who had never in her life but of her own free will
either put together a sandwich or touched her fingers to a
typewriter, recognize that she could empathize completely
with their feelings?

Soon after, she had lunch with an editor in a publishing
house who was showing some mild interest in her career. The
editor was a woman, with a high-ranking position in the
company's trade department, a husband who was a very rich
and successful doctor, and two growing children. Less than
halfway through lunch the pretense of an editorial conference was abandoned and her hostess launched into an elo-
quent discourse on the position of women, which was partly
a pitch for some books she was bringing out on the subject
and partly a lamentation for the conditions of her own life,
particularly her working life.

Our heroine was both taken aback and intrigued: the
grievance of a woman like her own mother she could understand—a painter who had been unable to hang in and offer
the proper devotion to her art, and whose overtime concern
for the development of her daughter left her now beached
and flopping around to fill up her days—but this woman?
She would have supposed her to have reached the best of all
reasonable settlements: a highly successful career of her
own, a successful husband, children. . . . When she expressed
these sentiments to her lunch companion, the tirade only
intensified. Her husband, she said, for one thing had always
believed her incompetent to share his professional concerns
and for another thing did not altogether take her work seriously either, believing hers to be the major responsibility for
the upbringing of the children and any time left over from
that was for her to do with as she pleased. And as for her
work itself, while it was true she was a senior editor, she was
paid a smaller salary than many of her male colleagues on
the ground that since she was already well taken care of,
money was not the issue, and—what particularly irritated

her—she was never allowed to forget she was a woman. Just that very morning she had received a memo from the editor-in-chief asking for the "feminine point of view" on some manuscript or other. She was outraged as well for the younger girls who worked in her office, all of whom were far overqualified, by virtue of education and accomplishment, for the kind of ordinary routine work they were required to do. "And what about you?" She turned suddenly on our heroine. "Aren't you a 'girl' writer? Do you think if you were a young man they'd send you on the kind of assignments they do—always the 'personal side' of things? And pay you so little? Do you think, if the world had taught you truly to take yourself seriously as a writer, you would have the kind of trouble getting down to things or completing assignments that you described to me earlier?"

The agitation that resulted from this lunch ebbed and flowed in successive waves for nearly a week. She looked at the apartment she and her lover had set up and felt that it was not a writer's apartment at all. The smallest alcove in it, hidden from view by a bentwood screen, was the place where she had set up her writing table; her portable typewriter was kept in its case under the bed. The place was gradually filling up with domestic objects that required her attention, dusting or keeping up of some kind. She found by the end of that week that she had not once made the bed and that she was days overdue in getting her lover's shirts to the laundry. Finally, one evening in the process of clearing away the supper dishes, she looked down at herself and at her lover stretched out on the couch engrossed in a televised baseball game and startled them both by simply letting the tray full of dishes crash from her hands to the floor and slamming out the door to the movies.

The *coup de grâce* was delivered by her old school friend who worked for CBS. "I am into Women's Lib," she announced. "It's really straightened out my head. I want you to come to one of our meetings and do a story about it." The "meeting" turned out to be a gathering of about fifteen young women in someone's apartment. She and her friend arrived late, so whether or not it had had some ostensible purpose or agenda she never discovered. By the time of their arrival the group was well into the heat of a kind of group-therapy session, with each girl in turn bearing witness, as it were, to the outrage done her person as a woman. They talked mostly of sex. One denounced men in the street for assuming that because she wore a miniskirt she was a proper object for their humiliating leers. Another said she finally understood that all this talk about the sexual revolution and new sexual freedom was just men's propaganda to rob girls of an excuse for not going to bed with them. A third confessed, after a certain amount of verbal fidgeting, that she had never had an orgasm. She received a standing ovation. One or two spoke of their hatred for a family system that turned women into "walking wombs" and said they refused to be society's "breeders." All in all, the talk centered largely on the issue of the sanctity of the speakers' persons and bodies and of a great variety of violations being perpetrated thereon. Our girl reporter noted that a number of the women in the room were not wearing brassieres, with the effect of making them look either younger or older.

She herself did not take part in the discussion but knew from the excitement pounding in her breast, an excitement rising to and echoing every word being spoken, that she would not, not yet, be able to write about it either. These girls were ten times more extreme than the lady editor had been. They also seemed, anyway the most articulate of them, to have some theory linking their problems to the evils of capitalist society; this, she had to confess, largely bored her. She had in her time demonstrated with the best of them against the triple evils of war, racism, and poverty that her contemporaries had discovered to be running rampant over the United States today, but she did not take the prospect of revolution seriously, and real Marxists had seemed to her like members of a faith she was willing to tolerate but whose theology left her cold.

But never had she considered social evil as something being done to *her*—which accounted for her reaction to the story of the Columbia girls. She supposed that the kinds of emotion now coursing through her, as yet somewhat inchoate but with their main component a certain sweet bitterness, were the same kinds of emotion as are felt by blacks. She had never liked girls, or the company of girls, that much; though naturally, particularly at her age and in her circumstance, she had several close friends among them. Now she understood that liking or not liking them was beside the point, a smoke screen created by the illusion that she had many more free choices than in fact she had. They were her community. In their new responsibility to themselves as women and to one another as women, they were being responsible to her as well.

She began to read the Movement's documents. Each of them made her feel angry and made her feel good in that peculiar combination she was learning to take for granted. They told her that, like blacks, women were an oppressed class; that more than blacks, they had been oppressed throughout history. But what of the rights they had already won—to vote, to own property, to pursue careers, to move about, to have sexual experience before marriage, to have pleasure in such experience, to plan and control the having of babies? These were bogus, the literature replied. Voting, owning property, getting educated, going to work were all a sham that existed as theoretical opportunity only without true cultural sanction. What did it mean to vote or go to school or go to work for a living if the main assumption of the culture in which these activities took place, and which was shaping the actors themselves, was that they were creatures set apart, with special capacities and incapacities and with their own special roles to play? What did it mean, for instance, that no one would frown on a girl's becoming a doctor if all her life the world had told her, in attitude and word, that this was an ungirllike thing to do? Naturally she would—as she measurably did—show a lack of interest in the necessary scientific discipline. She had from the cradle been wrapped in pink, dressed in frills, encouraged to play with dolls, to read novels, to long for motherhood.

On the subject of sex, these documents, like the women at

the meeting she'd attended, were both outspoken and livid. Women were objects. Their so-called new sexual freedom was only the freedom to have sex, not *not* to have it. Thus the pursuit of this freedom placed them even more squarely under the thumb of male power. And the notion of *pleasure* in sex—this was, several articles went so far as to say, nothing less than an outright male conspiracy. For the very definition of a woman's pleasure now in currency—the attainment of orgasm by means of an act of sexual intercourse—was such as to equate it only with a man's pleasure. In sending women out after sexual equality, men had sought to make them even more dependent than before on the male's capacity to provide. Women without intercourse-induced orgasms had now to deem themselves sexually inadequate, failures. And being no longer required simply to withhold their favors as the true mark of feminine self-respect, they were left doubly the victims of the selfish brutality and inadequacy of others.

There were documents of another sort as well, but these again, like Marxist theory, interested her less. For one thing, they were boring to read, being not so much exchanges of personal experience or expressions of personal rage as laboriously gathered and documented statements of the inequities of women's occupational status. These tended to convert their subject from an oppressed class into a pressure group, like a trade union, a conversion which did not release in her all those good ugly feelings but instead merely oppressed her with the implication of a need to act, to lobby in Washington or something, in general to perform good works. She supposed they were all absolutely true—women such-and-such a percentage of the labor force but only earning such-and-such a percentage of the annual earnings; women PhD's (a subspecies which it had always both tired and intimidated her to contemplate without professional rank; women (this piqued her more) holding only such-and-such a fraction of top executive jobs in the major American corporations. But despite their truth, they did not speak to her.

The Movement, of course, in wide variations of intensity of commitment and grievance, extended far beyond Women's

Lib. At one end there was WITCH, an acronym for Women's International Terrorist Conspiracy from Hell. Its members were, as their name indicated, extremely shrill and from her point of view rather silly. They did things like picketing bridal shows and holding public brassiere burnings. (She continued to wear hers, in enhancement of as fashionably expensive a collection of clothes as she could afford.) On the other side were the kind of women she thought of as old-fashioned feminists, women who followed the lead of Mrs. Betty Friedan, say, author of *The Feminine Mystique*. Their program was to continue to demand in more or less traditional terms rights for women equal to those of men and to harp on such things as the need for young girls to prepare themselves for the securing of their rights, on the need for reordering women's education, and so on. Some few, but by no means all, of the new liberators were lesbians—her one college experience with lesbianism having made her extremely sensitive and accurate in the detection of these. Some, but very far from all, were as her lover had at first attempted to charge: homely, misfits, whose adherence to the Movement represented only their will to avenge themselves on the men who had always ignored them. There were those who, à la the blacks, thought to stage demonstrations against employers, demanding a quota of places for women in the echelons of management; among these there was even a subgroup who, in the staging of one such demonstration against the male editor of a national woman's magazine, insisted on smoking his cigars and using the men's room. She would not have known precisely where to place herself in all this. Demonstrations like the last were certainly not her dish of tea; nevertheless, she supposed they were all in aid of the struggle to call attention to the problem. In any case she was, she had amply demonstrated to herself from college days, not cut out to be a joiner, only a supporter.

Her lover's first response to the Movement had been to giggle—somewhat nervously, she thought. She and their other female friends soon gave him reason to stop giggling. His contention that Women's Lib was nothing but a bunch of lesbians and homely girls grateful for their advances vanished in the discovery that not only she but most of the young, attractive, sexy girls she knew were being strangely roused by its propaganda. Next he tried to reason with her, advancing the arguments of human history, of innate biological difference, professing himself fully and forever liberal on the issue of equal pay for equal work, claiming his own virtue on the score of encouraging and allowing for her career, finally and in exasperation pointing out to her that as a husband he would still be expected to be the breadwinner and that, moreover, in his contentions both with the world and with her at home, he was the one not permitted to cry in the face of mistreatment. (Being a frequent and easy weeper, she was particularly infuriated by this last.) But all to no avail; for as he quickly found out, there is no appeal in argument from the absolute relativity of a position based on culture. Even granting that everything he said were so, she countered, it was still all his fault, since his very argument bespoke a passive acquiescence in the culture that made it so. They did not yet speak of these things as intimate individuals but rather as spokesmen for positions—about the act of sex, concerning which they both knew it impossible with the best will in the world to remain spokesmen, they spoke not at all—because they were not prepared to separate.

The blowup between them over her liberation, when it came, was not about sex either: the possibilities for damaging one another by a head-on confrontation in this area were still too great for either of them to bear. Nor was the quarrel violent. It was, instead, an icy, steely, two-hour conversation which began with a complaint that she had forgotten to buy wine for their dinner; ranging from there across such topics as the unmade bed, his unlaundered shirts, her evident envy of a prize he had recently won for a newsphoto, his having interrupted her in the telling of a story at a recent dinner party; and ending with his assertion that if she were a writer, she would simply write, as he simply took pictures, rather than spend half her time telling anyone who would listen about all the things that made writing difficult for her, and with her counterassertion that if he had been secure as a man, he would have wanted her to be successful rather than being merely permissive about it, which was just a way of withholding his support while pretending not to. They lay in bed that night back to back, each staring out into his particular half of the room and wondering how long, for the sake of one's spiritual health, their affair ought to continue.

They were not to split up right away, for daily habit is powerful. They were possibly not in the end going to split up at all. But between them now, from breakfast to bed, would be the consciousness of a necessary, inevitable enmity and of the need to protect themselves most of all in the very place meant to be a haven from enemies—at home.

III

What had brought this girl to such a pass? She was the pride, if the puzzle, of all who had a hand in her growing up. She was the envy of childhood friends. Even the society against whose "values" she had inveighed was eager to pronounce her, through all its media and honored spokesmen, a superior being to any it had heretofore produced. Nothing either—not even the once operative but now vanished notion of the beginner's apprenticeship to his elders—had stood externally between her and her personal ambition. Moreover, out in the real world, as in school and at home, nothing produced by this ambition would go without at least its due measure of attention. The question of marriage, the question of having children, were now entirely in her own keeping. Yet she saw herself, felt herself, believed herself to be, oppressed. Oppressed by the parents who had always stood in awe of the possibility of her unhappiness; oppressed by the schools which had tracked themselves according to the contours of her particular capacities; oppressed by the working world which had issued her its most solemn invitation; and oppressed above all by the men who had wished to enter with her into some more or less negotiable pact of mutual advantage.

Partly, of course, she felt oppressed because she was invited to do so by the expression all around her of the same feeling in others. Movements like Women's Lib always have some degree of that circularity about them. Which is to say, in addition to being expressions of a deep dissatisfaction, they do themselves constitute a culture of dissatisfaction, which gives it style and sanction among the semblables and *soeurs* of their leaders. And who would not, enjoying something less than divine happiness, be both soothed and excited by the idea that he was indeed a victim?

Still, there must have been, had to have been, a very fertile ground in her own anxieties for all those public discontents to have taken hold there so quickly. A good deal of that anxiety had to do with her need to make a mark in the world. She had for the first time in her life suffered its very real pangs during her freshman year in college, when, bereft of a public identity, she had found herself quite unexpectedly with the need among strangers to, as it were, introduce herself. Such a demand must have existed for college freshmen everywhere and at all times, but no one had been less prepared for it by life than she. Convinced by the attitude of those around her that there would be no let or hindrance to her achievement, she was given to feel, on the other side, no corresponding pinch of necessity. Her condition in fact approached not the least workable definition of freedom: a state in which all the options are open. She could succeed or get by; she could prepare herself to be fully self-supporting, to play some luxuriously "creative" if dependent role, or to enhance herself culturally and spiritually for a life of marriage and homemaking. She could stay in school or she could leave, to the disappointment of family and friends perhaps, but with none of the opprobrium attaching to what for a young man would have constituted the very definition of failure, future as well as present. Therefore she had to choose and in choosing, stake something voluntarily on a definition of herself. This crisis as it was first enacted in school was, as we have seen, short-lived. Not only because she took the option to succeed but because, given her charm and the school's commitment to the idea of what would be the best for her, the institution itself became implicated in her making the "right" choice. There was, then, no genuine settlement, only a deferral of the problem.

Her one brief job counted for very little in this particular connection. For one thing, she had not got herself this job, it was given to her. For another, in her almost immediate decision not to throw in her lot with the magazine's lay the possibility to disregard altogether the question of her performance there. So what she actually knew of jobs she knew from hearsay. First, there was a crucial childhood memory: women sitting in the kitchen mornings over coffee, complaining of the dullness of the days with nothing but children for company while "he" was off in the city, mysteriously but no doubt profitably—and certainly no doubt pleasurably—spending his time "among people." The men who returned home each night had looked in the ordinary way of things tired from a day's work and often worried. Their conversation bespoke anything but a life of far-off adventure—they spoke of money a good deal, of problems, of enemies and allies. But the impression had been fixed: jobs were some kind of preserve of the privileged, they were meant to be interesting.

Then there were the jobs of her friends. Those among them who had been best—*i.e.*, most liberally—educated seemed to have the least satisfying of these. Either, the complaint ran, the job was too routine and boring, or it involved too many worries about things its holder preferred not to have to worry about—too much attention to precise detail, say, or being answerable to too many angry people when something went wrong. Funnily enough, though it was one of the cardinal planks in the feminist platform, very few of the complaints aired in her hearing had to do with money, except as an aspect of the appreciation or lack of appreciation being shown by management for the true qualifications and talents of the complainant. Nor did she ever hear a tale of someone's demanding more money at the risk of her resignation and being turned down.

What she heard most about, though she did not articulate it to herself in so simple a fashion, were problems of status.

The girls she knew who were secretaries resented being
called secretaries, they would without hesitation trade ten
dollars a week for some title that to a hearer would gloss over
their exact position in a hierarchy, and they seemed to resent
most bitterly of all those (to their mind) housewifely services they were expected to provide, such as procuring coffee,
buying gifts, making reservations. And most of them refused
absolutely to work for other women. For it was difficult
enough to "serve" a man, but someone differentiated from
them only by position and title was nearly intolerable. Those,
on the other hand, who had jobs carrying independent responsibility tended to be even more restive, for either the
work was found to contain too large a component of
drudgery or the pay to be insufficiently honorific or—and
this a very common complaint, she'd so briefly made it herself—the purposes of the enterprise for which they were
asked to assume some measure of responsibility were uncongenial to them.

She never heard men issuing such complaints as these, except for that special breed of men she had always in her
mind's privacy dubbed "losers"—who, no matter what they
did, archly or self-righteously pronounced themselves superior
to it and thereby were justified and ennobled in their failure.
And putting all these things together—the "interestingness"
of work to men, its obvious drudgery and lack of dignity for
women—the conclusion was inevitable: the status of women
was that of inferiors, they were not being handed a fair portion of that which had been preempted by and was being
desperately held as the nearly exclusive preserve of men.

She had, to be sure, known men whose every day on the
job involved them in a swallowing of pride, or at least the
resignation to a good deal of unpleasantness, and who
claimed to have no choice on the grounds of their need to
support themselves and others. At college she had even met
young men whose choice of studies and future career had
hinged on some consideration of what was likely to yield the
best return in terms of both money and conditions of work—
though there were clearly many fewer of these than there
had once been—and for them she and her friends had

tended to feel a certain contempt. If there was, then, something of a logical flaw involved in training oneself for a life of monied leisure, in the study, say, of the English novel, only to find oneself bitter about being thought unqualified in spirit as well as training for valuable work, such a flaw was not taken by her friends to be their own. The world had been misrepresented to them, they said; or, more commonly now, the world, precisely in its unwillingness to make proper use of their superior endowments, was an evil place and must be forced to mend its ways.

For herself, a free-lance writer, the problem posed itself somewhat differently. She could not, in the actual conditions of work, claim to be discriminated against. She must inevitably sit down all by herself and face her typewriter. The product of this confrontation had to be judged immediately and found adequate or inadequate. Both the level and quantity of her production were up to her. But her difficulties were immense. She found she could not always do what she intended, and there were times when she would not meet her assignments at all. She often had to undergo that extremely painful experience for writers of having her work emended, altered, questioned, under what she came to feel was an altogether arbitrary editorial eye. In high school, then college, she had heard nothing but priase for whatever she was able to do. Now she was often criticized: editors rejected her, or people took exception to, umbrage at, something she'd published. She started to tighten up more and more at her typewriter. Once, for a period of four or five months, she was unable to write a sentence.

She began to tell herself that the real difficulty lay in the world's expectations of her. The people around her, thinking of her inevitably as a wife and mother, did not care if she wrote or not. Her lover, pretending sympathy, demanded that he have clean shirts and a made bed—her contribution to the upkeep of their common household thus being made equal to her attention to her own concerns. Editors, pretending interest in her, seemed to keep raising the ante on her performance, asking her to take on more and more ambitious projects and to be responsible to more and a wider range of subjects that intimidated her. To this last, she responded with an ever greater concentration on those subjects where her expertise might not be challenged. Finally, with a large assist from Women's Liberation itself, she found it most satisfying to write only about herself.

Primary among the things she wrote about herself was a continuing discussion, carried on through symposia in virtually all the major national magazines, of her attitude to men and sex. She might have suspected there was something slightly redolent of the exploitation of women in the sudden spate of requests to discourse in public on the facts and circumstances of her own sexual temperament, but she did not. In the light of the overwhelming importance the matter had come to assume in her own eyes, she took its importance for others as a matter of course. Whatever reservation she might have had about exposing not only herself but all the men she'd slept with or refused to sleep with vanished under the impact of the knowledge that her experience, far from being private, was exemplary. She told of her unhappiness as a sexual object, of the lack of satisfaction with her so-called freedom; she described the humiliations of her abortion. Her declarations began to feed on themselves, and she truly warmed to her subject.

No one, not even her lovers, was as likely to be taken aback by her revelations as her own parents, particularly her mother. The sexual freedom she had been granted since early girlhood was something that not only had cost them the guilt of discovering in themselves a certain old-fashioned emotional resistance to it that had to be suppressed in the name of principle and fairness of mind, but had brought them considerable pain of simple envy. The freedom so largely denied to and so valiantly striven for by her mother—which striving formed the basis of a vow that her own daughter's sexuality would not be distorted by adult hypocrisy and purposeless social punishment—had been her generation's very definition of sexual equality: the right to live within a single standard of sexual conduct and the corresponding right to demand, as well as to give, sexual pleasure. Now here was her daughter, untortured by the longings that had once imposed upon herself the need for deceit and deviousness, assisted and supported in the realization of her true nature, claiming that it was precisely the possibility to have a wide sexual experience that constituted the major block to women's equality. For, said her daughter in effect, for a girl to be sexually active entangled her all the more with male egos and desires. And to seek pleasure in sex was to involve oneself in judgments of success and failure that were essentially male, and not female, in character. A woman permitted honestly to seek her own needs, as men had since time immemorial been permitted to seek theirs, would be demanding love and respect for and consideration of her person, rather than the direct satisfaction of a lust she was in any case not sure she had ever felt.

Her lover's response to this was not so much to be taken aback as to feel a curious relief mingled with rage and guilt. His boyhood, too—and until this moment he had not realized to how great an extent—had been held in thrall to the myth of the new sexual freedom of women. His success with girls, for instance, had been measured not by the number of them he could bring to submission but by the degree of sexual satisfaction he could bring each or any of them to. Each sexual encounter had been a test of his prowess not as a hunter but as a provider. So to have stalked and overcome his prey was not the end but only the beginning of his labors. To this end, he, too, had been successively monogamous, disciplining the lust which now need shame him only by its most flagrant weaknesses—its impatience and its reluctance to differentiate individuals. With the result, as he said to himself bitterly, that the woman to whom he had given most of himself—to the point, if she had asked it, of marriage— was now telling the world what she had never in deepest intimacy told him: that it had all been for naught. As his rage was that of having been betrayed, so his relief was that of knowing what it was, finally, that stood at the center of those delicate negotiations on which he had lavished so much anxiety, so much deluded consciousness. His guilt grew out of the suspicion that, withal, her problem was his responsibility, that had he but succeeded with her . . . mental habits, especially with respect to sex, after all, die hard; he thought, however, that if she called him selfish oppressor long enough and often enough, he might yet rid himself of that guilt.

As for her, the satisfactions of her new burst of self-expression blinded her to the fact that in the act of announcing women to be the equals of men, what she was really saying was that women were very different from men and that they wanted fundamentally different things. Nor was she aware that in her denunciation of men for keeping her from her true freedom what she was really denouncing them for was their having submitted to an earlier set of female demands, demands which had failed to bring her true happiness, demands she felt enslaved to rather than liberated by, and which she would abjure but knew not now in the name of what.

It is virtually an axiom of human nature that we will not know that which we are not forced to know. Thus given her upbringing and education, our heroine has attained to womanhood knowing very little about men and women. She need not know, for an elementary start, that the sexual revolution which oppresses her is a revolution made in her behalf by other women, wrested from men and assented to by them— as is always the politics of such cases—in the face of the power of the revolutionaries, and not from some notion of particular advantage to themselves. Nor need she, child of a marriage whose manners bespoke equality of husband and wife, know that marriage and children are not things imposed on women by men but quite the other way around. She would in fact be outraged by the proposition, taught in no school either of learning or life ever attended by her, that marriage is not a psychic relationship but a transaction: in which a man forgoes the operations of his blind boyhood lust, and agrees to undertake the support and protection of a family, and receives in exchange the ease and comforts of home.

Above all, being a creature of the sixties rather than the fifties, she need not know that freedom is an end in itself, a value whose strongest connections are thus not with happiness but with responsibility. The freedom granted her by society is, in so short a time as it has been demanded, remarkably equal to that enjoyed by men. It is the freedom to make certain choices and take the consequences. If she wishes to devote herself to marriage, she may do so. If she wishes instead to pursue a career, she may do so. If there are difficulties put in the way of the latter—of which her sex may or may not be one but is certainly not the only one and is often indeed not the one she complains of—she is free to attempt to overcome them. If she opts to have both marriage and a career, she will put herself in the way of certain inevitable practical difficulties, the managing of which will on the other hand also widen her options for gratification.

Perhaps most important, if she wishes not to be a sexual object, she may refrain from being one. What, after all, is to stop her from setting her own social and emotional price on her sexual complicity and then simply waiting for the man, if any, who is willing to pay it? If the price should be deemed too high, that also would be a freely chosen consequence. Or she might accept the implication of most of the pronouncements of Women's Liberation and simply remain chaste, thereby restoring to herself that uniquely feminine power over men which many women so cavalierly made light of in their struggle for equality. Freedom, runs a social theory thought by her educators too stodgy to trouble her pretty head with, can only be granted by others in theory; its realization can lie only in one's enactment of it.

To judge from what she says and does, however—finding only others at fault for her predicaments, speaking always of herself as a means of stating the general case, shedding tears as a means of negotiation—the freedom she truly seeks is of a rather different kind. It is a freedom demanded by children and enjoyed by no one: the freedom from all difficulty. If in the end her society is at fault for anything, it is for allowing her to grow up with the impression that this is something possible to ask. Even the good fairies who attended her birth would never have dared so far.

1970

TWO:

Being a Liberal

1

Thermonuclear War on Film

a. Stanley Kramer's *On the Beach*

At some moment during the course of *On the Beach,* the movie adaptation by Stanley Kramer of Nevil Shute's novel about the end of the world, one of the characters remarks that people must have an instinct for getting indoors and into bed to die. It is this idea which becomes the film's most effective cinematic device for portraying the last days of the last men on earth—after the atomic holocaust, when huge radioactive clouds are sweeping away what the war has left behind. The year is 1964. It is not clear how long the war has been over—a few months maybe, or weeks—or quite how it took place; somewhere there is a hint that the Russians attacked and "were expunged" by an American counterattack. To the best of anyone's knowledge, only Australia (where most of the movie takes place) and New Zealand still boast human habitation, and the scientists are predicting that radioactive dust—moving from the Northern to the Southern Hemisphere—will close in on these places in five or six months and wipe out the whole population in a matter of a few days. There is only one "hope": a scientist has a theory that the Arctic region may for some reason or other have escaped; this theory is exploded in a reconnaissance trip to the Arctic made by the one remaining United States submarine. A strange, unintelligible radio signal from the vicinity of San Diego is investigated, too, and turns out to be the result of a Coke bottle's knocking against a radio key. So the remnant of mankind settle down to die, which, by the end of the film, they have already begun to do—disappearing quietly from the streets.

In fact, everything that happens in *On the Beach* happens quietly. There are countless long slow shots in which the characters go about their final bit of living: fixing the morning tea and warming baby's bottle; sailing wordlessly in a racing yacht; preparing to make love in a country retreat against a background of monotonous drunken singing; even an auto race, with only the steady roar of the cars going around and around the track, becomes a quiet occasion—a handful of unexcited onlookers stand watching, and when the cars crash and burst into flame, to whom can it matter? In the submarine sequence we see American sailors lining up at the periscope for a glimpse of San Francisco (they were in the Pacific during the war, and this is their first sight of home). There is one jittery blast of music, and then San Francisco flashes onto the screen: a ghost city, perfectly intact and totally empty. Everything stands as if it were left but a moment ago, the seamen have nothing to say. For the audience this scene is perhaps more shocking than a heap of burning rubble. Nevil Shute's vision of the end of man by radioactivity has found its most powerful possible expression in Mr. Kramer's notion that only a cowed silence will serve as a response to his scenes of annihilation.

Mr. Kramer's technique depends a great deal on his restraint, his refusal to make any explicit comment about what the movie has to show. There are, for instance, only two real "speeches"—one by Fred Astaire (playing a nuclear physicist) and one by Gregory Peck (the submarine commander) —and even these are made reluctantly, as if they were being dragged up through layers of repression. But beyond restraint there is a refusal to be concerned with the business of how people would in fact behave when faced with the pros-

pect of their own extinction. No one either appearing on the
screen or sitting before it can possibly believe from the evidence of Mr. Kramer's camera that something enormous (to
say nothing of terrifying or awesome) is about to happen.
People walk or ride through the Australian summer streets,
have a party or a picnic at the beach; a wife hopes for a
promotion for her husband; a lady drunk is reclaimed by
love; a man whose wife and children had been left in America turns down the lady's advances on grounds of fidelity.
Here and there someone mentions bravery or "being realis-
tic" or his inability to comprehend what has happened, but
the movie never really makes the point that the last men on
earth must carry on "no matter what" or that they are too
bewildered to do otherwise. For nowhere is there a gesture
to suggest that someone, even for a moment, has been seized
with the knowledge of his certain death.

Radiation sickness, we are told, begins with vomiting and
weakness, then becomes painful and utterly debilitating, and
may take several days to kill. The death it brings is not pic-
tured as particularly ghastly, at least no more ghastly than
several other common forms. No one expresses fear at the
prospect of suffering; and in any case, "when the time comes"
the government distributes a pill to everyone that will effect
a quick, painless suicide. People are seen lining up patiently
in front of the hospitals, stating their names, the names of the
members of their families, being checked off on some mysterious list, receiving a little box containing the proper
dosages. (This is a piece of carrying-on-as-usual that strikes
one not as unreal but as utterly insane. What possible in-
equity—hoarding, say—must such a system be set up to
eliminate?) Suicide is doubly painless here because it doesn't
even have to be committed. When there is no hope for anyone, getting up some morning and taking one small pill becomes a matter of convenience and aesthetic taste.
And since most of mankind has died as a result not of
bombing or starvation but of radioactivity, *On the Beach* is
not upsetting in the way one might expect; on the contrary.
Though it asks us to contemplate the end of the human race

—and though to do so, as we must in this case, through the offices of a group of vital, glamorous people is rather un-nerving—the movie creates a series of images that work to soothe rather than heighten our sense of personal horror. The war is barely mentioned, except as a kind of great be-wildering "it" (whose fault was it? what started it?) and naturally cannot be described since by definition the only survivors are those who never even came near. The two American cities shown, San Francisco and San Diego, were not touched; they were only—and literally—cleaned out: there is not a single corpse to be seen anywhere, not even that of a dog or cat. The stark, oddly thrilling shots of "the destruction" on the West Coast lead us to suppose that ev-eryone, even without the benefit of pills, had enough time to die decently and arranged to do so. Nor is the life in Aus-tralia "postwar" in the usual way. There are some shortages, material and spiritual, but not enough time is left for any of them to become acute. The last community in the world will be allowed to cross over—as the camera assures us most of the already dead have done—instantly from total life to total death.

Now, there may be a certain intellectual horror in knowing that in one moment—or even within the space of a few days —all life on earth will cease. It is, however, not this aspect of a hydrogen war that lies at the base of our deepest anxiety: what we all really fear is the pain, terror, and suffering that would undoubtedly attend such a war, and perhaps even the possibility that we ourselves would be left after it was over, sick and maimed, to pick up the pieces of a contaminated world. A man, moreover, would have to be deeply, even madly religious to suffer *personally* from the idea that in future there will be no men on earth.

Yet this is precisely the idea that *On the Beach* expresses and would presumably stir us into action about. At one point in the film we are shown a Salvation Army meeting: a huge banner hangs in the public square announcing THERE IS STILL TIME . . . BROTHER. Later we see the scene again. This time the square is virtually empty, the preacher's box deserted; the banner which had earlier summoned the Australians to salvation is flapping in the breeze, and now its message is for us. But what is there "still time" for? When Fred Astaire, the nuclear physicist, is called upon to explain why there was a war, he tells his companions it was the result of the existence of weapons that man had learned to manufacture but not to manage. By 1964, then, there are no such things as policies, decisions, responsibilities—only the atom and its inevitabilities. Perhaps for anyone who actually came out on the other side of an atomic war, this view would be right. What would it matter then if the war had been caused by "justified" actions or tragic mistakes? But as for us, is the movie saying there is "still time" to turn back or divert the uses of atomic power—and in favor of what, peace at any price or conventional armaments?

The answer to this question makes no difference. Whatever meaning Mr. Kramer intended the message on the Salvation Army banner to have, the real effect of his movie is not to stir one's fears about anything, least of all about the bomb. If *On the Beach* avoids imagining what the world would really look like after an atomic war and if it never makes an attempt to portray how the last men on earth would behave while waiting for death, this is because Kramer has fallen victim to the most insidious seduction of our time—the seduction of the apocalypse. What he has given us is a fantasy in which all problems are solved by a single explosion. His Australians have achieved that perfect peace in which there is nothing more to do and nothing more to worry about; our life in the cold war seems full of strife and death by comparison. The world they leave behind is portrayed in the sweetly sad images of San Francisco and San Diego and the elegaic last days of Australia rather than in a picture of what must have become of New York or Moscow. There are scientists who say that a *real* atomic war would kill 55,000,000 Americans and leave another 10,000,000 sick or injured. In such a prospect lies the true horror; to imagine that 200,000,000 Americans will be killed is like reading a fairy tale and has much the same effect on our feelings.

Watching *On the Beach* stirs a momentary longing to

achieve what Mr. Kramer claims to be warning us against: a small world from which has been obliterated not only a life of responsibility but even death itself. It is doubtful that anyone leaves the theater thinking about how to prevent an atomic war.

1960

b. The Strangely Polite *Dr. Strangelove*

The most memorable comic elements in Stanley Kubrick's brilliant and impudent movie, *Dr. Strangelove, Or How I Learned to Stop Worrying and Love the Bomb,* are an assortment of visual gags: two airplanes copulating in midair in accompaniment to the screen credits; an infantry battle raging in the focus of a KEEP OFF THE GRASS sign; two hydrogen bombs mottoed "Hi There" and "Dear John"; Peter Sellers in a vaudeville-style battle with a right arm uncontrollably intent on raising itself in a Nazi salute; Slim Pickens flying through the air astraddle a bomb waving his ten-gallon hat; and several others. These gags have undoubtedly done more than anything else in the film to earn Kubrick and his collaborators on the script, Terry Southern and Peter George, their current reputation in some quarters for being radical social healers and, in other quarters, for being tasteless sick-joke makers. For to watch images like these being imposed on a story about the onset of nuclear war—indeed, even to acquiesce in the idea that such a story is a possible occasion for them—is bound to bring with it a *frisson* of overwhelming impiety.

The plot of *Dr. Strangelove* by now probably needs only the barest summary. A psychotic Strategic Air Command general, Jack D. Ripper (Sterling Hayden), convinced that the Russians are poisoning all our "vital body fluids," orders his planes to attack the Soviet Union. The bombers cannot be recalled except by a prior signal of three code letters known only to Ripper, and there is less than two hours' time before they strike. Washington dispatches infantry troops to the SAC base to wrest the code from Ripper, but he declares the troops to be Russian and gets his men to fire on them. By the time the code is finally discovered and the planes called back, a Russian antiaircraft missile has crippled one of them. The damaged aircraft does not receive the countermanding radio signal and continues on to the nearest target. Consultation over the hot line between the President and the Soviet Premier reveals that the Russians no longer have any control over the matter either, for they have recently put into operation a doomsday machine which is triggered to go off automatically the minute Soviet territory is attacked. And so, simulating a conventional suspense by moving back and forth from plane to SAC base to Washington, the film proceeds tautly to the montage of mushroom clouds with which it must inevitably end. Perhaps the greatest tribute to the brilliance and nerviness of Kubrick's impiety is that *Dr. Strangelove does* end with the mushroom clouds, that Kubrick, in other words, did not blink the logical necessity of his creation, and that he succeeded—partly with the aid of background music and partly by sheer cinematic sorcery—in making the sight of one nuclear explosion after another the funniest visual gag of all.

There is also a good deal of verbal joking in the movie—not all of it, however, quite so successful. Many of the jokes are in fact rather more banal than might be thought seemly in a production so insistent on its "advanced" taste in humor ("He is a man of the people, but he is also a man," says the Russian ambassador by way of suggesting that the President might reach the Soviet Premier at a certain unlisted number in Moscow). *Dr. Strangelove* may, as its admirers assert, be bringing fresh air into the murky regions of our social and political insanity, but it certainly does not do so by opening itself anarchically to the possibilities of madness as, say, the Marx Brothers did in *Duck Soup*. On the contrary, within its own confines the movie remains surprisingly careful and measured, with much of its comedy dependent on the simple and time-honored device of having the characters talk and act at cross-purposes. Everything is kept just slightly out of connection with everything else, and the final result is a sort of burlesque on the breakdown of communication, like one of those old Abbott and Costello dialogues. While the pilot of the bomber is promising his crew that they will all be promoted for their part in this historic occasion, President Merkin Muffley (Peter Sellers) and Premier Dmitri Kissoff are arguing over the hot line about which of them feels more truly sorry for what has happened, and a British officer (Peter Sellers again) is in a phone booth with the secret code trying desperately to reach Washington—without change for the phone. And at the center of all this confusion stands the boyish, gum-chewing patriot, Air Force General Buck Turgidson, who suffers from an almost constitutional incapacity to focus on whatever is the issue at hand, and who, as played by George C. Scott in a thoroughly subtle yet muscular performance, becomes the movie's main source of comment on the comedy of mismatched intentions that it conceives the international political situation to be.

A spoof *Dr. Strangelove* certainly is, but the spoofing is neither pure nor perfect, for other impulses are also at work in the movie. No more than Peter Sellers's Dr. Strangelove could control his right arm, it seems, could Stanley Kubrick control his love and great gift for movie making—even when that gift was helping to undercut the movie being made; possibly in a film that makes so much of men's powerlessness, the camera, too, will have its way with them. For example, breaking into a ridiculous picaresque battle at the SAC base, a nervous hand camera suddenly brings a vividly real infantry war onto the screen—which has the momentary effect of destroying the atmosphere of fantasy which is so essential to the comic force of this movie. Similarly, just as Sterling Hayden is making one of his most insane speeches, the camera stops to catch and play over his face (a face to which Kubrick's art has made love before), looking almost statuesquely beautiful and anything but villainously insane.

But apart from such considerations as these, the purity of *Dr. Strangelove* as an anarchic spoof is also compromised by the political partisanship it subtly expresses. Robert Brustein has praised Kubrick for achieving a rare freedom from the "stink" of ideology, right or left, but *Dr. Strangelove* is not nearly so liberated from politics as Mr. Brustein would have it. In fact, the movie throughout plays a curious game with its own political attitudes and with those of the audience, calling on responses to ideas it neither admits to having nor assumes any responsibility for.

About one-third of the action, for instance, takes place in an immense, airless chamber called the War Room. It is here that the President and his advisers confer about whether and how the war might be averted, and it is on the scenes in this room that everything else hangs. The War Room is bare and extravagantly modern, seemingly put together of onyx and plastic and walnut; it is the perfect visual setting for what takes place there—indeed, it is Kubrick's best realized cinematic invention, in a young career that has already produced many. What makes the War Room perfect, however, is not that it is a satiric caricature of nuclear-age government (though at times it is pushed into serving as one), but that it is a brilliantly conceived utopia, a nightmare utopia, the Nowhere of hypothetical speculation inhabited by the minds of the experts on nuclear war.

The War Room is supposed to be in Washington, but it could really be anywhere, underground or even underwater. No one is ever seen entering or leaving (the one person who arrives there in the course of the movie, the Russian ambassador, simply materializes between camera angles). Only a lighted wall map and some telephones on a huge circular conference table bespeak any connection with what is going on outside: as the planes under Ripper's orders advance on and subsequently retreat from the Russian borders, some person or electronic device on the other side of that wall records their progress on the map; the phones establish a few extremely hard-come-by points of contact—with Moscow, with the SAC base, with Turgidson's impatient girlfriend. Inside this nonconnected, nonexistent place, the deliberations carried on fall very naturally into the terms first presented to the world by Herman Kahn, who, as the author of *On Thermonuclear War* and *Thinking About the Unthinkable*, is perhaps the most thoroughgoing negative utopian of our time. The President and Turgidson and Dr. Strangelove, a sinister German nuclear physicist (also played by Peter Sellers, who is so terrifyingly plastic an actor that by himself and in his person he very nearly constitutes a statement on the obliteration of man), discuss precisely those questions that have been outraging the sensibilities of the American liberal intelligentsia for the past several years: questions like, Can the nation survive a nuclear war? What is an "acceptable" number of casualties? Would the survivors of a nuclear war envy the dead? The truth of the matter is that although *Dr. Strangelove* is an adaptation from Peter George's novel *Red Alert*, the movie could very easily have been written by Herman Kahn himself; he outlines just such plots in his books and even calls them "scenarios." To be sure, Kubrick and his collaborators set up all this discourse to poke fun at it, but then—for those who have known how to read him—so does Kahn, who never fails to imagine all the possibilities for chaos in the positions he offers. And where *Dr. Strangelove* is at its best, it most resembles Kahn in the way it rubs the hypothetical up against the real (as, for example, in the character of Buck Turgidson, the movie's most incisive parody of ordinary speech and thought).

Dr. Strangelove, then, bears witness to a curious politico-cultural reversal. Not very long ago (though it feels as though it was very long ago), we were told that every addition to public awareness of the unthinkable—the possibility that there might actually be a nuclear war someday—would serve the evil purpose of making nuclear war thinkable. Now we are invited, for the sake of the very social health that the nuclear strategists were supposed to be jeopardizing, not only to think about the unthinkable but to laugh at it. One must be grateful for every new admittance to the realm of acceptable thought, particularly public thought. But all public reversals, it seems, come with strings attached, even when they are given such a genuinely inspiriting form as a "way-out" movie. *Dr. Strangelove* makes no overt political gestures in the end, but it does make a few covert ones. Indeed, for a work that so obviously regards itself, and that has been so readily taken, as a radical disruption of the going complacencies, *Dr. Strangelove* is strangely polite in its choice of enemies: Jack D. Ripper is not only crazy, he is right-wing crazy; Buck Turgidson is not only sappy, he is sappy on the side of established military power; and the mad scientist Dr. Strangelove is a Nazi. No liberals are ridiculed in this "anarchic" movie, unless one considers President Muffley a liberal, and even then he comes off relatively well. Nor was Kubrick quite daring enough to have risked portraying his nuclear strategist as a Jew—not a Nazi but a refugee, in fact, from Hitler, as so many real-life nuclear strategists are. But to have made Dr. Strangelove a Jew—or on the other side, to have poked as much fun at the inadequacy of pacifist thought in the face of the nuclear danger as it does at the absurdity of strategic thought—would have involved the movie in a complexity—and an anarchism of spirit—quite beyond its basic intentions. And Kubrick in that case would probably not have been extolled for his courage by everyone from Robert Brustein in the *New York Review of Books* to the editorialists of *Life*. Everyone, after all, is against psychotic generals and Nazis.

Several people have remarked that watching *Dr. Strangelove* was as enjoyable to them as it appeared to be to everyone else, but that on leaving the theater, they felt depressed in a way they could not quite understand. Perhaps they were depressed because they had been seduced into feeling they were running free and then found themselves being hurled smack up against an invisible but solid wall of conventional political piety.

1964

2

A Visit to Dachau

With what expectations does someone like me go for the first time to Germany? I am a Jew, an American—and old enough to have spent my adolescence on the passions of World War II. During the war and after, I was a member of that now all but vanished collectivity called the Zionist youth movement. Thus, confronted by issues of life and death, even from so shadowy a distance as the American Middle West, I was a Jew foremost. I still am.

What, then, did I expect? And what did I want? To see a country full of once frenzied and now lobotomized madmen held in check only by the gluttonies of a great prosperity that one would not resent so much if it were indeed serving *that* purpose? Probably there was something of this, some small corner of an earlier primitive vision still left at the bottom of consciousness. But I was too old, too subtilized by the turning of questions this way and that in too many arguments, to believe in satisfactions derived from the refinement of hatred.

Was it, therefore, to "discover" on the other hand that Germans are merely ordinary human beings? In other words, to "forgive" them? Probably there was something of this as well. One wants to forgive, not because it is virtuous to do so but because it is convenient, the lifting of a great burden. Forgiveness is the policy of my government, the habit of my friends, the unspoken assumption of the world all around me. And how tiresome to be forever resisting everything, to walk around with a purity of grievance to which I am not even, strictly speaking, entitled; in short, to be so predictably and so eternally this troublesome, boring, nagging Jew.

But whether these people were monsters or human beings, I had a fear of them, the kind of fear that one wrong word, one previously encountered intonation, one automatically set signal could turn to quivering, blood-pounding rage. The question, before I set out, was quite simply: Would I (and *should* I?) go through my entire first two weeks on German soil without making some scandalous gesture of retribution?

As it turned out, during most of the time we spent in Germany, our feelings about the country rarely came into play. The word had gone ahead to Hamburg; we were "somebodies" and to be treated as a most dignified delegation. We were trotted around, welcomed at hotel luncheons, greeted at *Rathäuser*, given tickets to opera, concerts, theater, introduced to mayors, municipal senators, professors and students, Bundestag members, and even Chancellor Kiesinger. We were left to no chance encounters, no accidental, untidy experiences.

Thus no gestures of retribution, no assertions of any kind, rose to one's impulses. One's purpose got located, so to speak, outside oneself: in the struggle against fatigue and the violent stomach disorder that afflicted each of us in turn, and in the need to make some preliminary sense out of the incredible muddle that is current German speech and thought, public and private. For after all, if you cannot understand what a man is saying, you cannot even arrive at the point of testing your reaction to him. And the Germans I found to be in a muddle about themselves that made my own muddle about them seem as nothing. Their confusion seems to cover everything from the future of German foreign policy (which, as enunciated, seems to me to be based on a theory that one overcomes contradictions by multiplying them) and the meaning of democracy, to the nature of individual, personal aspirations. Germans, even the most sophisticated and clever of them, seem to be drowning one another beneath outpourings of moral, social, and political language whose terms have no precise referents in any conceivable experience. If Nazi Germany was, as they used to say, the land of Wagner, Fichte, and Nietzsche, then present-day Germany is the land of Hegel turned sour. To hear sincere and responsible people maintaining sincerely and responsibly that the elevation of a Nazi Party member of twelve years' standing to the office of Chancellor in effect constitutes proof of Germany's repudiation of Nazism because people did not then take Nazism seriously and do not do so now; or to hear, as we did more than once, an earnest and educated young person attempting to make a distinction between Nazism in the thirties and Nazism in the forties for the purpose of reflecting some sort of credit on the former; these are experiences so baffling that they take hold of one at a place far below the level of judgment or even of emotion. I found myself thinking, What is the *matter* with these people? quite forgetting who they were, or who I was, or the possible meaning of the relation between us.

One thing, at least, was made clear about "these people" from the first moment: they are obsessed with Nazism. Some few Germans that I met would agree. Most would, and did, respond to mention of the Nazis with extreme irritation, self-pity, claims of innocence, attacks on the sins of others, references to their sufferings during the war; and the young, of course, by announcing the year of their birth. But what they say they feel does not matter. Only two things can liven up a truly boring conversation in Germany, make the silent voluble and the phlegmatic lively—a question about reunification or a reference to Nazism.

There was, what with the perpetual round of polite occasions and the effort involved in just pinning down the denotative meanings of words, no time to get further with this obsession of the Germans than merely note it. In fact, I did not want to go further because it occurred to me that this must be a very complicated matter, and what I was *not* seeking above all was a sense of complication.

Nothing, as I was to learn only two days before leaving the country, could have been further from the case. Nazism all of a sudden became a simple phenomenon to understand, and the Germans' inability to cope with it even simpler. This is what I learned, or let us say, relearned, during a one-hour visit to Dachau concentration camp, which is a twenty-minute drive from Munich.

We had planned to go to Dachau, my husband and I, from the first. Before we left New York, our German hosts had thoughtfully and methodically provided us with a checklist on which to make known our particular interests among things to do and see; at the bottom, where the blank was left for "Other—Please Specify," we had, with a slightly unpleasant feeling of triumph and more than a little aggression, scrawled "Dachau and Buchenwald" (the flourish in the act revealing itself through our failure to remember the fact that Buchenwald is in East Germany). You wish to know what kind of people we are so that you may more appropriately entertain us? Very well, then: we are concentration-camp visitors.

Gestures of this kind define one only abstractly. When it came to it, I was not pleased to be making the visit. For where can one go after one has visited a concentration camp (not the worst, we were told, not really a killing camp, not really gassing, mostly shooting, and only, so far as we know, around a hundred thousand killed there)? How does one make conversation with the Germans one has yet to meet? Or perhaps one would feel nothing and so have to confront the problem of whether one was not oneself "dehumanized."

But the visit turned out to be easy. You could feel nothing (and in truth one felt very little) and still get the message. Let me describe the place, what is left of it. Dachau, like, I suppose, all the other camps in West Germany, has been "cleaned up"; its barracks taken down; a chapel of each of the three major faiths constructed on the grounds; its mass graves marked with tasteful memorial plaques, planted with good lawn, and bordered with neat flower beds; its gallows replaced with a marker; its administration building converted into a modern, well-lighted museum of horrors; and everywhere the memorial wreaths with ribbons identifying their donors.

The camp abuts a highway, not a main artery, to be sure, but not a backwoods dirt road either. Your car goes along the road, and right there, just beyond the shoulder, are the barbed wire, the watchtowers, and the ditch, now drained of its water. Beyond the neatly graveled enclosure in which once stood thirty barracks housing some eight thousand men, a pathway takes one across a little footbridge (over a second canal of water) and into the killing area. Here there are two one-story structures, one tiny, one about the size of a well-equipped stable (the size is crucial). The tiny structure houses only a single oven, Dachau's first crematorium, later superseded by three ovens in the other, clearly newer building. This building contains three small gas chambers, one larger one, the three aforementioned ovens, and a small antechamber to same.

My first reaction was disappointment. The other members of our party, there were six of us in all, were offended by the way the camp had been fixed up, prettified. I was far more taken aback by how unimpressive it was, really, to be there. The camps, I realized then, had come to loom in my imagination as vast, seemingly endless places, commensurate in some way with the amount of eternity they had brought to pass in those few short years. (I am told that Auschwitz does, topographically and architecturally, somewhat approximate its own nature.) But Dachau is small, one might almost say cozy—in any case, completely and terribly accessible, traversible, at a brisk pace, in ten to fifteen minutes. Driven by that urge that has something about it of the pornographic and certainly a great deal of the obscene, I was in a hurry to see the gas chambers and the furnaces. These, too, I imagined to be vast, my mind pulled out of proportion by a jumble of figures once at my command: so many hundreds, thousands, in a day, a week, a month. But with all the talk of German efficiency and order, I had not reckoned on German efficiency and order. No space or elaborate equipment was needed, not even for the dispatch of millions. The gas chambers are not great halls into which thousands marched, expecting to take showers: ceilings at most 7 feet high, the smaller ones less wide than the spread of a man's arms, the larger one—I had to think it—about the size of my own kitchen. Passive or resisting, people had to be *pushed* into those chambers—in order to fit. To be sure, Dachau was not a major killing center; it is said the gas chambers were not even used. But they were designed to be used. Clearly, if it is done properly, killing need not take up more than a minimum time or space. And the ovens are just exactly that, about the size of old-fashioned bread ovens. The real point about these ovens is that each body incinerated in them had to be placed, by a pair of human hands, onto a sort of cradle and then slid through a very small door.

All of this is something I was quite capable of imagining about murder Nazi-style when I was twelve years old, and no longer capable of imagining by the time I had reached the age of "reason." It is also something the Germans know, no matter what they did then or say now. They were there. Or their mothers and fathers were there, which is more than good enough. And there is nothing incomprehensible about it: under the Nazis a great number of Germans were beastly people who murdered millions of their fellow humans and took some kind of pleasure in doing so. They also tortured them and took some kind of pleasure in doing so. And for so much murder and so much torture there had to have been a great lust for hatred.

Which is to say that Dachau was not the product, as our theories of totalitarianism have so persuasively had it, of a monstrously rational "system" in which those obedient to the "system" set out to "exterminate" classes of abstract "unpersons." It was the penal institution of a society given up to the blackest urges of mankind, in which men were permitted to starve, torture, shoot, gas, and incinerate other men who had fallen under their power—and in which they did so, *had* to have done so, with gusto.

The proof of this lies in Dachau itself, in its intimacy and personalness. The machinery of Nazi killing is a machinery devised for men to use on others like themselves, and not, as the special explicators of twentieth-century terror have maintained, for the riddance of a pest, the establishment of a "new order." Nowhere in the process was there a provision for the distance, the detachment, necessary to create even so much of physical euphemism as can be found in an ordinary hospital.

Nazism, then, was not some shudder in the great march of history, not even, as the usage is properly applied, a real ism. It was, exactly as we were told by the most lurid movies and nonfiction best sellers of our childhood, an outbreak of madness. *Walpurgisnacht.*

Perversely enough, I left Dachau feeling easier than at any time during our trip about the future of Germany. My rage at the Germans was now direct and, in an answering way, of human proportion. With a madman one knows how to deal. He is to be restrained, and then one day he will die, leaving those after him concerned for the health and happiness of his children.

1967

3

Popular Jews

The career of Mr. Leon Uris tells a curious literary and cultural story. It might at first not seem worthy of note that a gifted writer of hard-core trash should three times out of the last four have made the best-seller lists in America—even though the times have accustomed us to somewhat different standards of book popularity. It might also seem quite natural that sooner or later such a writer would turn his talents to blood-and-thunder novels about illegal immigration to Israel and Jewish resistance to the Nazis in Warsaw; these are exciting subjects which only, as it turned out, needed someone of sufficiently strong stomach to make fictions out of them.

Mr. Uris, however, has done a great deal more than merely wax rich and famous—possibilities, after all, open to any American whose commodity finds its proper market. He has become the master chronicler and ambassador of Jewish aspiration not only to the Gentiles but to the Jews themselves. His commodity has, in fact, found a market far out of proportion, numerically and sociologically, to its special quality. By now it is unlikely that more than a handful of literate Americans have not either read one of his Jewish novels or been engaged in at least one passionate discussion about him with someone who has. I am referring particularly, of course, to *Exodus*, whose early sales were modest though steady and then somehow suddenly mushroomed beyond a publisher's wildest fantasies—and the power of whose effects, both on Jewish morale and on Israel's public relations, was witnessed by a staggeringly varied mass of readers.

In his review of *Exodus* in *Commentary* (June, 1959) Joel Blocker pointed out that the novel took its form directly from the movie it was meant to become. That is so, but somehow the observation does an injustice to the workings of Mr. Uris's genre. Movies, after all, have available to their manipulation the actual physical images of beautiful and glamorous people, movie stars. Mr. Uris's prose *writes* movie stars, which is no simple matter—especially in view of the postures these stars are given to assume. The muscles of every hero must threaten to rip through his clothing; adolescent heroines must awake to the stirring of strange new feelings within their budding breasts; Christian (possibly frigid) ladies must throw themselves at their brooding Jewish fighter-lovers; foreign correspondents and free-lance pilots must lose their hardened cynical hearts; etc. And all through a vast number of pages and carefully researched historical details.

Mila 18 is an account of the Warsaw ghetto uprising of 1943 and is at this writing third on the best-seller list. The book will certainly never achieve the colossal triumph of its predecessor—if for no other reason than that it *has* a predecessor. It is, however, undoubtedly consolidating Mr. Uris's position with the readers of *Exodus*: for it is the same book, covering slightly different ground—the Jewish heroism of *Exodus* carried retroactively, as it were, to the Warsaw Ghetto. The author intends, as he says in a foreword to the paperback edition of *Exodus*, ". . . [to write] about fighting people, people who do not apologize either for being born Jews or the right to live in human dignity." Left "where they rightfully belong, on the cutting-room floor" have been ". . . all those steeped in self-pity . . . all those golden riders of the psychoanalysis couch." Such an intention is foolproof. Who in this world would not happily accept an honest-to-God fighting man in trade for someone who rides couches?

This reviewer must confess that she sat down one evening not long ago with a copy of *Exodus*—after adamantly refusing to read it for two years—and did not move from the chair until morning and the last page. Not only is one, with a book like this, relieved of all the nagging, whining, doubting of most current literature, and provided instead with the refreshment of characters who think simply and act, act, act all the time; one is also on every page succumbing to an irresistible kind of titillation. For Mr. Uris's work is pornographic—not in the sense of being about or arousing sex, but in applying the kind of prurience usually associated with sex to the other human passions. Like the ladies' magazine fiction from which it derives, it is a pornography of the feelings; and this, while perhaps not as universally affecting as true pornography, has much the same power to set off pure fantasies:

> Christopher de Monti held his head between his legs and began to vomit. He vomited until his guts screamed with pain. Page after page it went. The full report of Andrei Androfski, the reports of a handful of survivors of Treblinka and Chelmno and the labor camps.
>
> "God! What have I done?" he cried in anguish. "I am a Judas! I am a Judas!"
>
> The puke and the tears and the pain and the liquor crushed on him and he fell to the floor in a dead faint.

Nevertheless there remains the riddle of why these books by themselves have seemed to accomplish what years of persuasion, arguments, appeals, and knowledge of the events themselves have failed to do—why people have claimed to be converted to Zionism, uplifted, thrilled, enthralled by them. A standard answer, of course, is that novels make facts and ideas vivid. But to get involved in comparing the "vividness" of *Mila 18* with that of, say, a Swedish documentary film called *Mein Kampf* would bring us to subtle and technical questions of social psychology.

The real answer to the riddle lies in the unwitting revolution Mr. Uris has wrought: he has for the first time brought off genuine trash about Jews. I say "unwitting" because Mr. Uris writes as he writes; whatever the subject, his sensibility remains what it is. But for his readers, particularly his Jewish readers, he has created the possibility of seeing Jews not as the troublesome and incomprehensible heroes that decent social conscience has always demanded but as the kind of heroes that middle-class dream life has conditioned us all to make our most immediate responses to. This is of course not to say that nothing bad has ever before been written about Jews under the Nazis or in Israel; in fact, almost nothing good (in a literary way) has. It is to say that nothing has been written about them before without the depressing demands of an inarticulate piety for Jewish experience in Europe; even novels about plushy Jewish life in America are shadowed by it somewhere. "Jewish fate" is always a hint to remind you that this is no easy or pleasurable matter—like the broken glass that is supposed to commemorate national destruction at every wedding. Plunging right into the heart of that Jewish fate at its most terrifying, Mr. Uris has nevertheless created a fantasy that all Americans can at the very least understand and at the most be considerably excited by. It is as if for years and years people who read about Jews had to keep one eye on the next world and now they have been paid off with something for this one.

1961

4

A Good Man Is Hard to Find

And I should hope that I should never cross a picket line; when men are cold and hungry, it takes someone more principled than I to insult them for no better reason than that they are wrong.

—MURRAY KEMPTON

Not the least funereal aspect of a New York City that has come during the past few years to seem ever more distinctly ashen is the disappearance of Murray Kempton from the pages of the New York *Post*. Mr. Kempton's musings on the political and other comedies of our time are still available, to be sure—though in a somewhat altered format—in the *New Republic*. But the very special place they once occupied in the daily life of New York now stands depressingly (perhaps the word is "shamefully") empty. Three times a week, in the bleak years between 1949 and 1963, he broke into the afternoon with a momentarily heightened sense of the reality of things. Sanity has been known to depend on a good deal less.

In spite of the very great comfort of having him around, Mr. Kempton at the time did not always seem to be reliably coherent—either from one event or character under discussion to another or, occasionally, even within the space of a single column. His prose may be the closest thing we have to what the eighteenth century meant by wit; but so much compression, when applied to the kind of subjects Mr.

Kempton was dealing with, sometimes made his observations sound gratuitously tangled or perverse. Moreover, his particular angle of social vision is fixed by the idea that in America what is deemed respectable and what shoddy or criminal is largely a matter of class style—an idea unifying enough, certainly, but one that when worked out in fragments of comment from day to day could look dangerously relativistic. It requires a rare flexibility of maneuver to lay aside the pieties through which, say, the editorial writers of the New York *Times* have been able to distinguish between such people as the labor racketeers and the business establishment that has happily exploited them. Thus in following the columns one often found the same figure being attacked at one moment and defended the next on the ground that his accusers, though classier, were no better.

Even Mr. Kempton's most devoted and admiring readers, then, are apt to be surprised by this collection of his *Post* columns put together under the title *America Comes of Middle Age*. It turns out that he was, in haphazard sequence, writing a *book* all those years. Between hard covers, these pieces do something more than collect well. Whichever of them seemed unduly compressed or strained by itself is now revealed as having suffered from a lack of proper context; and whichever of his positions seemed not altogether consistent can now be seen as having been firmly taken, only with respect to a different problem than the one going by the same name that everyone else was concerned with.

America Comes of Middle Age, as its title makes obvious, is a chronicle of the period that historical shorthand symbolizes as the fifties; in Mr. Kempton's view, "the saddest because they were the most abject years in the history of the United States." And their prevailing atmosphere, he says, has been given a mistaken association:

The Fifties were not the Eisenhower years but the Nixon years. That was the decade when the American lower middle class in the person of this man moved to engrave into the history . . . its own faltering spirit, its self-pity and its envy, its continual anxiety about what the wrong people might think, its whole peevish, resentful whine. The Nixon years belonged to all the young men who had been to the schools which instructed them that they could not be too careful, to the graduates of those courses in how to influence people since it was no longer of value to win friends . . . young men ashamed of their origins and of themselves.

The fifties was the time when among other things our most interesting domestic life was being lived out in a string of Congressional committee hearings, and Kempton's rendering of the period naturally emphasizes the dramas and characters, large and small, that come to mind in connection with people like Kefauver, McCarthy, Velde, Robert Kennedy. Our ardor for official exposures has spent itself; much of this account, in anybody else's telling, might now seem distantly historical. But just as nothing was so typical of America's surrender to "middle age" as the disillusion of liberals with Communists and politicians and labor unions—brought to them weekly through the courtesy of Capitol Hill and the Justice Department—so nothing better represented the kind of wisdom supposed to come with grown-up experience than the writing of Murray Kempton. The events presented in this book are not something we once went through and have for the most part left behind; they are shown as constituting for America one of those moments of moral upheaval in which people have the opportunity to discover something of themselves—provided they have both the courage and plain sense to name what they find.

There were moments when I enjoyed McCarthy. That is why he was a serious figure; in his twisted way, he explained to me how I was not serious enough.

The first chapter or section (there are eight, organized by subject) is devoted to few all-but-forgotten Communists. Putting them first was an important gesture, one that in a way defines Mr. Kempton's mode as a liberal critic. He had learned, as thoroughly and as early as any of his political semblables, what was wrong with the Communists. The people he discusses here, however, were not the Communists featured in the intellectual discussion of the early and mid-fifties—the ones gone mindless and "dehumanized" in the service of the Soviet Union. They were Communists who had done such things as work on the *Daily Worker* for forty dollars a week or who went to jail under the Smith Act. They were, moreover, citizens from whom agencies of the federal government sought to protect our democratic institutions by depriving them of such paid-for privileges as veterans-disability and old-age pensions. Mr. Kempton was perfectly willing to risk being thought fuzzy and sentimental in making sad fun of the idea that a little old lady named Elizabeth Gurley Flynn was a menace to the fabric of our society. And he is willing to risk the same charge now by opening his bid to give an account of America in the cold war with the story of injustices done to some minor individuals.

Along with his anti-Communism, he had also learned that life is tragic and that art is long—and had learned it, what is more, as well and truly as the best of his serious contemporaries. But unlike so many of the latter, he did not carry the lesson to what were parading as its inevitable conclusions. He has always operated not by refusing or rejecting the finest justifications of his culture or by consciously defending them, but precisely by assimilating them to the point where he can admit that even they do not answer to what the heart of a decent and sensitive man demands. He wrote:

> It was a dear, kind theory, and I am only sorry that it did not prove useful for the long pull. I do not apologize for it; the late Philip Murray was the finest man I have ever known and any cause of his would still be good enough for me.

The above passage, describing his attitude to the New Deal liberalism that had proved for him and everyone else so cruelly inadequate, is neither flip nor frivolous. It locates exactly that quality of spirit that kept Mr. Kempton from the theoretical refinement and ideological coarseness into which, as a member of the American intellectual community in the period under question, he was entitled to fall. This is the very quality of spirit that permits him on the one side to discover the true sociology of the American worker in the fact that no one sees fit to clean the filth off a factory floor rather than in terms like "other-directed consumer" or "upward social mobility," and that prompts him on the other side to insist on the distinction between William Buckley and Robert Welch. To borrow the phrase he uses in his chapter of celebrations, Mr. Kempton has always known "the name of the game" he is in. It is a game that all liberals are committed to but that few were unabashed enough not to drop out of when things got complicated; it is called the Fair Shake.

He managed to get through the Nixon age without having given in for more than a moment or two to its almost overpowering seductions: the new theory of a classless America engaged in a religious war against evil; the all-extenuating "reality" of politics that beckoned, say, to an Arthur Schlesinger; or the retreat into literature that ended by defining only those writers who touched the small emotions as "important." He entered the period as a labor reporter and left it as our last best liberal voice. He was always a gifted and satisfying writer; cumulatively, he is a marvelous one. In Mr. Kempton himself, perhaps, more than in what he has communicated of them, lies the best lesson the fifties have to teach.

1963

5

Riesman in the Sixties

Reading through the collection of David Riesman's essays *Abundance for What?* is a peculiarly unpleasant experience. The pieces collected here were originally published or delivered as lectures during the past nine years, and though they fall naturally into four sections divided by subject—"The Impact of the Cold War," "Abundance for What?" "Abundance for Whom?" and "Social Science Research"—all together they comprise a single continuing enterprise: to define the new temper of American life brought about by the conditions of "abundance" or "affluence" or whatever term one chooses to characterize the postwar period. Now, this subject is one that no one living in America can long escape from or fail to feel himself implicated in. It is, moreover, preeminently David Riesman's subject; indeed one might almost say that in *The Lonely Crowd* he invented it. And yet far from providing illumination or even entertainment, *Abundance for What?* only wearies the spirit.

Why this should be so is not quite self-evident. It is not that Riesman has nothing interesting to say. He has all too much that is all too interesting to say. It was, after all, in a review of *The Lonely Crowd* that Lionel Trilling made his now-famous remark about sociology's having taken over the traditional work of the novel, and even in these essays one can see what Trilling meant: Riesman has the kind of imaginative concern for the styles and textures of social behavior that becomes all the more precious as it threatens to disappear (in, oddly enough, this age of sociology).

To be sure—as Daniel Boorstin so heatedly demonstrated in *Book Week*—the difficulty with *Abundance for What?* is partly literary. Riesman is not by any definition of the term a good writer, and this book was clearly edited by a process of agglomeration, by the addition of further notes and comments and explanatory prefaces, when what was needed was a sharply critical blue pencil. Beyond that there is the fact that the essays collected here are not essays at all but memoranda or, rather, hasty outlines for books. With most of the pieces Riesman does not seem to be exploring the subject at hand so much as trying out yet another angle of entry into some imagined new "classic study" of American society. The result of writing under the pressure of this constant straining for the definitive idea and idiom, this operating in a veritable frenzy of extrapolation, is a prose style that is at one and the same time gruelingly explicit and maddeningly general.

Finally, there is Riesman's unfortunate taste for working in collaboration. No fewer than seven of the essays in this book bear the name of a coauthor, and in most of the others one can find at least some touches of an alien hand. Riesman and his collaborators seem to regard social "insights" as so many bits of raw ore that can be refined together in any combination; the broader the combination, the grander and more durable will be the alloy. In the midst of a discussion of the American obsession with being tough, for instance (offered apropos the cold war), one suddenly comes upon the observation that England has produced no figure like Reinhold Niebuhr. Obviously this idea occurred to somebody in passing and was stuck in to enrich the argument; it is the sort of thing—the book is full of them—that makes one want to weep for the demise of narrow pedantry.

If the problem were only—or even centrally—literary,

however, one's discomfort with *Abundance for What?* would be parochial and mean-spirited. Riesman has of course, probably far more than he realizes, been taken over by the rhetorical barbarity of American social science. But unlike most of his colleagues, he has a generous mind and a genuinely playful one. He is also in some way a good deal more modest than they: while he uses pretentious and trashy phrases like "anticipatory socialization" when he means "upbringing"—a habit of social science about which there is nothing left to say—he never quite permits his plain meaning to be clouded over. Riesman really means to discover for us big things, important things, which is the kind of high personal ambition that always demands its measure of humility.

What he means to discover for us are the nature and quality of our discontinuities from the American past. He wants us to see and understand all the ways in which we are new men living in a new society—that just as our fathers' way of life is no longer ours, so their characters and aspirations are no longer ours. There seems to be no need to rehearse his main theme, which was set down in *The Lonely Crowd* and has become almost a platitude of serious social thought since then: that technology increasingly shifts our basic relation to the world's goods from that of producers to that of consumers and that this shift is bringing with it radical revisions in some of the patterns of our social behavior. Furthermore, these new patterns are, at least so far, attended by a curious feeling of malaise—call it apathy, conformity, "other-directedness." There is no educated American by now—thanks in great measure to Riesman himself—who cannot in some way articulate the effect on our national habits of the fact that we are richer than ever before at a cost of less human labor than ever before: that we do not save but spend, that we do not risk but play the odds, that we tend to seek our comforts and pleasures in a more or less uniform way. Though the "other-directed" man does not appear by name in the present volume, he nevertheless remains the author's main protagonist. In their politics, problems of work, leisure, education and family life, the Americans of *Abundance for What?* are the same largely passive creatures of social manipulation as the other-directed men of *The Lonely Crowd.*

The trouble is that the very intellectual quality that manifests itself as openness and playfulness of mind also serves to undermine Riesman's usefulness as an observer of other people's lives and behavior. In creating his typology of "inner-" and "other-directed" men, he was undoubtedly trying to extend into our own day some form of Max Weber's apprehension of the relation between Calvinism and capitalism. He was trying, that is, to analyze what he saw as the new American "religion" of sociability in terms of the pressing new need to have the profusion of goods produced by an advanced technology efficiently consumed. But there is this difference between Weber and Riesman: to Weber, religion and capitalism were *real,* as were the human beings caught in their toils. To Riesman, on the other hand, as his very choice of approach shows, the things of which he speaks are not real but have only the limits his speculation gives to them. Consumption, after all, is not an institution, it is an activity and an ephemeral one at that; sociability is not a belief nor even a clue to character, it is a style of behavior. Riesman's data, in other words, are not institutions or ideologies but *styles.* When he talks about the middle class or the working class, for example, what he conjures up for us are images of the fashions that have prevailed among these groups for the past twenty years. Fashions can tell us a good deal about the economic and even the political conditions of a particular society. But what about the men who are given over to them? For Riesman the members of society are not men whose lives and strivings are ransomed to forces over which they have no control—the forces of nature or the forces of history; nor are they even (like Max Weber's Calvinists) men who really believe what their roles in society have required that they believe. They are mere semblances shaped now this way and now that by conditions that are themselves only semblances.

The story of what happened at the Hawthorne plant of the Western Electric Company is a perhaps minor but exemplary illustration. In the late twenties, as Riesman tells it, a group of psychoanalytically oriented social workers set up in the plant a program for nondirective interviews with the workers. The workers were invited to come and air their gripes. However, since the interviews were only intended as therapy —a time for the unburdening of grievances and problems— the interviewers made no report to the management of what they heard and did not intercede on behalf of their complaining subjects. At first the employees believed that the social workers were there to help effect changes in the plant, and morale was given an enormous boost. But by 1948, when Riesman went to visit Hawthorne, the workers were of course fully aware of the practical futility of these interviews and were quite indifferent to the whole interview program. Their indifference might have seemed the most natural and obvious response of sensible people to something that was getting them absolutely nowhere. Riesman, however, found a different explanation:

> One factor which might be important is the shift in the impact of permissiveness. When the program began, many employees at Hawthorne were poor, isolated immigrant women who were intimidated by their bosses in the plant, at home, and in the precinct. . . . *As* the milieu is now less aggressively directive, *so* there's a different breed of girls working there now [italics mine].

Riesman simply cannot *see* the manipulative attempt being made on those workers. He cannot see it because his very description is part of the same attempt writ large. The social workers were engaged in a shoddy—and all the more shoddy because unwitting—effort to do the Hawthorne employees out of their grievances with a "therapy" that had no reference or relation to the actual content of those grievances. Riesman's treatment of the problems besetting his contemporary Americans, like his "explanation" of the Hawthorne workers, is similarly "nondirective." For him, attitudes and forms of behavior—whether in relation to war, to the raising of children, to deprivation, or whatever—are never responses to real conditions Out There but always and exclusively the result of the conditioning of a man's milieu. If the postwar American malaise has indeed to do with people's inability to take the soundings of an independently experienced reality—as he himself has said it does—then his own work, to the extent that it succeeds in influencing American culture, must only serve to contribute to that malaise.

Reading David Riesman, then, is like being in a hall of mirrors. The literature that teaches us about "other-directedness" is itself totally other-directed. The essays from which we learn of a widespread acquiescence in the demands of the surrounding culture confirm themselves by their own acquiescence. The unpleasant experience one has in reading *Abundance for What?* is, finally, vertigo.

1964

6

Anti-Americanism in America

I have a gloomy premonition . . . that we will soon look back
on this troubled moment as a golden time of freedom and license
to act and speculate. One feels the steely sinews of the tiger, an
ascetic, "moral," and authoritarian reign of piety and iron.
—ROBERT LOWELL in a *Partisan Review* symposium

It is no insignificant trait of contemporary history that in
its rhythm of assigning epochs the decade seems to have
replaced the century. Who among Americans, and particularly among American intellectuals, cannot pithily characterize the twenties, the thirties, the fifties? Each of them is now
from our vantage point seen to have had its own unmistakable social flavor: its own politics, its own sense of life, its own
dictates of public and private comportment, its own literature. (Only the forties have been scanted in these characterizations, given over as they were to the war and its immediate
aftermath and thus to the strains of what was past and what
was coming.)

History, to be sure, cannot be so tidy as to mete itself out
in ten-year measures. The decade to which we have affixed
his name, for instance, did not find Dwight D. Eisenhower in
the White House until two years after its inception. Similarly
with the thirties, which in some important sense can be said
to have been over in 1937 or '38. Still, there is more than
mere convenience in describing certain patterns of American
life and thought in these terms. They do, after all, reflect the

rhythm, if not the exact chronology, of our spiritual development. In any case, everyone knows what one means by them. The twenties were the time—the Eighteenth Amendment to the Constitution notwithstanding—of the explosive, exuberant, and sureminded throwing off of American provincialism and small-town puritanism. The thirties were the time of a new, grown-up membership in the society of the Old World—a participation in the crises of what looked then to be its detumescence, a tuning-in to its intellectual currents, and, finally, a bloody and costly sharing in its salvation. And the fifties were the years when America self-consciously assumed the role of the world's major conservative power, with everything that such a position implies—including an internal atmosphere ridden with, on the one hand, high and righteous self-definition and, on the other, with a spirit of the most dulling prudence and caution.

An American adult of today, then, has in his ordinary lifetime virtually spanned ages. His mind and imagination have been confronted with the demand that they make room for, accommodate themselves to, five traditional lifetimes' worth of issues, movements, countermovements, revolutions, consolidations, and counterreactions. His life-style—the expression of his sense of social relations, his values, his aspirations —has been assaulted not only by a technology that continually renders itself and the issues it creates obsolete but by shifts in basic fashion that are, to say the least, unnerving in their rapidity. He sees himself separated by experience and attitude not only, as his modernity has prepared him to be, from his children but even from those five years younger than he. He struggles to incorporate a new system of thought which, somewhere, a new vanguard has already set itself up to discredit.

An exemplary serious and educated American has without yet becoming an old man had something like the following spiritual odyssey. He has, with the writers of the twenties, thrown off the repressions and hypocrisies of the traditional bourgeoisie. He has accepted the liberations and burdens of Freudianism. He has, with or without any of the party affiliations that might follow therefrom, taken over the Marxian critique of capitalism and the class society and, again regardless of party affiliation, on the other side been profoundly influenced by conservative warnings about the depradations against culture of the newly empowered masses. He has discovered the possibilities for totalitarianism—implicit in Marxism, explicit in Leninism—in the attempt at a radical reordering of society. Following on this, he has come to acknowledge the evolution of American capitalism into a variant system no longer comprehended in the categories of its traditional critics and, moreover, to grant its superiority to other economic systems as a means at least for the release of wealth. He has, largely through the agency of the Nazi episode in Europe, discovered in the heart of man an evil no mere social programming can hope to bring totally under control, much less eradicate. And he has discovered in turn that the preoccupation with such evil can be dangerously allied to complacency about those ills and inequities in the life of society that can, in fact, be remedied. Most recently . . . but of now later.

Taken all together, these ideas may sound like the very recipe for human "wisdom"—each view set off by another which softens, modifies, modulates it, and the whole, a balanced and "stable" amalgam. They have not, however, *been* taken all together but rather come into intellectual power in a series over four decades, each of them for a time supplying the central impulse to a new movement of thought. Nor in the end would the wisdom resulting from the judicious combination of ideas and the critiques of ideas probably be worth very much. If the description of his odyssey makes the exemplary intellectual* sound, with desperate injustice, a little foolish, it must be remembered that such views as he has incorporated are not purchasable by choice but are the hard-won coin of experience and the effort to make sense out of that experience.

---

* Terms such as these are as necessary as they are questionable and require their user to stop and state his case: by "intellectual" I mean quite simply a man whose life is committed to the direction of his thought. In his *Armies of the Night* Norman Mailer describes such a man as one deeply limited by the inexorable "logic-of-the-next-step." So be it.

Ideas are powerful things, requiring not a studied contemplation but an action, even if it is only an inner action. Their acquisition obligates a man in some way to change his life, even if it is only his inner life. They demand to be stood for. They dictate where a man must concentrate his vision. They determine his moral and intellectual priorities. They provide him with allies and make him enemies. In short, ideas impose an interest in their ultimate fate which goes far beyond the realm of the merely reasonable.

This is what accounts for the rabbitlike rate at which new cultural "generations" are produced in America. For a "generation" under these conditions represents not a new batch of the young who have come of age but a new preoccupation which has found its style and its rhetoric. (It is also what accounts for the fact that many Europeans, and particularly for some reason Englishmen, find American intellectual life to be so full of brute vitality by comparison with their own: the arguments they witness among us are often battles in which men are fighting for their lives.)

In any case, to have taken part in what Lionel Trilling once called "the life of the mind" has been a peculiarly double experience: energizing and enervating, offering promise and promising despair. Each succeeding decade has come to an end with its own record of disillusion and bewilderment. Each new decade has begun with its own hinted promise of a revised and corrected, perhaps this time eternal, vision.

Of course, simple stylishness has also played its part in these dizzying shifts of attitude and preoccupation: vogues in thought serve momentarily to brighten the life much as vogues in dress. The point was once brilliantly illuminated by the historian R. A. Nisbet when he observed that one of the most underrated social forces in history is plain boredom. And how could even the most dedicated intellectual community resist the hunger for the new that stalks American society in general and the insatiable media of mass communication in particular? But whatever the motive behind one's submission to them, ideas about the world, as we have noted, are consequential. Even slogans, whose original purpose— take two leading slogans of the sixties, "Black Power" and

"The War on Poverty"—is only to call people out of some impasse (or solace them while they remain there), can often turn the course of events.

II

And what of the sixties—which will soon be drawing to a close? What was their promise, and what will prove to have been their disillusion? Naturally, in one way it is too soon to talk of the sixties; something of their drama remains yet to be played out. Nevertheless, certain things are already clear. The first of these is that the sixties will—like the thirties, though in a rather different sense from them—be seen as a turbulent, a "radical," decade. And the second is that it will be known as the decade of the Vietnam war—despite the fact that consciousness of the war did not become keen or central until the decade was nearly halfway over.

Both of these characterizations would have seemed astonishing in 1960; for the decade, to begin at the beginning, opened not with the threat of ugly tension and war but, on the contrary, with the promise of a new series of triumphs for American liberal democracy. This promise was one which had lain dormant through the years of war and cold war, years in which the system was seen to be hanging on by its fingernails and was accounted well merely to have remained intact. A new sense of possibility was, now, not so much to be released as to explode—with all the energy of one of those historic revelations about what might be attainable if people only willed it to be.

The revelation was communicated in the main from two very different sources and in two very different ways. First, intelligibly, from the political reordering implied in the strategy of massive nonviolent protest which had recently been adopted by the civil-rights movement. And second, mystically, through the personality of John F. Kennedy. The meaning of the grand surge of protest that began with the Montgomery bus boycott—and that was obviously, despite whatever horrors along the way, going to make its effect—lay in the assurance that there was after all a simple, noble, and *aesthetically pleasing* way to bring to an end the age-old scandal of American society. (Criminally callow as this response seems today, what it most reflected was a longing to throw off that sense of social complexity which had since the onset of the cold war hung like a dead weight over all our imaginings of the future.)

The effect of Kennedy is considerably more difficult to define. It had to do with his youth, his beauty, his—odious word—style, his being unlike our—even more odious word—image of a politician. Norman Mailer, for instance, in a long essay describing the Democratic convention that nominated Kennedy, spoke of the quality of cold liberation that came off the man and predicted what did in some way happen, that Kennedy's candidacy and election would help to release a host of energies and impulses long storing up in the psychic underground. Just how this release came about must be a question for future historians of American culture to decide. The point is that Kennedy's presence in the White House did, in fact, have such an effect—almost without regard to his policies or record. (Just as his assassination three years later set off a widespread feeling of personal desolation that went much deeper than simply shock at the murder of the President.)

Meanwhile, that process in U.S.-Soviet relations which had been converting containment to coesixtence and coexistence into something called "the thaw"—however chancy or reversible it might prove to be—had begun to still some of the anxiety that seemed earlier to condition all of life. And perhaps even more important than the abatement of anxiety it afforded, the coming to an end of the cold war left space in the political thought that it had been so totally occupying for other and fresher problems. Americans suddenly "discovered" that some 40,000,000 of their number were still living in great poverty. It was rumored that in a number of universities students were no longer apathetically figuring the angles—as they had done in the decade preceding—but were returning to the passionate study of modern history, social justice, and Marx. The demand for nuclear disarmament was receiving a growing, and growingly respectful, hearing, at least in the major cities and possibly even in Washington. Popular entertainment, on stage, in films, and on the printed page, was being touched by a healing and invigorating new impiety. Books were being written and widely read which helped to explain why the fifties, after all on the whole a comparatively peaceful and comfortable time, had left so many people feeling so bad, their lives so confined and narrow, their young so cynical or delinquent.

The triumphs for liberal democracy that seemed forthcoming in the early sixties were not, to be sure, millennial ones—and perhaps not even material ones. They consisted largely in things of the spirit: public tones and postures, the terms and modes of public debate, the nature of the issues debated, the simple willingness to acknowledge the existence of serious national problems, the eagerness to pursue new thoughts and the hospitality bestowed upon those who thought them, a banishing of priggishness from high places, a new tolerance and even sympathy for the liberties needfully taken by the arts and by artists—in short, those things of the spirit which enlightened Americans, no matter how hard-nosed the times teach them to be, never really lose their abiding faith in. Combined with the proper legislation—not then, as it was usually not, given much searching attention—and the necessary adjustment of our posture toward the rest of the world —to some extent being undertaken by the Kennedy administration—the new spirit would be moving us a step or two anyway in the direction where the millennium might one day be discovered. Or if not the millennium, then at least the possibility for a reasonably stable world, a reasonably just society in the United States, and a reasonably attractive quality to life.

A great sigh of relief went up among the intellectuals (though that it did so would no doubt now be hotly denied by the majority of them) at the fact that they were, and once more in good conscience could be, liberals. The term "liberal" was not one that many people were to use. In the fifties

it had come to be something of a dirty word: one generally
used it with reference to oneself only in irony and reserved
it in its uninverted sense for others who displayed either an
unwonted simplemindedness or an unthinking loyalty to old
cant. Insofar as it had been known truly to apply to one,
liberalism represented a compromise with one's anxious
quiescence parading under the banner of the tragic: it meant
a highly articulate, sophisticated, and well-documented ac-
commodation to things as they were. Thus the word was to
have little currency in the new prevailing atmosphere; people much preferred "radical." Nevertheless, the early sixties
were in fact a moment when intellectuals could and did
dream of influencing the taste for change being expressed by
their government and by the society around them. This moment had arrived, moreover—it is a crucial point—within a
system still operating by the most ordinary give-and-take of
American politics. It had arrived without apocalypse, without even the help of most intellectuals in bringing it, and
without appearing to threaten those comforts the society had
already provided. The Negro, it then seemed, might at last
be integrated without any fundamental overhauling of that
system, the poor might at last be led out of poverty, the
peace of the world at least minimally guaranteed, the educational system revamped, etc., etc.—all through the workings
of a new spirit of willingness and the application of new and
as yet untried ideas ("new ideas" was a favorite commodity
of the Kennedy administration, and it sought experts to provide them in every field). Even the notion that an advanced
technological society like ours might simply do away with
money as the medium for the distribution of life's necessities
was advanced by a social thinker or two without any reference to the inevitability of political upheaval. It was the
imagination that was to be radical; the system would be
plastic enough to incorporate it. The new active liberals had
the comfort once more of knowing what there was to care
about and, somewhat more vaguely, what it was they wished
to advocate. People were beginning to have fun and con-
gratulated themselves.

III

Some seven or eight years have now gone by since the days described above. Their joyousness has been intentionally exaggerated (without a mention of the Berlin Wall or Bay of Pigs or a survey of the New Frontier's actual record on the issues of civil rights and poverty) because people who are committed to the shaping force of their ideas tend more than others to gloss over the texture of past experience—difficult in any case to keep hold of in the torrential rush of decades. *Of course* not everyone who expressed himself in that period was expressing enthusiasm unbounded. Of course such new political vitality as there was was braced by a hard-won and not so foolishly to be surrendered skepticism. Nevertheless, something of all this there was—I speak here not of the words alone but of the music, and the music said things are better for earnest men, better than they have been in a long, long time.

During seven years, then—five, really—the atmosphere in the universities and centers of culture has sharply turned from a new wave of liberal enthusiasm to a storm of reckless, nihilistic, and profoundly despairing radicalism. All the things that had seemed most hopeful at the beginning of the decade have become precisely the sorest spots in this new radical sensibility.

The desire for a relaxation of American moral fervor against some abstraction called Communism has been completely reversed into a powerful moral fervor against some abstraction called imperialism or capitalism (read, America) ; many of the people who most vociferously gave voice to the first now burn their ritual candles at the shrine of the second. The demand that the Negro be given his rightful place in the centers of white society has been muffled under a raucous cry of doom to that society; and many of the same people who applauded that demand and seconded it now applaud and second the longing for destruction that supplanted it. The poor whose release from the ugliness of poverty was to be the first order of social business are now exhorted by those who lead their cause to make a subversive

value of their poverty; and many of the people who once sought
to offer them some greater share of the nation's wealth now
seek to support their subversion of the values needed to create
that wealth. The cities that were to provide the centers for
America's new forays into a more graceful and vivacious life
now teeter at the edge of destruction as viable political and ad-
ministrative entities—and at the edge, some of them, of
destruction period; and many of the people who had been the
most eager to take part in the social experimentation they
promised to yield are now the most eager to pronounce them
hopeless. Hallucinogenic drugs have powered and ratified a
new youth culture that dictates disengagement from all forms
of social and intellectual discipline, a settlement into creature
existence, and a total, exclusive submission to the realm of self;
and many of the people who once cheered the emergence of a
serious, active, and disciplined youth—particularly after the
disengaged and self-full fifties—now sympathize with the claims
of that culture and, with a reckless disloyalty to the standards once imposed on their own intellectual formation,
support its products.

Nothing serves better to illustrate the tone and feel of this
shift than the career of Stokely Carmichael. That the man
who had once been a leader in a serious, determined, and
day-by-day attack on the unequal status of the Southern
Negro—an attack whose nonviolence was the mark not of
weakness but precisely of its determination to succeed once
and for all—should now be spending his days making futile
desperado announcements of a coming retaliatory terror
against white society seems to sum up a great deal about the
current decade. Future generations may one day blandly find
in this career merely a symptom of the inevitable dynamics
of the Negro Revolution caught at midpoint. For after win-
ning what there was to be won, or very nearly so, in the way
of Constitutional redress, the Negro's condition as a powerless minority was logically to require the transfer of his demands from integration to "black power." In the lofty and
distant view which the future, looking back, so properly ar-
rogates to itself, there will not necessarily be much attention
paid to the violent language and behavior through which the

Negro first set out to add his weight to the balance of American urban politics. Nor may the rioting in Northern urban ghettos be recorded as anything more than "incidents" in a certain process of political and social reorganization. Nor, certainly, may the use of the Vietnam war as the justification for the declaration of absolute, worldwide racial enmity—as Carmichael and his colleagues and sympathizers now use it—appear as anything other than the taking advantage of a certain historical coincidence to sharpen the pride and group consciousness of American Negroes. For many of his contemporaries, however, most particularly for those who share with him a coming of age in the sixties, Stokely Carmichael embodies something very large and real in their own current sense of life. He has become the very personification of their sudden total and implacable hatred for American society.

As a public spokesman, of course, Carmichael has to some extent been the victim of his listeners, and in this, too, he is peculiarly representative of the time. For they have not resisted him, have not even demanded that he make sense. They ask only that he speak to their mood, like people in search of entertainment. If and when he fails to thrill them, he will simply be abandoned, like so many before him, to the escalations of his own spirit. The role of "box office," like that of boredom, is one that modern social critics would do well to ponder.

But if the fate of civil-rights militancy illustrates the change in temper most dramatically, that is only because it is the most definable and containable of the present welter of public issues. The course from hope to despair has been run at exactly the same pace, and by exactly the same plotting of curve, in the realms of foreign policy, domestic politics, and the arts. The new position of "despair"* proceeds from one axiom: the American system has come to evil, it must in one way or another be undermined at its foundations.

The corollaries of this axiom are several, and stand in a

* I use quotation marks not because the despair is not real but because it is a despair of adopted posture rather than individual feeling; unlike personal despair, which counsels resignation and silence, it has brought with it a veritable whirlwind of energy, action, sociability, and noisemaking.

complicated relation to one another. The first corollary is
that any and all of America's difficulties abroad are of her
own making and are thus amenable to her own unilateral
unmaking. Supplying documentation for this view is a whole
new enterprise in historiography—undertaken by such historians as William Appleman Williams, Staughton Lynd, Gar
Alperovitz—which seeks to revise our theories about the
onset of the cold war and the assignment of responsibility for
it. The engine driving this enterprise and supplying its tone
is the notion that by the end of World War II the United
States had become the world's leading imperial power, in the
face of whose possibly blind but inevitable will to aggran-
dizement the Soviet Union had to move to protect itself.
Such a notion is, of course, not new, only the application to a
more recent history of the theory of "capitalist encirclement"
advanced in defense of the Soviet Union in the thirties. Many
of these historians' most ardent students had not even been
born in the thirties, however, and by one of those quirks of
the American educational system—which appears to teach
its students to maintain a proper skepticism only toward the
experience and earned wisdom of their elders—they seem
not to recognize behind all this merely the reversion to an
older formula of good and evil than the one their mentors
would have them discredit. In practice, the application of
this attitude means that while, for instance, in demonstrating
one's opposition to the Vietnam war one does not necessarily
wish to march under the flag of the Vietcong, neither does
one wish to be intolerant of or make open quarrel with those
who do. One might not necessarily wish to give aid and comfort to one's country's enemies, but it is, after all, only by
virtue of her own lust for power and profit that she *has* enemies.

Another corollary is that any and all of America's domestic
difficulties are the result of the ill will of white society. In
practice, then, while one might not necessarily wish for the
Schadenfreude of the anarchic destruction of our cities, neither does one have the heart to make open quarrel with those
who do. One need not necessarily favor the terrorization of
one's innocent fellow citizens—white *and* black—but after

all, no one of white skin, and no one of black skin willing to remain at peace in this society, is by one's own theoretical lights quite innocent.

Nor need one—in the realm of culture—take complete satisfaction from the evidence in one's own party of a growing illiteracy and a complacent disregard for all the hard work, hard thought, and hard spiritual discipline contained within the Western cultural tradition. But neither would one wish to oppose the spiritual freedom claimed by those who do make a principle of such disregard; to do so would be not only "square" but in some sense to affirm and perpetuate a curse on all mankind. For after all, that tradition has been placed in the keeping of heavy-handed and pusillanimous academic bureaucrats and has been made to serve the purposes of an evil status quo.

IV

What has happened to create so nearly seismic a reversal of spirit? Much of the answer can be covered in three words: the Vietnam war. To put the matter very flatly, the government of the United States has become involved in a military venture which to the vast majority of the educated, enlightened, liberal community of Americans seems at the very least senseless and at the worst evil. Implied by these three words, however, is a problem far greater and more thoroughgoing than a merely bitterly unpopular government policy. Any military venture of the United States, to be sure, would in these days be fearfully opposed by that community; the existence of a vast nuclear weaponry throughout the world has, as Hans J. Morgenthau many years ago predicted it would, virtually ruled out the waging of war as a means for settling foreign disputes or securing new arrangements of international power.

The Vietnam war bespeaks a much greater failure than the failure to—or even a foolhardy unconcern to—keep the peace. Coming as it did hard on the heels of a new belief that our foreign policy would at last replace the mechanical reflex ideology of the cold war with a flexible system of re-

sponse to individual local problems, Johnson's escalation in
Vietnam exposed the fact that the governing establishment
of this country placed no credit whatsoever in that belief.
Our "commitment" to the Republic of Vietnam could still be
thought of as one of a complicated leftover tangle of holding
actions and alliances; our direct and relatively large-scale
intervention in a civil war—even in countering an intervention made on behalf of the other side—spelled out America's
continuing determination to let no further inch of ground fall
to the Communists. The same determination was evinced in
our intervention in the Dominican Republic, but left by itself, the Dominican adventure might still have seemed only
an ugly blunder.

There was, then, to be no new American foreign policy,
only a new enemy—and an increasingly desperate application of all the old justifications for dealing with him. What
had appeared to be a genuine new adjustment of attitude
could now be seen to have depended entirely on the fact that
for three years our foreign dealings had been in the hands of
a man with a penchant for traditional civilized diplomacy
and a talent for operating without a full-blown policy. The
"new look" under Kennedy had been Kennedy's alone, personal to him and, as it turned out, to only a few of his advisers; it had not been established in government beyond his
person. Now, under Johnson, America was once more to return to being (or if you will, remain), in the accent of the
late John Foster Dulles, "anti-Commonist." In a sense, it was
to be more purely anti-Communist than in the fifties, since
the demise of a centrally controlled worldwide Communist
conspiracy now made it less easy for government spokesmen
to maintain their former confusion between the containment
of a single hostile power, Russia, and the defeat of a hateful
political order, Communism. Not that the attempt has not
been made to identify this new holding back of the tide of
Asian Communism with the containment of an aggressively
expanding China. But in a world which has learned to dis-
count the myth of the Communist monolith—and which is
anyway apt, in the face of all the evidence, to remain somewhat skeptical of the picture of China ready and able to

swallow all of Southeast Asia country by country—the analogy will not wash.

Thus though Johnson has personally borne the brunt of the blame for the mess in Vietnam, some opponents of the war, with considerable justice, find Johnson himself to be only the perfect representative of a larger, and as they would have it, reactionary ruling class. Enough talk of "aggressive Communism"—particularly in a period of hot, and unpopular, warfare—must sooner or later, it seems, breed its own corresponding talk of "aggressive capitalism." In any case, while a continuing sterility in foreign policy, as under Eisenhower, creates a feeling of acute frustration, the dashing of a promise for better things, such as Johnson was responsible for, creates a far deeper response of demoralization.

Beyond the war itself and what it means for the state of American foreign policy, this mood of demoralization has been even further deepened by the almost diabolical lack of public candor with which the citizenry has been treated on this subject. We have very nearly attained to that Orwellian nightmare in which "peace" means "war," "victory" means "defeat," and "consensus" means "individual will." If Johnson has at least an arguable case—and even some of his opponents might still be willing to believe he does—he behaves as if he does not. Senators who dissent from his policy, we are told, no longer have access to his person. Persuasion of the opposition consists almost exclusively of references to public-opinion polls which show them to be in a minority, or pronouncements, such as that given in a newspaper interview by John Roche, a member of the White House staff, to the effect that the President's opponents are isolated and unimportant people. Reports on the progress of the war consist almost exclusively of daily tallies of the enemy dead. And behind all of this there is an atmosphere emanating from Washington of ever-increasing petulance and bad temper—frequently, in this psychologically oriented age, taken to be the mark of an uneasy conscience.

Americans have of course—and with little benefit to the commonweal—had long training in taking for granted the disparity between government statement and government in-

tention. Had not the Eisenhower administration assured us
that it would not rest content with the mere containment of
Soviet power but would seek to do everything within its
means to assist in bringing Eastern Europe to full democratic
liberation? The majority of Americans were obviously quite
content not to have to believe it. Did not both Nixon and
Kennedy make stirring martial gestures in the direction of
Cuba during their respective Presidential campaigns? Again,
people instinctively understood the game and did not take
them at face value. Any keeping of separate public and private accounts by the government is bound to leave its citizenry with some measure of anxiety followed by or inter-
mixed with a certain creeping cynicism. Yet it makes a considerable difference whether official dishonesty is one which
speaks belligerently for the sake of remaining pacific—as was
the case under Eisenhower—or whether it is—as with Johnson—one which speaks the love of peace for the purpose of
intensifying war. Dullesian hypocrisy about the aims of
American policy in Eastern Europe buried us beneath a load
of distorting language that often made it next to impossible
to discuss or think about the problem at hand. Johnsonian
hypocrisy about the aims of American policy in Vietnam,
tied as it is to the destruction of a country and the killing of
its civilian population on the most questionable military and
political grounds, has served to call into question—particularly among the young—the very legitimacy of government
authority.

V

"It is enough," Franz Kafka once wrote in his diary, "that
the arrow fits the wound it makes." In a very large measure
the opposition to the war has come to reflect and be reflected
by Johnson's conduct of it. In this sense, perhaps, the disaffection that goes so far as to wish a defeat upon one's own
country is well deserved by the arrogance that dares pursue
its own privately defined terms of victory. In any case, the
radical, despairing nihilism that has ballooned among us in
the past few years shares a number of spiritual and intellec-

tual characteristics with the present atmosphere in the White House. Notable among these are an unthinking dependence on political formulas expressed in moral terms, a refusal to make certain necessary distinctions, a lack of candor, a shutting off of genuine debate, and an almost personal demand for loyalty, for the closing of ranks.

It would be silly, of course, to lay the entire current disaffection among the community of the enlightened at the door of Lyndon Johnson—or even of the war itself. Some of what accounts for that community's disgust with the state and nature of American society has to do with frustrations that were inevitable, particularly given the high, innocent expectation with which it greeted the early sixties. The single most important of these expectations, in fact, was not thwarted but, on the contrary, raised to fever pitch precisely by Lyndon Johnson: the expectation that there would be full-scale, orderly redress to the American Negro for his unthinkable treatment at the hands of his fellow Americans. Only the most insanely doctrinaire of his opponents would even at this heated point underrate Johnson's role as the foremost civil-rights President in history. The frustration arose from the fact that the Negro wanted and needed two contradictory things (contradictory, at least, within the particular legal and social tradition of the United States): individual rights and dignity on the one hand and group power on the other; and he could no longer wait patiently for the attainment of either. White society was prepared to give him, as an individual, the former. But the latter, because it would cost people something in the way of the diminution of their own power, was not to be given. Power was something that would have to be wrested. The problem very quickly became a grave one for the Negroes—and in a sense even graver for their white sympathizers—because the moral justice and urgency of their case blinded most of their leaders to the fact that they were pursuing two separate and contradictory ends which would require two separate and distinguishable programs of action. Thus long before he was ready for it—which is to say, long before he had forged for himself the necessary community structure to serve him as a base—the Negro had to confront the resistance of the already-structured communities into whose network of power he would have to make some incursion. The experience of the resistance and of his unpreparedness for it understandably left him in a rage. His white sympathizers, who had dealt only, and guiltily, in terms of morality and so had refused themselves the right to make any cool judgment of his political behavior, were then split into groups willing to share his rage or frightened by it. Having failed on both sides to understand the mechanism of power in which they had involved themselves, angry Negroes and angry white liberals and radicals fell back for an explanation of the new difficulty on a theory of American society as hopelessly and irremediably racist. This theory was perhaps as inevitable as the frustration that gave rise to it. Other things being equal, it would have surrendered some of its simplicity to the exigencies of a day-to-day struggle in which not all would be defeat and not all victory.

But other things did not remain equal—the country was engaged in a war which these same activists deemed to be an unjust one. And not only engaged in this war but engaged in it beneath the clouds of an official temper which left very little open to the spirit of public consultation or influence. So the war, while it did not create the frustration of the civil-rights movement, helped harden that frustration into the atmosphere of a beleaguered camp and provided real fuel for the idea that "orderly political process" was a snare and a delusion for the complacent.

The same can be said for the sense of futility that now surrounds the war on poverty. The poor, too, were caught in a contradiction—very nearly the same one—and in this case without even the élan or drive which supports people who are making a fight for themselves. But the realization that even so little money as had been spent on the poor could not now be spared from the requirements of that other, realer, war once again hardened ordinary frustration into unheeding bitterness.

And so partly fairly, partly not, all the issues that had roused a spirit of opposition—mainly war and poverty and equality for Negroes, but not only these—were fused into one; and in that fusion much of the opposition—enough of it to leave an ineradicable imprint on the entire culture of this decade—was funneled into a single piously articulated attitude of anti-Americanism.

It is this attitude, and not adherence to any particular school or schools of radical political ideology, that earns one admittance to that precinct of the intellectual community called the New Left. It is this attitude, and not the chronological accident of one's birth date, that entitles one to claim membership in that exclusive and intimidating generation Under Thirty. It is this attitude, and not a commitment to the free adventure of the mind, that now accredits one as a truly free spirit beyond the taint of having sold one's soul for pleasure or profit.

Thus we have, within twenty short years, come full circle. The word "evil" hangs heavy in the language of intellectual discussion, just as it came to do in the years after World War II. Then it was applied to the Soviet Union, now to the United States, but the refusal to countenance political complexity that it bespeaks remains the same. Now, as then, dissent from the prevailing currents of fashionable opinion is adjudged to constitute moral failure and places the dissenter beyond the pale of argument. It is astonishing—and more than astonishing—appalling—to realize that the developments of two decades, in a rapidly changing world, have not deterred many of America's most intelligent, most serious, most talented people from their appointed round.

VI

With all due respect, then, to the trials and frustrations of the sixties, the response of the intellectual community to those trials and frustrations has been both disastrous in itself and a depressing omen for the future.

At precisely a time when the values for which this community believes itself to stand—the enlargement of intellectual possibility and the devotion to standards of excellence—are being most threatened from the outside, it has responded only in kind, by threatening them further from the inside.

When a historian like Staughton Lynd proclaims Hanoi to be the model for the achievement of freedom by small nations, he is perverting both the use of his intellectual discipline and his mandate as a thinking man.

When the organizers of a movement to withhold federal income tax in protest against the war draw up a statement which identifies the United States with Nazi Germany, they are, while pretending to appeal to the moral sense, perverting that sense.

When Susan Sontag, wishing to express her horror at the fruits of modern technology, launches an attack upon the Faustian spirit of the whole of Western civilization, ending with the observation that "the white race . . . [is] the cancer of humanity," she undermines the very ground on which she herself is entitled to speak or write.

When Andrew Kopkind, a highly talented young journalist, finds in the fascist tactics wielded by a group of Negroes at a conference of radicals a necessary—finally even a hopeful—experience, he reveals a carelessness toward the virtues of freedom that a writer of all people may indulge in only at his peril.

When Robert Brustein, dean of the Yale drama school, indiscriminately and in a tone of deepest self-gratulation lends his sponsorship to any and all works of art whose intention is subversive, he is, in fact, subverting nothing so much as that artistic integrity to which he professes devotion.

The examples could multiply. They abound in the liberal weeklies, in the highly influential *New York Review of Books*, in some of the quarterlies and are to be heard from the platform of every forum, symposium, teach-in, and round table on peace.

What is sorriest about this present climate is that it witnesses yet another betrayal for which yet another high price is sure to be exacted—in disillusionment and bitterness and violent reaction. An intellectual temper which has not the patience to sort out the illegitimate from the legitimate cannot long sustain itself. We learned this from the fifties; it will be this decade's lesson, too. The seventies will very likely bring a turning back—a turning back from the value of all social passion, as well as from the futility of violence. And may we not expect that the disillusion of tomorrow will become the hard, cold, oppressive philosophy of day after tomorrow?

1968

7

The Stevenson We Lost

It comes as something of a shock to discover how little, in the event, one wishes to read—or, as the case may be, reread —the speeches of Adlai Stevenson. Speeches, to be sure, with only a few exceptions make extremely unsatisfactory reading; separated from its occasion, particularly from the precise sentiment of the occasion, and from the solid present vitality of its deliverer, a speech stands exposed and thin as the conscious or unconscious manipulation it was intended to be. Probably anyone over forty can remember the exact emotion connected with hearing the voice of Winston Churchill, through the ocean roar of shortwave, intoning, "We shall fight them on the beaches. . . ." To read those words today makes one wince—though after all unfairly—at the shameless bravura in their cadence.

In the case of Adlai Stevenson's speeches, one's reluctance goes a lot deeper. It goes deeper even than the standard and predictable fear that the scrutiny of something which once seemed marvelous and important will yet again prove not to have been so and thus disappoint us in our past and in ourselves.

For this collection of speeches (*An Ethic for Survival,* edited by Michael H. Prosser), published and read as it was meant to be in the year 1969, is to the reader at least a funerary act. Far more funerary, indeed, than any or all of the inumerable pious biographical portraits of Adlai Stevenson published since his death in July, 1965. A biography, no matter how operatic or clouded with incense, and even if only by implication, in the end must make the assertion: This was a life. Reducing to print the spoken words of a man now dead only serves as a fresh reminder of his death. There is nothing quite so final as the act of establishing, fixing, the ephemeral.

And while Adlai Stevenson alive was a figure about whom one could beguile oneself with many different thoughts and feelings, Adlai Stevenson in death has become a memory in relation to which it is necessary to *do* something—make some decision, come to some conclusion. The bothersome question is: What? He is, among other more happily avoided things, a nuisance to the conscience.

He is at least for this reviewer and, I would presume to say, for many others like her who supported Stevenson ardently far beyond the point of his having any real chance to maintain political leadership, and then did not even so much as turn against him but simply paid him no further heed. By the time he fell dead in London it was no longer possible for such as we to take any measure of what, if anything at all, had been lost to us. For one thing, the country had just passed through nearly two years of cataclysm: the assassination of a President, an avalanche election, and finally the large-scale commitment to an unpopular war. More important, however, was the fact that Stevenson's supporters had already lost him, and long since, and in three different guises. The first loss was in 1952, when a majority of Americans (who knows? perhaps wisely) declined his call for a new politics and a new drive toward national greatness and opted instead for the postwar calming respite of Eisenhower. The second was in 1960, when a bare majority of Americans did seem ready to take up their dreams of glory but only in the atmosphere of breezy confidence created for them by John F. Kennedy, not in the careful, careworn spirit personified by Adlai E. Stevenson. The third was in 1961, when he became U. S. Ambassador to the U.N. and underwent a final transformation into that most unmemorable of all species of famous men: the useful and self-disciplined public servant.

Not, however, that the slight but persistent feeling of guilt toward him—the guilt that makes even so unritual a funeral as a book into an occasion one wished one didn't have to attend—is in any way personal. Seen personally, the story of Adlai Stevenson is quite simple, and if a little sad, one has heard many sadder. He was a politician and, as the public shorthand has it, a leader of men. He risked becoming President of the United States and lost. Near what turned out to be the end of his life, he was offered a rather painful choice —to retire from his career, or to take a lesser job than he was entitled to and so be humiliated—and he chose the latter. Along the way, he had some good, if insufficient, part of celebration and honor and power.

Still, his career and he himself demand to be dealt with in some other way, or in a variety of other ways. In the editor's introduction to the volumes under review, for instance, Michael H. Prosser, who is a professor of speech communication at Buffalo University, tells us that the project of bringing together and annotating these utterances on foreign affairs grew out of an earlier project, Mr. Prosser's doctoral dissertation, which was a close textual analysis of Stevenson's speeches. It is only a hunch—one would have oneself to be a scholar of Stevensoniana to know the figure—but it seems likely that Mr. Prosser's dissertation was only one of dozens of academic essays devoted to this curiously suitable subject. After all, PhD candidates in the fields of American history, politics, and sociology are numerous and public figures serious enough to lend themselves to serious analysis are all too few. But *why* does it seem so right that this man, who never came to power except briefly and almost by accident in the State of Illinois, should be subject even before his death to so much academic scrutiny? What is there that needs to be explained about him?

Mr. Prosser describes an afternoon in December of 1964 in which he stopped off at the U. S. Mission to present a copy of the dissertation to its subject. The Ambassador was harried; Che Guevara was across the street with the General Assembly, about to address that body, and the Mission staff was busily polishing up and deploying the Ambassador's defenses. Stevenson had just time enough, though, and heart enough for a hurried gesture of acknowledgment. Prosser was carried across First Avenue in the Ambassador's car and given a seat from which to watch the afternoon's proceedings. Some weeks later he received a note from Stevenson which was at once gracious and a little overhearty, saying:

> I was overwhelmed with the enormous research you put into [the thesis]. I am moved, therefore, to send this further word of thanks for telling Stevenson so much about Stevenson's speeches.

Now, this little anecdote is depressing, though for reasons having nothing to do with the conduct of either Mr. Prosser or the Ambassador, in both cases perfectly proper and purely conventional. What makes it depressing is the incursion of those infernal speeches again. They seem to describe an arc, from the beginning to the end: Stevenson had come to glory on them and in the time of his humiliation was delivering them still. As if everything for which he was ultimately to be remembered resided in what he did not do, which is to say, in what he said.

No, the guilty feeling with which one contemplates Adlai Stevenson is not that connected with personal betrayal or even that of witnessing a hero brought low. It comes from the realization, not quite articulated or articulable, that those among us who valued him most did so for the wrong reason and those among us who came to decry his political fate did that, too, for the wrong reason, the two reasons in fact being one and the same.

Those who in 1952 were to become, and for eight years to remain, his most loyal and vocal constituents were delighted —and startled into an amount of ordinary political activity previously deemed unthinkable for people like them—by

Stevenson's early campaign announcement: "Let us talk sense to the American people." Talking sense meant talking to *them* in particular—a thing that no politician in living memory had ever done—for they, after all, were the men of sense in American society. These were the members of a rising and newly self-conscious class in this country—the *intelligentsia*—and had been wholly taken for granted in the Democratic configuration put together by Franklin D. Roosevelt (perhaps like the Negroes, they were known to have "nowhere else to go"). For the first time, then, in 1952 and for a brief illusory moment in 1956, they felt themselves to be on the brink of genuine influence. Almost immediately, however, they—I must say *we*—displayed an inclination to disregard the sense and concentrate instead on the talk.

Stevenson, of course, had his share of responsibility for the ease with which Stevensonians turned their attention from his real, and occupied themselves with his symbolic, substance. He too, little less than they, seemed to be deeply smitten with how well he talked. He appeared to be, as perhaps all Illinois politicians must at some time be, haunted by the shade of Abraham Lincoln—who among other things has undoubtedly earned a place for all ages to come in the history of American prose. Moreover, he was a man whose lesser vanity was subject to the highest temptation in modern American public life: someone fussily, even prissily, literate forced by circumstance to make his mark through the media of mass communication, where even the slightest show of elegance and wit puts one instantly by the side of Alexander Pope. We are told that he hated to have ghost writers even when, as in his Presidential campaigns and later at the U.N., they were an absolute necessity; any final draft of an address delivered by him could with justice be called his, regardless of where it originated. Mr. Prosser describes and even tabulates for us the numbers of corrections and revisions in his hand, of tone and phrasing and formulation, to be found on the original manuscripts of the speeches. No doubt a man's distaste for having others compose the words to be ascribed to him is as honorable as it is rare in these times. No doubt, also, Stevenson's unease in this regard was compounded by the fear of giving his image as a man of grace of mind and bearing into the keeping of writers who might prove incapable of doing it full honors.

But whatever Stevenson's own responsibility for it, the attachment to his—finally the word will out—style, at the expense of the meaning of his commitments, led his followers into a kind of political self-betrayal that has held them in its tangled toils ever since. What they sought from him first and foremost was a public token of their superiority to their less educated countrymen. When he failed to capture for them a majority assent to that superiority, the failure was taken to be his in the doing, not theirs in the being. As early as 1953, one began to hear it said of him that he was a "loser," that he was in some way "indecisive," that he lacked that final confidence-inspiring iron in the soul. Such talk was to intensify in the passing years until, with the bald and impermissible subversion by Kennedy of his entire position at the United Nations over the Bay of Pigs, it became the final summation of his character. The fact that certain decisions of policy, choices of action, did not come easily to him was seen as a deficiency in the essential quality once fashionably called "command." Thus from the very beginning, Stevenson's complexity of vision (what he actually meant when he spoke of talking sense)—whose *articulation* had made them feel him one of their own—was in itself of little more account to his own constituents than to anyone else. (The parallel that suggests itself between this and, to a much greater intensity, last summer's currency with respect to Eugene McCarthy might give one pause.)

In short, Stevenson was responded to less as a leader than as a virtuoso in public performance. And like all virtuosos in relation to their anxious, ambitious families, he was required to be an instant critical sensation, thus confirming them—or they would (secretly, to be sure) be content to see him retire from the scene. Positions in ensembles are not acceptable to the families of virtuosos.

It is good, then, if one must be subject to such reminder, to have the speeches on foreign affairs culled from all the rest. Many of these were, for one thing, delivered in the years before the Stevenson manner became a public institution, as it were: to such groups as the Chicago Bar Association, the Northwestern Law School Association, the American Association for the United Nations. (The ambassadorial addresses to the United Nations are in this context less interesting; they are clearly committee-crafted and may or may not be precisely what Stevenson wanted to say.) For another thing, they bespeak a simple and direct, though supple, and highly serious mind. They are not particularly witty or even very much touched by that self-conscious will to elegance with which memory associates his campaign oratory. As a stylist, of course, he does not even come near to the perfection of eloquence in Lincoln's plainness nor to the high polish of Wilson's brilliance. But he was adequate and sometimes more than adequate to the rarely assumed burden of holding two separate ideas in view at the same time.

Stevenson's message on foreign affairs, though not without a certain resolute good humor, was no fun. It seems terribly important now to see this in the light of all that has happened. He was an interventionist, if you will, a cold warrior, and he counseled patience, negotiation, and nonintervention. He had no new policy to offer beyond Harry Truman's but added to it a spirit of quiet empathy for the concerns of the other side. His fellow Americans, no matter how many of them responded to him as a figure, were in no mood for what he really had to say: not in 1952, when they wanted to talk grandly of right and wrong, sort out and win a moral argument, and do as little as possible and at as little cost to themselves as possible; and not in 1960, when they wanted to be on the move and to believe that the right formula for action on their part would bring a clean decision to all their problems. Nor certainly would they be in the mood today, when the very ideas of both talk and action hang suspended in the smog of Vietnam.

More important than his message, however, in making him

feel so long departed from us was his posture (a very different thing, if not the polar opposite, from style) as a rational,
doubting man. There is very little reason, and even less
doubt, being admitted into the public arena today.

People cannot be blamed for wanting to have fun, particularly Americans. The burden of America's majority in power
was one thrust upon us; we did not, truly we did not, seek
it—all we ever really wanted was a little pleasure and profit.
And this burden has proved a nearly intolerable one to a
nation of, on the whole, fairly amiable pleasure and profit
seekers. Stevenson subliminally communicated to us the outlines of that burden and grew, himself, a little prissy and a
little stuffy with its weight.

But people in pursuit of fun, as even Aristotle knew, are
apt to get pretty bored, and their boredom apt to lead them
to be pretty careless about their genuine interests. One of the
early acts of President-elect John F. Kennedy was no small
outrage against the principle of promoting the public welfare: he did not appoint Adlai E. Stevenson to be Secretary
of State. Reading these speeches—precisely for their failure
to promise easy good times or anything other than a long,
costly, painful, prosy give-and-take with the world—more
than anything else reinforces the long-forgotten belief that
Kennedy ought to have, *must* have, done so. Yet when he did
not, but appointed Stevenson instead to speak for us in just
the place of open diplomacy where no real confrontation and
no real settlement had ever or could ever be made with the
Communist world, Stevensonians made no real protest. They
were weary of the tender-mindedness that being followers of
Stevenson had imposed on them for so long. They "understood" that Kennedy wished to make his own foreign policy
unhampered by the presence of so important a figure with so
acknowledged a position. They even "understood" that in
politics such factors as personal vindictiveness against a rival
are to be taken for granted.

So they got Dean Rusk. At what peril to the psychic safety
of this Republic we may never know.

And when Kennedy subjected Stevenson to a humiliation
the dimensions of which had not been witnessed in our time,

permitting him to lie in ignorance, and then be belied, in front of the representatives of virtually the whole world, it was the thereafter broken Stevenson, and not the shamefully brutal Kennedy, who bore the brunt of the disgrace. To have viewed the matter otherwise, just as in the case of Stevenson's appointment, would for men of up-to-date sensibility have been hopelessly square.

Unfortunately, the lesson of Adlai Stevenson is a square lesson. It is that in a free democratic society which values its own nature as such, men of real quality, no matter their bad luck or shortcomings, are not expendable. This lesson is one America may yet live to learn.

1969

8

Kennedyism

Can it be only ten years now since American society stood ready to be acted on by the Kennedys?

Well, and if we find ourselves inclined to the utterance of such banalities as this, we cannot be entirely to blame. So much of everything connected with the two brothers—young, graced, and doomed—came to us in an aura of domestic "triumph" and "tragedy"; so much about them was larger on the scale of drama than we were equipped to lend our workaday credence to; so much event, public and private, so much public and private passion—and so concentrated in time—that we could almost not respond to the Kennedys at all without calling on the prescribed and stylized sentiments shaped in the childhood reading of fairy tales and in that adult sense of existence whose ultimate, and ultimately banal, expression is paranoia.

Nor can one take the measure of how we were affected by those two victorious penultimate Kennedy moments we witnessed with our very eyes, both of which ended in a death by gunfire. To put it simply, Dallas, November 22, 1963, happened to a nation unwilling to believe in the reality of political assassination. No matter that Americans had within a century already lived through three successful Presidential assassinations and several other attempts (philosophy has long stood humble before the problem of the workings of experience on belief). And Los Angeles, June 4, 1968, left behind a significant part of the nation—if not, secretly, all of it—ready to believe very nearly anything in our political existence possible. If the Kennedys have provided us a permanent legacy, this suspension of disbelief might well be it.

And what indeed—inescapable banality again—of those to come? What will they make of a decade so much of whose political fact and fancy must depend on the by then forgotten? How will they understand, for instance, their vast inheritance of highways, bridges, airports, monuments bearing the name of a President in office for less than three years (in the course of which embroiling the United States in the most unpopular war to date) and of a former Attorney General who had served out not quite four years of his first term as junior Senator from New York? Very likely there will be no problem; people tend to accept the heated pieties of the past as simply a given of the historical environment.

For us, however, there is still a settlement with these ten years to be made—sanity itself may demand one, certainly any kind of perspective on what has actually been going on in this country does.

I

Though they have not been all of the decade just ended, and though the settlement with them is by no means the only one to be made, the Kennedys have hovered over the sixties in a unique way. Many of our public pleasures were determined by them, many of our greatest public problems were bequeathed by them, and many of the period's attitudes— including those assumed by Lyndon Johnson—had reference to them. For the brief time they were in power, John F. Kennedy and that circle of family, employees, political allies, and friends who after his death were to be dubbed the Court-in-Exile did a good deal more than constitute themselves a new administration. In fact, they swamped the national consciousness. Their arrival in the White House in January, 1961, very quickly came to be seen not as a changeover but as a breakthrough of some kind. Out of power, they succeeded in becoming a sword of Damocles hanging over Washington. Johnson's most dangerous opposition, for example, was understood to be not the Republicans, not the Southern recalcitrants, but the Kennedys. Out of the mess of an assassination that might have been thought to spell the demise of much more than their now fallen leader, the Kennedy clan somehow managed to impose his two surviving brothers as a certain token of the future. Being a company town, Washington is a fine web spun out in an incredibly delicate tangle of personalities and professions; and many, we may imagine, were the politicians, publicists, and hopeful bureaucrats assessing the width and depth of the channel that now separated them from the waiting pretender.

In a way, the Kennedys' peculiar hold over the times became all the more potent as it receded into the realm of the potential. Both remembered from the past and portending the future, they could serve as a general, highly flexible standard of invidiousness with the present.

This last point is an important one. American history will have little call to thank us for the decade past, particularly its second half, and more particularly, I believe, that area of it where in the end the Kennedys made their most powerful effect: its social imagination. How would anyone engaged in the effort to place them be able to establish their centrality to the period and at the same time leave them without responsibility for any of its nastiness? This very problem has been occupying many minds, ingenious, ingenuous, inflamed, or just plain vulgar, for some time now.

Actually, the first serious attempt to establish the Kennedys as at once decisively influential and in the literal sense of the word inconsequential—it seems now a truly prophetic attempt because who could then have foreseen how very much nastiness there would be for which to be blameless? —was launched immediately after the death of JFK. In 1965 we were presented with two mammoth inside accounts of the

Kennedy administration: Arthur Schlesinger, Jr.'s *A Thousand Days* and Theodore C. Sorensen's *Kennedy*, which invited us to believe that the United States under JFK had passed through three decisive years in which everything, and yet strangely enough, almost nothing, happened. Both books frankly admitted to partisanship (although Sorensen's somewhat more frankly than Schlesinger's) —after all, both men had been employees and intimates of the President they memorialized. And both, though in very different ways, set a pattern of apology that would prove of lasting value to the Kennedy movement in the years ahead.

That Schlesinger and Sorensen should have been rewarded with best-sellerdom was to be expected: never in living memory had people been so obsessed to know the inside story of a serious public figure, transmogrified from tough politician into movie star into faery prince into martyred hero in hardly enough time for anyone to have arrived at a measured judgment of even one of these personae. In addition, there was a secondary point of great interest, in the authors themselves. For they were precisely a part of what seemed most significant and novel about their subject. In other words, they were Kennedy intellectuals, among that breed of men who had not found their way into the heart of government affairs since the early thirties (and even then, it was suggested, not quite the same breed and not quite to the same extent). The authors' relation to Kennedy was one of the very things everyone wanted to know about him.

Schlesinger and Sorensen reported with absolute unanimity on the essential characteristics of Kennedy's Presidency. It was a Presidency very nearly unprecedented in its power to rouse, to mobilize, to harness, to initiate, talents, hopes, energies, ideas, and commitments. Kennedy's Washington, moreover, was a place which had virtually overnight been swept clean of its Eisenhoweran cobwebs, so depressing and enervating to the whole society, and flocked to by some of the cleverest, most adventurous, and best-trained minds in the country—minds to be seen at work through lighted office windows night after night until the wee hours and at play in the ambience of the most exquisite *décor,* food, and conversation since, easily, the end of the eighteenth century. Thus Schlesinger:

> Intelligence was *at last* being applied to public affairs [italics mine]. Euphoria reigned; we thought for a moment that the world was plastic and the future unlimited.
> Never had girls seemed so pretty, tunes so melodious, an evening so blithe and unconstrained.

Though unanimous in what they wished to evoke, the two authors were operating from very different literary purposes. Sorensen's book is purely the work of an earnest servitor and ends less as a real memoir than a kind of open-ended campaign tract, with candidates and offices left to be designated. Schlesinger—being the far more intelligent of the two, and a historian with a theory of American politics—evinces some awareness of the prior question to which his book must supply an answer. He sets out to answer in advance, as it were, future objections to his having assigned John F. Kennedy a place in that great Democratic Party pantheon of Andrew Jackson and Franklin D. Roosevelt.

One thing becomes absolutely clear in both accounts: to run a government is great fun, maybe the best fun on earth. This ought to be a point too obvious to need making—at the base of any mythology of human existence there being the knowledge that men will kill and die in order to be so privileged—but it is a point often obscured in the cant of those who have already been given their turn. A special quality of the Kennedy administration was the way it took its pleasures openly and was thus able to communicate them to the rest of us. We thought of Washington, *mirabile dictu,* as one of the gay places.

But if Washington had been transformed, we were not on that account to have expected any ensuing wonders. For Kennedy's Presidency as described by Schlesinger and Sorensen was, on the other hand, a perpetual process of discovering its almost unbelievable powerlessness to make a material effect with all the talents, energies, ideas that it had roused, mobilized, and so on. In the face of public prejudice and Congressional hostility—simply, as Schlesinger put it, "how intractable the world was"—Kennedy was found to be a man beset and crossed at every turn. (Sorensen, who unlike his fellow author had no benefit of years of solid work on the New Deal behind him, was able, in a series of lectures delivered at Columbia University while Kennedy was yet alive, to ascribe this powerlessness to the office of the Presidency itself.) His first important lesson in this regard, of course, came with the Bay of Pigs. Many others were to follow, particularly in the fields of civil rights and poverty. Correspondingly, his bright new Washington was also a nightmare of bureaucratic prerogatives and traditions, entrenchments, and resistances, which fairly clanked at the least whisper of an unaccustomed motion. Thus all the sound and fury created by Kennedy and his new talent in the years 1961–63 was an earnest of how our government was being restored to the plane of high principle; all the nothing it concretely signified, as far as new legislation, new federal programs, or— something for which we have not even yet begun to assess the price to be paid—foreign policy were concerned, betokened the inevitable obstacle of practical politics.

To boil the proposition down to plain language, we were asked to judge Kennedy as President by his intentions rather than by his achievements. Now, this is not a particularly outrageous request, especially coming from two employees of his administration and in the aftermath of his bitterly premature and shocking death. Nor does it much matter that this claim upon the world's trust is normally pressed in behalf of the weak, almost never in the name of someone wishing to be regarded as better and braver than the average run of men. Elective politics is a field whose highest wisdom is thought to reside in the art of navigation between announced intention and actual behavior; voters are as conditioned to the idea as politicians. In the case of John F. Kennedy, however, his supporters were asking something for *themselves*, something of which this instance was only to be the first of a long series: that we take their word for it.

II

The truly interesting question about the Kennedy administration, though, is not what did it accomplish but what, in the words of Oscar Gass, "did these people want."

For besides elegance and gaiety, that which preeminently characterized the New Frontier was a kind of swashbuckling, an arrogant lack of principle. By "lack of principle" I do not mean that anybody was an especially unprincipled individual. Anyway, only children or idlers level such charges at political leaders. What I do mean is that Kennedy and his "best and brightest people in the country" swooped down on the White House and tackled its problems in the spirit of the belief that these problems continued to persist only because the "right" people had never before been let loose on them. How much there was to be undone and cleared away: the work of Truman hacks and Eisenhower dullards, an inert State Department, not very bright generals, a bunch of small-time tacky Congressmen. And who could conceivably be better for the job? This spirit accounts in part, probably in great part, for the enormous new élan they brought to Washington. ". . . They aspired," Schlesinger tells us, "like their President, to the world of ideas as well as to the world of power." "Ideas," in Kennedy parlance, meant proposals for programs to initiate—a perfect technocratic definition of the term— and if there was a distinction to be made in anybody's mind between a new proposal and a genuinely new policy, Schlesinger, who normally does understand such a distinction, gives no indication of it. (There were, of course, those study sessions in McLean, Virginia, with guest lecturers offering their views on philosophy and art. This, too, was "the world of ideas" about which—*nil nisi bonum*—the less said the better.) The Alliance for Progress—the adaptation of a new posture and a new rhetoric to Point Four—serves as a notable example of one such program; the Peace Corps serves as another—a genuinely original but hardly earth-shattering move in the same direction as above; and a third, painful at the moment to mention, was the tooling up of the American military for counterinsurgency warfare.

Lack of respect for, lack of imagination of, the genuine difficulties—and, yes, even the genuine convictions—of one's failed predecessors is the first mark of what I have termed arrogant lack of principle. Its base lies perhaps in snobbishness, perhaps in a parochial lack of that curiosity which for educated men spells cultivation of spirit, certainly in a hunger for a kind of power that can be fluidly and comfortably wielded. Among other things, the New Frontiersmen swept through the offices of duly elected representatives of the people—some of them duly elected and reelected for nearly as many years as their interlocutors had been alive—and, with a tough-minded political-science knowledge of the low calling of the legislator, made a shambles of White House-Congressional relations.

The other side of the swashbuckling was a deadly caution. Nor was caution a contradiction, but rather in the fullest sense a complement, of New Frontier auto-intoxication. Any possibility for a greatness of record, as distinguishable from high style and intention, Kennedy avoided. He took no real leadership except in foreign policy, and even there it was largely a matter of making a personal impression and establishing personal relations. He was instead an avid reader of the temper of the times. In some cases he badly misread that temper—for example, the degree of impatience among Negroes with the pace of progress in civil rights and the degree of impatience in the country at large with anti-Communism as a guiding principle of foreign policy—and lost opportunities already prepared for him. He had attained the White House by the narrowest margin and naturally wanted to stay there through his allotted eight years. What tiny margin of popularity he had, had followed on a campaign in which the major stated issue between him and his opponent was that he was the better man, that he would "get the country moving again." His mandate was thus undefined, and he set out to fulfill it, as he incomparably did, exactly as promised: by being the better man. And his New Frontiersmen in turn set out to fulfill their mandate from him by constituting themselves, throughout the Executive, a group appearing to be the most dashing and creative public officials ever. Here, indeed, was where the fun lay, for all of them, and, directly and indirectly, for the rest of the country.

What the Kennedy administration wanted, then, what it sought to do, was to impose an image of itself on American society and American history: an image of itself as the rightful, by virtue of intrinsic superiority, American ruling class. And in this endeavor it was unquestionably successful.

III

The Kennedys out of power, by which I mean, of course, out of Washington—and by which I also mean not only the two surviving brothers but their family connections and respective and intersecting retinues—are in their way even more interesting than the Kennedys in power. For at this point intention becomes all, and the only measure is that of intention against intention.

If the New Frontier had established itself in the public mind as the vanguard of our rightful ruling class, then John F. Kennedy at Dallas was our fallen king. New Frontier Washington had ceased to be London or Paris and had, with a hint from the now dowager queen, retroactively become Camelot. In a funeral egregious for its well-researched pomp and full panoply of made-up historic gestures, from the televised widow's kiss bestowed upon the decked coffin to the lighting of a permanent gas flame at the grave (after all, we had never buried a king before), we buried him and set about speculating as to whether and when the heir apparent would make his move.

Later we learned that for some months after his brother's death Robert Kennedy had gone through a "crisis"—which seems, from what one can gather, to have been a depression. How, then, could we have known about Robert Kennedy that which he himself may not have known or acknowledged to himself at the time: that he would inevitably, sometime within the next ten years, make a bid to take his brother's place? I do not think it was mere cynicism in us. Thoughts of Robert Kennedy's Presidential possibilities, usually in the form of insinuating jokes but perfectly serious for all that, had begun to circulate soon after John Kennedy's move into the White House. The Kennedys had been brought up to be President. That much we had known at the outset. Their father had decreed it—if not one son, then another, and maybe all in turn. These extraordinary brothers were obviously quite unlike, and yet we knew, though how dreadful and precise a prediction that knowledge would turn out to be no one ever dreamed, that they could if necessary be interchangeable. Robert was the second oldest eligible Kennedy, therefore clearly the next Kennedy attempt at the Presidency would be his.

This is not at all a "nice" idea, neither about the Kennedys nor about us as citizens and voters; nor does it even provide a pleasant family picture—quite the opposite; nevertheless, the idea that the name Kennedy was a collective, a dynastic name was not without its own very powerful appeal. For one thing, it was honest, and honesty about the dream of being superordinate, particularly when personified in so aesthetically acceptable a way, can have the effect on people of freeing them from one of their grosser anxieties. For another thing, this vision of the family with its ranks of retainers closed all about it—it called itself, or we called it, the Kennedy Machine, the most efficient instrument for conducting election campaigns in memory, many experts said—had a longed-for quality of intimacy. Sitting Presidents have no doubt always been subject to the public's curiosity about the details of their private lives. But the process by which they became candidates for the Presidency had come to seem very distant and baffling, the arcane manipulation of party factions and leaders whose terms of negotiation could only be sorted out by those highly trained and experienced, like anthropologists translating some elaborate native ritual. The Kennedys with their Machine made it all seem simple and personal again. Getting to the White House, or anyway getting the chance to get to the White House, was the result of the absolute determination to do so combined with the means to bend whatever forces necessary to one's will. "No damned nonsense," as Lord Melbourne once happily remarked of the Order of the Garter, "about merit."

And so by the time Robert Kennedy—certainly a far more important and singular figure at the start of his candidacy than his older brother had been at the same stage—was only two months dead, there was hardly a whisper of skepticism about the necessity for brother Teddy's being next to try. The only question was: Now, on such short notice, in 1968— or four or eight years from now?

IV

On the day Lyndon Johnson announced his decision to withdraw from the 1968 campaign, Senator McCarthy is reported to have said, "Now Bobby will have to run against his brother Jack." This remark was thought by many to have been nasty and bad politics as well. But like so many things the inscrutable Senator has said, it sounded merely clever and was profoundly true. Except, of course, that Bobby had actually been running against Jack, probably by instinct, since at least 1965.

How could he have done otherwise? The issue at stake was not simply Vietnam (which had been left by the New Frontier at least in an arguable condition). The issues were the new black militancy, urban blight, poverty, guns or butter, the spreading insidious influence of the military: all matters that a Democratic junior Senator from New York had to make his political property—if not he, who?—and several of which had been preempted by Lyndon Johnson with a speed and effectiveness that must have been, to put it mildly, embarrassing. Robert Kennedy had staked out his claim on the New York Senate seat in virtue of his name and his need for a base of operation. To those among his future constituents who had come to revel in the stylistic glories of Kennedy Washington, his campaign had smacked of the promise that Camelot would for as long as necessary be relocated in Manhattan. To others it had promised an infusion of spunk and energy into a state party crippled by inanition. There was in the very nature of things nowhere for Robert Kennedy to stand, or at least to appear to stand, but to the left of Lyndon Johnson. Which meant, since Johnson was already so busily and so successfully dispelling the myth of the powerless Presidency, two steps to the left of his brother—and of his own former self.

Robert Kennedy is a far less easy figure to deal with than his brother: because he was in himself less easy; because he died only a candidate to be a candidate; and because, running against himself and therefore needing some mythic explanation, he provided such perfect material for the wholesale mythicizing of others. Upon meeting him after he became Senator, one's leading impression of him was that of a certain unnameable vulnerability. Several of those who knew him well pronounced him shy. But to call a politician shy cannot have reference to the same quality called by that name in ordinary people. In the case of Kennedy, suspiciousness was probably the better word. Though as a future Presidential contender he was found by his well-wishers to be a tender, suffering, reflective man, in his earlier role as JFK's right hand, he was said to be ruthless and rough-playing, a watchdog ready to spring at the slightest scent of an unwanted intrusion. Neither of these characterizations seems apt somehow, though something of each was visible in him. But a high degree of suspiciousness would fit, and account for, both.

Possibly the watchful vulnerability to be read in Robert Kennedy's face was the result of his discovery in Dallas that politics was a more final and serious business—as final and serious as war itself—than he had been taught to bargain for. Electing his brother President had been a thoroughly professional enterprise. Step followed step, plan followed plan, without any real hitch. Electing himself Senator had proceeded in the same way. But in between had come the knowledge that one could be killed; the profession had become a vocation. He must at this point have needed to believe that there was some reason beyond the mere reinstitution of jolly times for him to offer himself up to it. What must that reason be?

At any rate, he was not lacking for people with reasons of their own to help in the supply. Most of the original Kennedy court, one by one resituating themselves outside the precincts of Johnson's fiefdom, became available to him. For many of these, there is some evidence to suppose that he had but to take up where they, as a group of associates, had left off, only this time from the further vantage point of Lyndon Johnson's mistakes. For some whose overriding passion was to settle the war he was a logical figure around whom to organize a crusade: for he could command the numbers and the national political machinery to turn their still amateur movement into a seriously contending force. Finally, and perhaps decisively—though now, of course, we will never know—there were those who sought for him to become America's new prophet of social change. His connection to New York, with its inevitable leftward drift, brought into his entourage young men self-consciously speaking for the so-called radical culture of the young. Preeminent among these were two named Adam Walinsky and Peter Edelman, having in common with each other and with what sociologists would call their age cohort that peculiarly serene assurance about the correct wholesale application of the epithets good and bad, moral and immoral, progressive and reactionary, which has come in the aftermath of 1968 to be the sole divining rod of something termed the New Politics.

It has often been said of the young Robert Kennedy that he hated liberals and hated above all to be thought of as a liberal. No doubt the term was associated for him with all the prissiness and sissiness for which one's life could be made pure hell in the American prep school (not to mention in the household and on the playing fields of Joseph P. Kennedy). History had blessed him, then, by presenting him with the need to move left at precisely the moment when to do so would place him in a company highly congenial to his old contempt for liberals: the young, the militant, the righteous, and the generally restless.

V

Now once again, as we were with his older brother, we are left with a rich posthumous record of Robert Kennedy's personality and intentions. In the brief year and a half since his assassination, book has followed book in a seemingly regular succession: the story, ending in the midst of a primary campaign, is briefer, easier to summarize, and even more susceptible to the superimpositions of the tendentious. Once again, that is, we are asked to take the word of those in a personal position to know.

But unlike John F. Kennedy, Robert Kennedy has been handed on to us in, roughly speaking, three personifications: Bobby the dutiful, Bobby the suffering, and Bobby the bold. Each of these is, naturally, the protagonist of a separate book, in keeping with the author's own politics. There is the portrait by Theodore C. Sorensen,* who wishes to claim Robert Kennedy for the greatness of some ongoing Kennedy tradition—and in which the author (again) enjoys some small measure of reflection. There is the one by Jack Newfield,† who wishes to claim Robert Kennedy for the militancy and moral virtue, if not the precise ideology, of the New Left. And there is the Robert Kennedy of David Halberstam,‡ a Bobby whose wit and wisdom have carried him beyond the stale and corrupt conventions of Democratic Party politics into the promise of some new national purpose.

About Sorensen's book one hardly has the heart to speak, for it is not, as was his book about John F. Kennedy, a serious piece of work. As its title, *The Kennedy Legacy,* implies, it is merely an attempt to establish the apostolic succession; and thus in his account Robert Kennedy is simply a man who grew older and bigger and finally old enough and big enough to receive the holy dispensation. Sorensen does not scruple to announce, for instance, that the rather elaborate network of personal styles and talents and public postures he chooses to characterize as the Kennedy "legacy" is nothing less than "the most important body of ideas in our time." Apart from what this reveals about Sorensen's notion of an idea—let alone an important body of them—the passage signals that in

---

* *The Kennedy Legacy,* Macmillan.
† *Robert Kennedy, a Memoir,* Dutton.
‡ *The Unfinished Odyssey of Robert Kennedy,* Random House.

1969 its author feels no more need than he did in 1965 to justify the Kennedys by much more than the mention of their name.

Informed gossip has it that Sorensen's was the main negative voice in the Kennedy court's discussion as to whether or not Kennedy should enter the race against Johnson in 1968. Now there is no reason to doubt, as certain very angry Kennedy defenders do, that in urging him to be moderate about the war and to stay out of the race, Sorensen had Kennedy's own best interests at heart. He was not, after all, hired to be a confessor but a political adviser. As it turned out—as it turned out for many others in that fateful year—he was a very bad one. Political-mindedness at that moment in history was not only not an inspiriting or uplifting spectacle, it was not clever politics either. Sorensen devotes a good deal of effort to exculpating himself for the mess that was made of the peace candidacy by Kennedy's behindhandedness, and the results of this effort are also not only not pretty but not clever. For in what has now become established New Frontier tradition, he cannot simply admit a mistake—surely the cleanest and surely also the most unanswerable way of disposing of a bad record.

Sorensen's mode of dealing with the past is worth dwelling on because it is not his alone. His formulation with respect to his role as a Kennedy adviser follows exactly the formulation of most of the other denizens of Camelot—and not the least among them Robert F. Kennedy—with respect to U.S. involvement in Vietnam: namely, I was right to begin with, and when I changed my mind, or had it changed for me, I was right still. Any opponent of the war who happened into certain enclaves of the Court-in-Exile as late as 1966 is bound to remember the absolutely withering jovial contempt in which he was held as the woolly-minded adherent of a politically hopeless position.

An early and consistent opponent of the war might also, had he been ingenuous enough, have experienced some puzzlement at the idea of a successful alliance between Robert Kennedy and certain factions of the Young Left. He was, as Jack Newfield recounts, the Attorney General against whom they organized civil-rights demonstrations. He was by his own account one of the architects of the Cuban missile crisis, whose successful negotiation by the Kennedy administration the peace movement could not ever really find it in its heart to forgive. He made no forthright public statement on Vietnam until 1967. And surely, if any man had been seen working within the limits of the "system" that the young professed so mightily to abhor, that man was Robert F. Kennedy.

For his left wing, then, those rallying behind the Kennedy who could "turn the country around" with his special gift for communion with the disaffected young and blacks, the dilemma posed by Eugene McCarthy was especially poignant. And its resolution is given the crudest and therefore the clearest exposure in Jack Newfield's book. Being perhaps the most dedicated contemporary practitioner of that very old-fashioned art called agitprop—whose most salient characteristic has always been its utter unembarassment either with fact or with niceties of perception—Mr. Newfield is able in a perfectly unembarrassed way to make of Kennedy a man with no relation to his own history. Once upon a time, Mr. Newfield's story goes, there was a bad old Robert Kennedy who had worked for and been friendly with the late Senator Joseph McCarthy and who had been Attorney General under John F. Kennedy. Then, quite suddenly, there was a new Robert Kennedy, taught by the assassination of his brother that there is evil in the world, especially in the United States, taught by his own suffering to care about the sufferings of the poor and the young and the black, learning to read poetry and becoming—in the phrase that offers a just tribute to the level of Mr. Newfield's literacy—"an existential hero." Actually, this new Robert Kennedy is a man no serious person in his right mind would wish to vote for. He is full of moral certainty and, on the other hand, troubled with painful indecisions, insecurities, and dark nights of the soul; he is precipitous in the adoption of new ideas and, on the other hand, pushed this way and that by the judgments of those around him. Above all, he undertakes to seek office not out of a keen appetite to have it but out of a sense of deep moral obligation. (That is, I think, precisely why the book was so warmly greeted by many of Kennedy's professed admirers: Mr. Newfield evoked for them a man very much as they themselves might wish to be—a perfect antipolitical fantasy.)

Not that Kennedy could have been anything but profoundly affected by the assassination of someone so close to him and someone so obviously beloved. Even just the experience of being suddenly cast out into the cold—of being, as it were, orphaned—and having to make one's way back into the world again would teach any man a profound lesson about the arbitrariness of fortune. Nor could anyone operating merely from political motive have succeeded so consistently in being a white hero to the blacks or an adult hero to the kids. But the discontinuity between the two Robert Kennedys proposed here serves another purpose than merely to further our understanding of the self-evident. It is the key to a much more general assertion about the nature of political virtue: that is, that no man can be lacking in virtue, as in Newfield's view Kennedy was in the fifties and early sixties, and still have deep human feelings; and conversely, no man can opt for such virtue and still conduct himself as an ordinary political animal.

In this conception, the radical Robert Kennedy was continuous with his former self in only one respect: his freedom, early and late, from the taint of liberalism. This freedom, bred precisely in Kennedy's original conservatism of temper and outlook, makes it possible for him to attain to a politics "Beyond Liberalism." Never having struggled against the Stalinists in the forties and fifties, as did "Hubert Humphrey, Walter Reuther, Irving Kristol, and Irving Howe,"* Kennedy was free to operate with a mind uncluttered by a lot of stale cold-war claptrap.

Nor is there any evidence of discomfort at offering such an analysis of a man who had worked for Joe McCarthy and had participated in the decisions to invade Cuba and to contain the Vietcong on grounds of the domino theory. For the purpose of this analysis is not so much to excuse the past as to

---

* The list, I swear, is Newfield's own, reproduced in full.

sketch a present in which Robert Kennedy and his most
prominent constituency might be liberated from any of the
standard liberal claims of the organized labor movement, the
responsible civil-rights movement, and even the group of his
prematurely dovish fellow Senators.

Finally, there is David Halberstam's Robert Kennedy, the
central figure not of a politics beyond liberalism but of liberalism redefined. This Kennedy is most assuredly a man one
would wish to vote for. To begin with, he is attractive, vital,
and sure enough of his powers never to be unduly solemn.
Then, too, he is actually a politician—he comes from somewhere, has a history which remains his own, and makes
decisions on a balance between commitment and political
advantage. Like the hero of Sorensen's account, this Kennedy
is a man who had grown; but the growth was not into worth-
iness to occupy an already prepared position but rather into
a new position based on a concern for new issues.

The new issues to which the newly grown Kennedy ad-
dressed himself are not quite precisely specified. Yet it is
impossible not to know what they are, for they constitute—
Richard Nixon notwithstanding—a significant part of the
temper of this time: in addition to Vietnam, there are the
blacks and the poor and there is the unrest of the middle-
class young, and the orientation derived from them is toward
a "new" militant localism.

Yet the truth is that the Kennedy who as Attorney General
was found wanting in sensitivity to the urgency of Negro
demands and the Kennedy who as Senator rushed in to reconstruct the Bedford-Stuyvesant ghetto—in the process
very nearly destroying the recently developed and delicate
political tissue that might at last have brought that community some genuine political leverage—were not so very far
apart. Both were acting mainly from advice as to what would
and would not wash. And both were unable, partly from a
brash unconcern for the needs and experiences of others,
partly from what might have been a simple shortcoming in
intelligence (if indeed the two are not the same thing), to
gauge the likely consequences of their policy. (It is interesting to note that nowhere in the accounts of him over the last

six years is there the record of an attempt to assess, quite simply, the measure of Robert Kennedy's intelligence. Even now, perhaps, the observation sounds a little shocking: after all, an informed and experienced mind has not for well over a century been among the requirements for even a great American leader. But these are, as the past six, and particularly the past two, years have amply illustrated, extraordinary times.)

VI

The "new" issues in American society, and the New Politics they are widely believed to have generated, extend beyond the problem of Robert Kennedy himself. The term "New Politics" came into currency more or less about the time of the 1968 Democratic convention and at first provided a useful shorthand symbol for the Young Turks of the combined Kennedy–McCarthy camps in their dealings with Hubert Humphrey and his backers and allies: an outgrowth, no doubt, of the name New Democratic Alternative, itself the polite term for "Dump Johnson." To begin with, then, a New Politician was a Democrat opposed to a Democratic war and hoping to take sufficient control of the party to bring about a reversal of its Vietnam policy. Today, of course, a New Politician is something different. He is a man engaged in proving himself worthy to inherit the Kennedy mantle— the setback suffered by Teddy Kennedy at Chappaquiddick having left the position at least temporarily open.

Exactly how the term was enlarged and subtilized to include some and exclude others would make a fascinating study in the manipulation of public speech—a subject that has long been begging for study. Suffice it here to say that Eugene McCarthy, for example, is not really thought to qualify for New Politician—those followers who did not completely defect in effect having constituted themselves a separate party—while Edmund Muskie is, by latest report, being considered. In any case, the Whig court appears to be assembling to import from other shores the monarch who will prosecute their Glorious Revolution.

Insofar as anything is genuinely new about the new issues, it is that they constitute the sleight of hand by which everything but the last few ugly scenes of the decade—the riots since Martin Luther King's assassination, revelations about the corrupting power of the Pentagon, above all, Chicago—is made to disappear in order that we may start over again. The new of 1972 is to be the new of 1960.

The 1968 campaign of Robert Kennedy served both him and his fellow New Frontiersmen as a means for dissociating themselves from the actual record of John Kennedy's administration (a) without experiencing any loss of the *mana* attached to it and everyone in it and (b) without, by definition, being disloyal to it. Ted Kennedy's 1969 campaign against the military served the same purpose. Even the memory of JFK himself has been dissociated from that record without any very noticeable public outcry. About Vietnam, of course, the reply of the Kennedyites is: under Jack, if he had lived, things would have been different. Perhaps indeed they would; such speculations—though it is a crude and brutal thing to remind people of—are the single advantage of standing on the platform of a dead candidate. What matters, however, is that ten years later, and in the face not only of Kennedy's disastrous decision to hold South Vietnam as a friendly power but of the overall decision behind it to pursue seriously a policy of containment in Southeast Asia, we are offered nothing more than a variation on his original campaign promise: he would have been the better man.

As part of their sleight of hand, the Kennedyites have managed not only to lift any vestige of blame from themselves but to lay rather handsome portions of it elsewhere. Arthur Schlesinger mounts an attack on Dean Rusk as if unconscious—certainly as if the reader were to remain unconscious—of just whose appointee Dean Rusk actually was. A former highly regarded Kennedy State Department official, and an intimate of Robert Kennedy's, attacks the labor movement—"not worth the powder it would take to blow it up"—for being hawkish: seemingly unconscious—certainly as if the listener were to remain unconscious—that it might better behoove some opponent of the war other than a former State Department official to disdain this particular use of explosives. A former Assistant Attorney General under Robert Kennedy expresses outrage at the refusal of the American working class to shoulder the main burden of a program of speedy and costly reparations to the Negro. A former Assistant Secretary of Defense under McNamara scolds a conference of concerned liberals for showing too great a concern about the inequitable distribution of wealth in the United States and too little about the economic depredations of our huge military budget. And these examples are far from exhaustive.

In fact, the current campaign against the military-industrial complex merits particular attention. Our first warning against this encroaching blight on American economic and political life came, of course, from Dwight D. Eisenhower as he left office. It seems to have become a dire threat once more. Somehow the New Frontiersmen, in the vanguard of the movement to control the military, have been allowed to forgo mention of the fact that in the years 1961–63, under the tutelage of none other than Robert S. McNamara, that same military-industrial complex enjoyed an enormous if not a geometric rate of growth. Moreover, the reason it did so was that the Kennedy administration, upon taking office from its brinksmanship predecessor, found that our military force was not adequate and adopted what was called the "2½ war" strategy. This strategy called for a military establishment (and budget) adequate to the simultaneous waging of two major wars and one minor one.

VII

Thus the New Politics is simply Kennedyism afloat without the anchor of an individual Kennedy. The line seems to have run out, at least for the moment, with the youngest son. In attempting to apply to a matter of personal scandal the public-relations techniques by which his brothers had remained perpetually blameless for their errors of public policy, Teddy and his retinue discovered for us the limits of those techniques. He called together the soldiery of Camelot and made a speech to the public about courage; but he was no longer the darling princeling, having after his brother's death become the liege and lord—and America was, momentarily, no longer a monarchy.

Many adherents of the New Politics would dispute its inevitable connection to Kennedyism. David Halberstam, for instance, would apply the categories of old and new by the standards of 1968 and primarily on the issue of the war; he would thereby be inclined to find much of the New Frontier old. But the war will one day be over, and the Democrats will one day make their bid again, and things will then be divided in a rather different way. Members of Robert Kennedy's and Eugene McCarthy's youth contingents would surely dispute the connection of the New Politics to Kennedyism, holding the old Kennedy court to be just another manifestation of the establishment they affect so to despise. But the innocents among them neither understand properly what the phenomenon of Kennedyism is nor wish to analyze the implications of what they themselves are currently advocating.

Kennedyism is the assertion of the right of those properly endowed—by education, upbringing, leisured high purpose, and, yes, by birth, if need be—to rule. The New Politics, even for the "kids" who find other names for it, is the assertion of the right to be ruled by attractive men, morally attractive, aesthetically attractive, in a morally and aesthetically attractive society. Both create the political ambience in which it is more suitable to speak the language of class: to speak of an individual man's "instincts," his "style," his "sympathy for," rather than to engage in a hard and clear examination of whose interests are being served by a given political impulse. And both create, though their adherents refuse or pretend not to know it, the vision of a political future which for a democracy cannot be a vision of openness, fluidity, but just the opposite. Theirs is the stuff from which establishments are really made.

The demand to be ruled in an attractive way is a reactionary demand—regardless of the radical rhetoric in which it may be couched. The alliance it bespeaks between the privileged and the *Lumpen* and against the coarse-grained and sometimes brutal equalizing of the middle is nothing new to the history of Western politics—though the extent to which it has taken hold is new indeed to the history of twentieth-century America. This alliance was only prefigured in the elegant romp of John F. Kennedy through Washington; it attained to a full embodiment in the Presidential primary campaign of Robert F. Kennedy. In between spanned most of the sixties, a decade not the least of whose ironies will turn out to be that in the midst of a reckless turbulence sometimes called "revolutionary," and explicitly egalitarian in its ideology, American society was solidifying within itself as never before a body of sentiment more properly attached to a truly hierarchical social order enjoying the grandeurs of empire. The furthering of social welfare came to reside in the call for such things as a religious change of heart, or the application of special standards of conduct and competence to our colonial wards, the blacks, or private philanthropy to the poor. Men of the common stripe were called to return to their former happy status as villagers, looking out for their own affairs and resting content without the undue interventions of government. The children of the upper middle class cried out in their universities for some institutionalized mark of their privileged estate.

Perhaps America is indeed settling into the spiritual condition of a great conservative imperial power. If so, the lesson of the sixties and of the Kennedys is that it has taken no bloody-minded or profit-greedy class of imperialists to lead her into that condition.

1970

THREE:

Being an American

1

"A Good Piece of Goods"

My mother, who lives in the Midwest, spends a good deal of time during her visits to New York shopping around for bargains. Through the years she has managed to find an impressive number of those places where, "they say," you can pick up all sorts of special buys in hats, shoes, bags, linens, and whatnot. With her it is mostly a matter of sport: her hometown, which is not small, can offer her everything she might possibly need or want in the way of stores and goods, but the formality and the stodginess of its business traditions leave unsatisfied her basically Arab instincts. And then all the hustle and bustle that gives her so much fun also serves to feed her Midwestern patriotic sense of superiority over life in New York. She never actually buys very much, but she always has a story to tell.

Just recently she was regaling the family with an account of what happened that day at a dress sale in one of our notoriously typical stores. She had taken from a rack one dress she liked very much, which was being sold at a great reduction in price. Only, a couple of the buttons were missing. She approached the salesgirl about it, but the salesgirl was indifferent to her problem. So she asked to see the manager. The manager was a young man in shirt sleeves. He said they hadn't any extra buttons. My mother said in that case how about giving her something additional off the price.

"Lady," she mimicked him in her own special version of a New York accent, "we're giving away the dress now. Look at the ticket. It's marked 'As Is.' "

"But I'd like to buy that dress very much."

"Lady, you're an intelligent woman."

"But those buttons are half the dress—they make the whole effect. How can I wear it without them? And it would cost me a fortune to replace a button like that!"

"And what do you think he said to me then?" she asked.

"He said," I answered quite without thinking, " 'Darling, do what you want. But I'll tell you one thing. You'll leave the store right now and you'll take a walk over to the Ritz Plaza, and that dress will get there before you—without the buttons.' "

"No," she said, "Waldorf. Not Ritz Plaza. He said the Waldorf. But how did you know?"

"I would have said Ritz Plaza myself. But then, times do change," I told her. "You've forgotten that I'm an old pro."

I had almost forgotten myself, but her mention of the young man in shirt sleeves brought back all at once the time four years ago when I took a job as salesclerk in the Queens branch of Jays Department Store (main headquarters Brooklyn). It was in November, sometime before Thanksgiving, and the stores were all hiring temporary people to help out in the Christmas rush. I happened to pick Jays because the store was within walking distance from my home. I might have made more money than the barely minimal 85 cents an hour Jays offered by getting on some bus and riding to Jamaica, say, or Hempstead. As it was, I simply walked over to the store one Friday morning, presented my credentials (which were, by the going standards of Christmas sales help, considerable: several years of after-school clerking in my father's ready-to-wear) to the personnel department, and walked home again with instructions to appear the following

Monday, a round lapel button with my name stamped on it and a key which entitled me to half the space of a coat locker in the basement.

Jays is one of those serve-yourself ladies' wear stores—whose progenitor, I guess, is S. Klein—that specialize in manufacturers' closeouts, special buys, "name" merchandise with torn-out labels, cheap copies of expensive or high-style items, and assorted leavings and giblets from the cutting tables. It is well known among inveterate lady shoppers that at Jays or Mays or Klein's or Ohrbach's you can, but with a little patience and perseverance, buy everything at from $3 to $50 cheaper than in the Fifth Avenue stores—a piece of common knowledge sturdily reinforced by the merchandising technique that crushes hundreds of unlike things together on small racks or piles them shoulder-high on counters, provides almost no salespeople and absolutely no salesmanship, and permits the preying instinct of shopping women its full scope.

I had heard much about Jays from friends and neighbors —though I had never had the occasion to shop there myself —but I did not stop to connect the nature of the store with the nature of my future employment. I simply assumed that all clerking was like that I knew so well from my father's small store, where every good sale was a personal accomplishment and where such things as goodwill and service were essential to a business reputation. I told the personnel manager of my vast experience with coats and suits (which was a lie) and expected that Jays would exploit my talents to the fullest. I was assigned, however, not to the Fireside Room, with its reputed $200 models for $89.50, but to Budget Slips, main floor.

Jays Queens, after the fashion of all suburban branches of big department stores, was a rather new two-story structure with a bus route before and a gigantic parking lot behind. Budget Slips was a square-shaped counter on the aisle directly in line with the back doors. Our merchandise was laid out on counter tops around the four sides, with shelf space for extra stock below the counters and inside the display case that stood in the middle. We sold full slips, half slips, some nightgowns, and (then in the first flush of a long-term vogue) crinolines.

Monday was a great day at Jays. The store was open until nine o'clock at night and teemed with bargains. Almost every department put out Monday "leaders" that served to keep hordes of women milling through the place from the opening bell to the closing. There were nylon stockings at three pairs for $1, cashmere sweaters for $7.95, hand-finished all-silk blouses for $2.99, and countless other standard specials. Our own contribution to the fracas was $1 slips. These slips were thrown out hurriedly before opening on the counter end that faced the rear entrance and parking lot. So that when the doors finally gave way beneath the weight and force of the at least five hundred early comers, we were the first department to be swooped down upon. The ladies used literally to tear through the intervening Menswear (a small and unimportant department, a bone, really, thrown to Jays' claim of being a family store) in order to get first choice on our sizes and colors. Those Monday mornings are like a dream to me. I can hardly remember anything about them, except the pure physical sensation of stooping, squatting, tearing open boxes, and handing up tons and tons of rayon acetate into grasping outstretched hands. I very quickly learned how to crouch below the counter where the cartons of reserves were kept and yell "Call your sizes!" throwing up the goods in the direction I thought I heard the requests come from. It was easier this way, for me and the customers, than trying to find the needed 44-pink or 38-blue in the chaos of the counter. I cannot imagine that those poor, fragile rags ever made it in one piece to the cashier's counter, but, then, anyway they could never have survived their first wearing. The ladies knew this about them, too—they would joke about it as they reached for their second or third slip—but nothing mattered: the Monday fever was upon us all. We at Jays took our eminently successful stand on the principle that "for a dollar you can't go wrong."

*   *   *

On my first morning, then, I was directed to my station, introduced to Pearl and Hazel, my counter mates, and hurled straightaway into my Monday dream. There hadn't even been time to give me some orientation in practices and procedures. All that could come later (though by the time it did, it was no longer necessary). The first thing I realized was that as a salesclerk it was not my function to complete any transaction. Jays was organized, as are all such stores, like a supermarket. The customer walked around taking whatever she wanted and carried it to a cashier, who took her money and wrapped up her purchase. Obviously in such a system the problem of theft is enormous, but so far as I ever knew, it was handled at Jays with brilliant success. You could roam about as much as you pleased and pick up as much as you pleased before buying, but you could not go from one floor to another with unwrapped merchandise, and no cashier could complete a sale on anything that was not properly ticketed. Any item that came to a cashier without a price ticket or with the ticked pinned loosely or looking in any way suspicious (where there might be the possibility of its having been "switched," that is, taken off something cheap and fastened onto something much more expensive) was taken immediately to the floor manager—the clerks were never permitted to touch a ticket and would have been fired on the spot for doing so—and correctly priced for sale. After the day's sales had been totaled up for the entire store, the ticket stubs removed by the cashier and deposited in the register were sorted and returned to the departments from which the merchandise had been taken. These tiny tickets contained in code a precise description of the items they priced, so that without any duplicate sales slips whatsoever, each department knew exactly how many of what had been sold the day before.

My job was merely to direct the customer to what she wanted, provide the correct size (or talk her into buying the available size-too-small), and if I had time, try to interest her in buying the stuff we had a hard time getting rid of. The prices in Budget Slips ranged, with one or two exceptions, from $1 (on Mondays) or $1.99 (on all other days) all the way up to $3.69, so there was generally very little any of us had to do but keep a mechanical watch on our stock, maintain some kind of order, and hop around continuously, handing things to people. Pearl was as new to the store as I. She had previously worked in a small dress shop in Forest Hills but had had to quit, she confided to me, because the sudden death of her husband had left her too shocked and too "nervous" for all that responsibility. "You call this retailing?" she grumbled to me when there was a moment of quiet (always to be utilized for folding and piling). "Why, my boss used to go to Florida for a month every winter and leave me with his store. Why, he used to come to me every other day with some horror of a dress he had bought and say 'Pearl, what am I going to do with this dog? Pearl, you're the only one who can make this dog walk!'" Pearl always wore a long, freshly sharpened pencil stuck through her chignon as an announcement of her former superior dignity. Hazel, a quiet-spoken spinster who had been working in the store for two years, was bitter, too, but from the other side. Hazel was a careful and conscientious woman, clearly intended to be one of the producers, not distributors, of this world. Her complaints went to the very heart of the enterprise, the necessity for having customers at all. "They're a bunch of animals," she told me. "For two years now I have been straightening around this place, putting sizes together and styles together, stacking things diagonally with the tickets all showing, so you'd think they could find exactly what they want and just take it. But, no, they have to flip through everything, pull it apart, and change their minds a thousand times. And wait till you see that Manny!" she finally exploded. "He's the buyer. He has no manners at all!"

We were given a half hour for lunch and a half hour in reliefs, fifteen minutes in the morning, fifteen in the afternoon: all duly recorded by timeclock and card. The rule was you could not leave your counter without having in your possession a little white slip stating your destination and time of leaving the floor, signed by your section manager (a

young girl whose sole function, it appeared, was to keep tabs
in this way on the personal urges and habits of the help). I
was reluctant to leave the counter that first day. For one
thing, in putting my coat away when I arrived, I had cast my
eye over the lounging facilities provided for our relief time:
two wooden benches subtly placed beneath the timeclock;
and I had also caught a whiff from the other side of the
locker-room wall of the cafeteria vegetable chowder and
creamed canned corn and stewed tomatoes being prepared
for lunch. But my inability to survive for three hours without
a smoke finally drove me downstairs. (Later on, when I was
feeling quite at home in Jays, I learned several techniques
for sneaking a puff or two in the stockroom—at a fearful
hazard to life and goods.) There I took my place on one of
the benches with several weary-looking women and listened
to lurid tales about customers' abuses, the main source of
sociable conversation among Jays' employees. One of the
women, who worked in Childrenswear, sat rubbing a bruised
shin. The children, she said, monster offspring of those mon-
strous mothers, all kicked her.

"That Manny," about whom Hazel had so passionately
warned me, was our buyer. His domain was lingerie: Budget Slips, Better Slips (our modest, self-effacing sisters across
the way), Robes (a couple of standing racks near the front
door), and Panties (a big open table three aisles over).
Manny appeared after a couple of days. He had been away
"at the market." The first thing he did was run his hand
through the open slips and bellow, "Too thin. Too thin. Fill
out this goods. Get the stuff out here on the counter. Let
'em see it, let 'em have it. Pull out those crinolines there.
Give 'em sizes, give 'em colors." He was a big man and
heavy, put together with a peculiar combination of obesity
and athletic hardness. His face was rather coarse but not
mannish coarse, girlish coarse: too much lips, too soft; too
large eyes; too pink cheeks, too soft again. He spoke with the
heavy dentalization of east Brooklyn and had a voice commensurate. There were several customers at the counter. I

saw Hazel flinch and then caught the cold stare, from over
by the escalator, of Miss Hardman, the floor manager, the
forces of law and order.

To say that Manny was a buyer and had been at the market might be misleading. These words tend to conjure up
images set by ordinary retailing, images of a carpeted office,
of four-times-a-year attendance at merchandising shows, of
expense accounts and tickets to *My Fair Lady*. The buying
for Jays was a week-by-week affair (sometimes, when the
rush got heavy, it was day-by-day). Since a store of this sort
depended entirely on the goods that were immediately at
hand when the hands were there to snatch them, and on the
grandiose claims that could be made for them, the buyers in
fact ran the business, you might say, *were* the business. They
had to know at every minute what was being bought and
why, even what was being said by the customers that might
augur something for the future—and the future at Jays was
tomorrow, not next season. Every woman who walked away
from a counter not having found something to please her was
accounted a sale lost for all time and represented the buyer's
personal failure to provide. Though the table of organization
at Jays might have looked very much like that of Macy's or
Altman's—it boasted clerks, section managers, floor managers, a display department, and so on—there was a crucial
difference of weight: the buyers were in effect tenant-propri-
etors. Manny's office, not to be too romantic about it, was a
packing case in the stockroom, with a telephone and a clip-
board holding the data sheets on yesterday's sales. Most of
his time was actually spent on the floor, rushing around from
one of his wards to the other filling in the dwindling stock
and seeing that the girls handled it right, often stopping to
help out with the customers.

It took about five minutes to see and understand the nature of Manny's irascibility with the girls, part of what Hazel
called his bad manners (the other part was simply his intensely personal interest in the business, something startling
in a place that pretends to be a respectably systematic world
of employees). He wanted them to love his slips, to love his
business, to be unhappy, not relieved as they were, when

things got slow, and, above all, to keep him accurately informed about what they needed in the way of stock. He
wanted them, in short, to be retailers. The first thing he said
when we were introduced was "Ask me questions—for Chris-
sakes, keep on asking questions!"

His name was Emanuel Lisitsky, and we were, in a compromise gesture toward the awkwardness and time-consum-
ing nature of "Lisitsky," to call him Mr. L. We never managed to. Hazel coldly and scrupulously used his full name;
Pearl and I slipped into "Manny."

From that very first moment on, Manny's presence involved us in a special kind of battle on main floor. Do not get
the impression, from the descriptions of cashiers' counters
and crowded racks, that the store was an honest and forthright "shlock" enterprise. It wasn't. The fittings and arrangements and displays, while not elegant, were sufficient to give
the illusion that this was a department store like all others.
The building was new and bright; our floors shone and our
mannequins all had freshly curled hair. And the managerial
forces, so efficiently impersonated by Miss Hardman and her
platoon of hangers-on, persisted, against both the frank behavior of the customers and the pressuring tactics of the
buyers, to uphold Jays' dignity. Four times a day Miss
Hardman came and instructed us to clean up the counter
that had just been thrown into a tousled intimacy by Manny,
or to tape up the boxes he had just ripped open. "Your stock
will get soiled!" she would glower in Fifth Avenue consterna-
tion. She was capable of talking about our bits and pieces
with crooked seams, mismatched fronts and backs, and
sewed-up rips with the hauteur of a Ceil Chapman, and I
had to admire her for it. Instinct told me, though—the customers themselves told me, who regarded soilage as only additional psychological reassurance in their game of getting
something for nothing—that she, and the poor frenzied
Hazel, represented the wrong principle. But instinct or no,
she was one of the bosses. We had no choice but to shuttle
back and forth between Manny's sincerity and Eleanor
Hardman's pretensions, throwing stock out and putting it

back: Pearl moving around with firm deliberation, brandish-
ing her useless pencil, and Hazel bursting into tears at least
once a day. A certain shortness of temper always underlay
relations at Jays—from bosses to clerks to customers and
back again; this split personality of ours accounted for a
good part of it.

As Christmas came closer and closer, things reached an
unbelievable pitch of intensity. We were open every night
and busy every single minute. Still more help was taken on
for the afternoons, mostly school kids. We tripped over one
another in our confined quarters, now rendered even more
confined by the presence of piles of boxes in our little back-of-
the-counter corridor, and new shipments were arriving every
day. Our stock and our custom changed composition
slightly: we were doing a huge business in the size range
from 42–48 and in such formerly dead items as long-sleeved
flannel nightshirts, camisoles, and wide-strapped cotton slips
—Christmas gifts for old grandmothers and cleaning women.
For the imminent approach of New Year's Eve, our crinoline
section was mobbed from morning till night. Through it all
the public address system, ordinarily used to announce the
store's closing in ten minutes, was piping music—Christmas
carols and currently popular recordings.

And Manny was blooming. Shirt sleeves rolled up, face
flushed, mountains of boxes balanced on his shoulders, he
literally danced from counter to counter, yelling at the sales-
girls in great good humor and urging on the customers.
Christmas was clearly Manny's great season. We were doing
a fantastic business in our little corner (he once told me the
average daily figures; they meant nothing to me, as I had no
standard to judge by, but my father, when I repeated them
to him, clapped both hands to his cheeks) and that was supposed to mean a great big bonus. But money was not the
main thing with Manny. When, the week before Christmas,
the Queens buyers were informed by Jays' owner, Jay Gold-
stein, that there were to be no bonuses distributed that year
—in Queens we were flourishing, but the Brooklyn store had
had a bad year and there was no money in the till for extras
—the boys were all thrown into a terrible funk. For days

they walked around quiet and petulant or stood around on the floor in groups of two or three whispering angrily. All, that is, but Manny. He continued his waltz through main floor, commenting only, "I do all right, I do *all* right. Uncle Jay'll take care of me some day. He'll be good for it."

Success in the organization did not immediately matter, either. You had but to see him in the lunchroom sitting with the smartly dressed, pale counterparts of himself (the buyers always ate together at a special table) to understand that Manny had nothing to worry about and that he knew it: eating fast, talking expansively—I can still see him at that table, shouting about something and gesticulating with a fork from which there always dangled a floppy uncut lettuce leaf. He understood, and just looking at him you understood, that everybody else in the whole crazy world of retailing could be dispensed with and Manny would go on standing by a slips counter or some other counter, any kind, somewhere, chanting "Here they are, girls, right here. Call it out and we got it. They're fabulous! Fabulous!"

That Christmas rush was for him its own meaning. He was a man whose business was to do business, and he was doing it. "Look at 'em, Dex-tuh," he would coo every morning before opening time, pointing to the huge crowd already pushing against the doors. "They're all ours. A sure thing, sure as the roses in May, sure as a pregnant woman at a shorty nightgown count-tuh." Or he would come by later in the day and say, "Listen, Dex-tuh baby, my own true love, I'm getting sick of that line of rayon tricot we carry. Let's clear it out of here by tonight. To hell with nylon this afternoon, and let's push the tricot, huh. Will you do that for me, baby?" "Take my hand," some crooner was pleading through the loudspeaker, and Manny chimed in with a surprisingly sweet voice, "I'm a stranger in paradise"—all the while spattering the corals and aquas of the rayon tricots up and down the length of the counter. He was in paradise, all right, but to this particular selling-man's dream of a paradise no one could be a stranger for long. Even Hazel got infected. She stayed close to the crinolines, laughing at the sight of herself covered with the sparkly stuff that was supposed to decorate the net underskirts but that long before lay in little piles over everything, or recounting in mock horror case after case of some 250-pound woman who insisted on buying one of the stiff petticoats to give herself that "bouffant look."

Pushing the rayon tricot was easy. (We never did sell it out, of course, because the minute Manny saw that it was moving well, he hurried into the stockroom and telephoned the manufacturer for more.) Pushing anything was easy during those days, but anyway I had been taking lessons from the champion. I could never bring myself to begin shouting at the passersby, as I had seen him do so often, things like "Right over here, girls!" I had tried it once or twice and had been defeated by the sickly, uncertain sound of my voice. But hawking wasn't really a necessary part of Manny's system, just something that happened to suit *his* style. The secret was conviction. Bargain hunters are a breed of people in search for conviction; this fact is the very meaning of a store like Jays. A woman who intends to buy a black dress, size 16, will walk into any dress department, go to the rack marked 16, and choose a black dress if she finds one to her liking. But a woman who is "out shopping"—even if she has the pretext of some specific quest—will naturally gravitate to the kind of store whose goods are all lying out in readiness and shrieking for her recognition. Because what the shopper, as distinct from the mere statistical consumer, is really looking for is anything at all that will relieve the terrible pressure on her to take possession of some of this world's goods and pass others by.

It is hard to describe concretely how a salesclerk communicates the conviction needed to draw customers to her wares (at Jays you only had to pull three or four customers together; that was enough to create the ensuing mob). She need not, as I said, actually call to them. But there is a way of suddenly beginning to put forward an item, to fold and unfold, to shake it out, to be busy and intent over it, and there is a way of looking—knowing, superior, as if one had just discovered the importance of something neglected—that no free-floating buyer can resist. The women would begin to squeal at me, "Oh, is it *really* a bargain?" and I knew I had them. "Oh, honey, please give me one from the bottom!"

Pushing dead stock at Christmastime was easy, all right; it was being pushed by the living that got to be a nightmare. I tried to avoid the crinolines as much as possible. Because the women weren't taking those petticoats (stiff ones to flare at the waist or tight ones to flare at the knees or soft ones with ribbons and spangles to provide "a tantalizing glimpse of color beneath the lifted skirt") from us; they were killing us to get their hands on them: kids in bobby socks, elegant ladies in Fireside Room finery, and Hazel's pets, the 200-pounders, elbow to elbow. The crinolines were kept in large deep cartons, standing up so as not to lose their shape, and once I was actually tumbled head first into a carton, my feet waving in the air.

"Attagirl, Dex-tuh," roared Manny, slapping my thigh in pure fraternal enthusiasm. "She really goes after the stuff. But I mean."

"That happens to be one stuff you couldn't get me after even for the Baltimore Cotillion!" I came up with a mouthful of spangles and paste.

"Now, now." Manny suddenly stopped smiling. "That happens to be a good piece of goods."

I shut up immediately. One kept forgetting about the irrepressible Manny that with him the joke always had a fixed limit, just at the point of his buying. He didn't care about the slips themselves—they could have been hardware—but he was dead-humorless about his claims for them. In Jays we had three classifications for our merchandise: ordinary stock was "fabulous"—fabulous was routine, nobody much minded about fabulous; something that turned out to be a pretty good buy was "mad"—for mad you had to have at least a modicum of respect; but a feat of buying, one of those real triumphs which by themselves alone could have justified our reputation, choked us into inarticulateness. "A good piece of goods," Manny had said. That was the highest. A cowed silence was the only acceptable response.

I do not mean to be laughing now, either. Manny was right: it was a good piece of goods. The thing might have crumbled to pieces in one's hands, it might have disappeared completely in the first strong wind, but that would not have altered its value for us in the least. When you stand behind a counter, you have to have your own true and your own beautiful that have nothing to do with any other systems of judgment. Something sells, therefore it is beautiful, and sells at a proper percent of markup, therefore it is valuable. You have to have them, not only in a flamboyant enterprise like Jays but in order to sell anything anywhere. Personal preference is a matter for the customers out there—and not even for them, poor beset creatures, because they end up buying just what is mostly being bought. Retailing, however subsidiary and dependent its function in the national economy, is an absolutely closed system: what is selling is what is good is what is selling.

The day of Christmas Eve, at about four in the afternoon, a peaceful silence suddenly descended on Jays. The orgy was spent. We knew the quiet would extend through the next few weeks; even our Monday-morning regulars would have neither the cash nor the energy to face us for a while. I received a box of Loft's chocolates, and in my pay envelope was enclosed a mimeographed letter that said: "Dear Temporary Employee: It has been a pleasure having you with us. Won't you please stay on to help us with our gift exchanges, which will bring your term of employment to January 15. Thank you for your help. Think of us next year," etc.

Manny wished me luck and said, "We'll be seeing you around here in the mob, Dex-tuh. I'm gonna get you into one of those petticoats yet."

"Oh, no"—I was shaking my head—"once I step out from behind this counter, I'm not coming back. I can't afford to shop in a place like this. Too poor. You guys would do me in."

I meant it, and I have never since set foot in the place.

1958

2

Novelist of South Africa

The Price of Diamonds is Dan Jacobson's third novel. In another time, perhaps, or in another country, the consistently lavish praise heaped on Mr. Jacobson's earlier works, *The Trap* and *A Dance in the Sun,* would have been enough to make the appearance of his third book a much awaited literary occasion. But he is, in this time of movements, trends, generations—when people get excited about new novels mostly in proportion to how much they reveal about the problems of our culture and what they predict about the moral and spiritual climate of our children—an intractably lone voice, and one that may seem too quiet to be heard above the beat and angry uproar. And then he writes about South Africa, a country which, for all its richness of political and social tension, seems to be rather far away from the center of our concerns. The *New York Times Book Review,* for instance, because *The Price of Diamonds* is about a crime and one of its leading characters a detective, saw fit to have the book reviewed by the man who runs the weekly column on mystery fiction. Once having been called a remarkable writer with a remarkable talent, Mr. Jacobson seems to present no further problems to his critics.

"Remarkable" is probably not the word for this work—it seems patronizing and improper when applied to a prose style so fixed and controlled and to a literary intention so concentrated, as do those other words for young writing, "promising" and "talented"—but Dan Jacobson is something better: a man whose character and intelligence grow into and out of one another, who has, in the service of that character and that intelligence, nothing left to learn about craft, and who says exactly what and as much as he means to say. These virtues (and put this way, they do seem austere ones) are precisely the virtues needed in the management of Mr. Jacobson's theme—which is, very crudely, the meaning of being an honorable man when to do so goes against the laws of the surrounding nature—and to convey the way he wants to look at things—which is with detachment and wisdom.

Mr. Jacobson was born and grew up in South Africa (he now lives in England), and South Africa is his subject and will probably continue to be so, under whatever name or location he gives it. For that country—which is a brilliantly concrete and specific place in his writing, full of landscapes, weathers, private languages—is also nothing less than the very special and pointed vision he has of the problem of being human. In no other country in the world, perhaps, do the conditions of everyday life make such an unending assault on the self-image of the man with a Western conscience as they do in Mr. Jacobson's homeland. This assault on the self-image comes not merely from the fact that South African white society oppresses and terrorizes black men—an individual, as individual, can at least partially dissociate himself from the cruelty practiced by those around him, can even find it fertile ground for cultivating a feeling of heroism or righteousness. The problem that pursues Dan Jacobson through his books and stories grows out of the peculiar mixture of a life that is genuinely comfortable, pleasant, desirable even, set squarely on the foundations of another kind of life almost inconceivable in its squalor and dislocation and suffering. To the outsider haunted by the record of white exploitation of the blacks, the situation in South Africa offers the relief of being potentially explosive. To Mr. Jacobson, it is the chastening experience of having lived, and lived well, and aspired to live better, by a system of crying injustice. Such an experience gives the problem of human decency its true proportion and keeps it alive and glowing. In *A Dance in the Sun* the narrator remembers:

> Time passed in the garden, in the stoep, in the back-yard, while we trudged to school or idled holidays away on our bicycles, and shyness and silence gave way to talk and stories of pleasures that were so distant from us that we knew they could never be ours, of griefs so great and distant that we could not understand how this person who had borne them should be standing in front of us with a spade or a broom in his hand, talking evenly, as if the earth had not swallowed up his mother's body, as if the farmer who had beaten him so that he could still show us the scars on his arms and shoulders were not still alive and perhaps doing the same thing to another. And already there stirred within us the first uneasy strivings toward guilt and pity that were later to hunt us and shame us in our own country.

To the boy looking back, the bicycles and backyards, the gardens (and they hint to us of pleasant suburban streets lined with big and comfortable homes) are as real as the stories of the once beaten and scarred kaffir. Together they make up the truth of his childhood, and neither can be remembered without instantly bringing to mind the other.

In the problem of reconciling the two memories and giving each its due, Mr. Jacobson has found his vision and his statement: man cannot aggrandize the proportions of his own small nature, cannot finally be altered, by the knowledge of evil. This is the kind of statement that comes to no conclusion but can only be the basis for a continual exploration. For the purposes of his exploration Mr. Jacobson has needed the discipline of a tightly, perfectly rounded incident or set of incidents—in the three novels thus far they have centered on crimes—to keep what he has to say from getting turned on its head. He has had to set up his story with elaborate promises of a neat denouement; for when a conclusion is made inevitable in this way, by such things as the motion of the plot and suspense, the author's refusal to draw it can be understood as the real point he is making, instead of as his failure to make a point at all.

In *The Trap,* the farmer Van Schoor discovers that he has been betrayed by his "good boy," the kaffir Willem. Van Schoor had been comfortably pleased with himself for his absolute faith in the black man—he had even, without investigating further, accepted Willem's story of a homosexual attack and fired another much-needed hand—only to find Willem in the hands of the police for stealing his sheep. Van Schoor pounds his fists into Willem's smashed and bleeding face; he is purged by his rage at truth. But afterward Willem's partner in crime, the white man who with Willem had been stealing from the farmer and who had been the one to betray Willem to the police, sits down at Van Schoor's table to have a cup of coffee with him. It is with this cup of coffee, not the "truth," that the book ends.

In *A Dance in the Sun* the narrator and his companion pledge themselves, through the operation of pity and conscience, to bear witness for the kaffir Joseph and against the white man Fletcher—which would have meant, in fact, to accuse Fletcher of kidnapping or murder. But Joseph has unearthed the truth about the crime Fletcher committed against him and his family and has asked the boys to support him, not to bring Fletcher before the law but only to blackmail him into taking Joseph back into his household. The boys go off to finish their holiday "smarting under the treatment we had just received, and the knowledge of how we had exposed ourselves to it . . ." and Fletcher is left dancing like a madman at the knowledge that for the whole life before him there would be Joseph's subservience and Joseph's victory over him.

Both the earlier books are about relations between black men and white men. Both take place on farms in the middle of the veld, with its hard cracked earth, its thorn trees and its furious sunlight—the perfect landscape for the promise of finality and, on the other hand, irresolution. *Diamonds,* which has moved into town (the veld is there only underneath the scrubby bushes and lawns of civilization and waiting silently all around the outskirts), represents a kind of relaxation into comedy and an abstraction of the author's problem. In the town, called Lyndhurst, things become more complicated. The town is a place of backyards and gardens and the middle classes. In the town, for instance, there are Jews and there are businesses and there is Legemco, a branch of the South African diamond monopoly. Lyndhurst is a place built, literally, on diamond mines; and diamonds breed crime—not social crime but crime for profit—so there is an underworld. But if things there are more complicated, they are also more abstract and can even be terribly funny: diamonds are, after all, dirty little stones that come out of the ground; the economy of Lyndhurst is founded on some laws called the Illegal-Diamond-Buying Laws, which have nothing to do with human values but are only a construct of the diamond monopoly, itself a construction, for maintaining high diamond values; and the question of a man's relation to some dirty little stones and the laws that protect them is really more like a question of his relation to himself, a very abstract question indeed.

Diamonds, is the story of how Manfred Gottlieb, husband to Riva, partner to Fink ("Fink and Gottlieb—Manufacturers' Representatives"), father to Irvine (off in Johannesburg learning to be a doctor), accidentally comes into possession of a few illegal diamonds and of how he holds onto them, not to get rich with, but in order to enact a fantasy of heroic lawbreaking and mastery. His fantasy primarily involves his partner, Fink: Fink the rebel, the radical, the lone wolf, who for years had been shouting his program for the destruction of the diamond interests and his threats that he, Fink, would personally fly in the face of Legemco one of these days. In the dialogue of their long partnership, Fink had become to Gottlieb the voice of the world "out there," a world that promised wonders in which he could not believe and then reproached him for his timidity and lack of faith. ("Fink, you are a kind of socialist." "Gottlieb, you are a slave. With a slave's mind.") When the diamonds are left with him, Gottlieb believes they are intended for Fink—that his partner has finally acted on his threats—and that by hiding them away he will, with one act, become superior to I.D.B., to Fink, to the whole, wide, beckoning, threatening world:

> "But I meant to test you by showing you these diamonds," Gottlieb then permitted Fink to say: "and here I find you have been even more severely tested than I planned, and, Gottlieb, you are unruffled. How did you manage it?" "I have my reserves, Fink." "I can see that you have reserves of iron, Gottlieb," Fink was then encouraged to say. "Thank you, Fink —but please—don't embarrass me with such praises." And with these last imagined words of his own in his ears, Gottlieb fell asleep.

In the end Gottlieb commits a crime, though not the crime he had thought himself prepared to commit (from which he is saved by seeing an enactment of its consequences, as it were, beforehand), and Gottlieb and Fink become reconciled to each other and to their respective lives. This story, with every one of its strands pulled into place and tied neatly, is just as inconclusive as its predecessors. That is, the two men end up where they started—except they no longer have the illusion that such things as diamonds afford them the possibility of heroic action—and the life to which they become reconciled is a life still caught in the same tangle of comforts and fears, of getting along, and of getting along well, while at the same time being dependent on a "system" that constantly threatens their sense of their own reality. The diamonds are indeed disposed of forever, but the dust they raise as they roll down the side of a great empty pit is the dust of South Africa.

Mr. Jacobson is a man who keeps his temper and his perceptions cool. He is a master at creating the "small" book, in which each and every detail must contribute to a strict accounting for the flow of events or the behavior of the characters but still have a convincing existence of its own. In *Diamonds*, for instance, the relations of Gottlieb to his wife and son and Fink to his daughters are dealt with and described only insofar as they are absolutely necessary to an understanding of the predicament of the two men and to furthering the process of the plot. And yet the author has

managed to create a whole live world of family that we can
see easily for its vividness and recognize easily for its rightness. Even the names of the children (Irvine, Althea, etc.)
become the clue to a story of humble, ambitious fathers who
push their sons and daughters beyond themselves and are
then left behind to nurse the fear of being abandoned. In
order to sharpen the meaning of the problem represented by
his main characters, Mr. Jacobson has made them Jews:
people not quite alien to the earth that gives forth the precious stones, but who cannot possess it either. (As Manfred
Gottlieb wanders through Lyndhurst on his nightly excursions to the underworld, the town is his home, yet he calls its
inhabitants "these people.") But quite apart from their
symbolic function, Gottlieb and Fink and Riva and their
children are more accurately Jewish and more meaningfully
Jewish than any other Jewish characters I know of in contemporary fiction. No particular point is made of their being
Jews, they do not have to discuss it, the author does not have
to mention its relevance to their situation or their feelings;
they just *exist* in the way they must. To make every single
element in a work of fiction serve its exact purpose, as Mr.
Jacobson does, and yet to make of each something that has
its own reality, that exists, that persuades, that moves, all by
itself—this is art of a very high order.

Still—with the proof of the pudding on one's very tongue
—it is difficult not to feel that the unfailing detachment,
precision, and self-control of all Mr. Jacobson's work (particularly this book, since it is the most "relaxed") point to
something more than the operation of his literary intelligence. In the whole of his writing there is not a single gratui-
tous detail—thrown in for love or even just because it has
occurred to him—not a gesture, not a response that does not
have its exactly defined place in the whole. And obversely,
not one thing any of his characters ever does or says is done
or said without being carefully accounted for and predicted,
not only by the kind of person he is made to be, but by
something explicitly referred to in his history. *Diamonds* is a
book almost frightening in this regard. It cannot be that Mr.
Jacobson is incapable of making mistakes; the kind of irony

with which he touches his material is as capable of mistakes as is passion. The truth of the matter is that Mr. Jacobson works almost as much by a principle of evading the "wrong" objects and perceptions as by finding the right ones. The principle of evasion is for him an honorable, not a cowardly, one, and one that must cost him a great deal of anguish and self-effacement; for clearly what he is pushing away, excluding, at every moment he writes is the chaos he does not yet feel adequate to—the chaos of things gratuitously ugly and mean and of the feelings in himself for which he has no respect. He does not permit himself, or his characters, the rage that might contradict his ironic, humane intelligence. At the end of *Diamonds* the perpetually angry Fink says to Gottlieb: "When all around us there is nothing in the world except what we make, Fink was busy making such jokes and such tricks. . . . That is why I tell you, Gottlieb, I am a man to be forgiven, not a man that you should ask forgiveness from."

But the gentleness of *Diamonds* is deceptive. There is a kind of fury in the close arrangement of the writing which comes not from the knowledge that "there is nothing in the world except what we make" but from the sense, the South Africa-born sense, that there is much too much in the world we have not made and can do nothing about. This sense, too, is part of Mr. Jacobson's vision, the part, if he let it, that could spur him to move beyond the limits he sets for himself to be a writer of "big" books—and a major novelist.

1958

3

Norman Mailer's Campaign

Norman Mailer's *The Presidential Papers* is a collection of much of his occasional writing of the last few years. There are the epic essays on the 1960 Democratic convention and the first Patterson-Liston fight; some poems; a couple of interviews, one real, one imaginary; a chapter from a novel in progress; some columns done for *Esquire* and *Commentary;* a speech delivered in debate with William Buckley; and a few assorted sundries. The pieces are of varying lengths, intensities, and postures, held together by the kind of introductory comments Mailer originally fashioned for *Advertisements for Myself.* Unlike the earlier collection—which spanned many more years and several turnings in his career —the *Papers* are all products of a single and ever-intensifying preoccupation: that vision of men and society for which Mailer has (not entirely arbitrarily) preempted the name of existentialism.

The book, like so many of its author's public performances, will not fail to outrage (and all the more since the assassination of President Kennedy). For one thing, because it is exactly that, a public performance, Mailer is a writer who has not for one moment allowed his contemporaries to forget the impulse to seduction by exhibition that trembles beneath the written word. But more important, I think, is that throughout the *Papers* Mailer's cheekiest and gaudiest moments are precisely his most serious ones; he therefore cannot be taken seriously except in his own way on his own terms—which is a form of tyranny that few writers are not either too timid or too well mannered to impose.

Consider the shocking liberty of these pieces. Norman Mailer sets out to define the application of his existentialist notions to politics; this definition is extracted and formulated out of his own writings; and the whole thing is then consecrated to the education of the President of the United States. What is more, his address to Mr. Kennedy is undertaken in no mere spirit of fun—with little of that ebullience which derives from the new dispensation to make clean sport of public affairs—but for the purpose of being listened to and even wielding some influence. He has himself photographed for the dust jacket seated on an old-fashioned platform rocker; even this is only half a joke, one can see it in his eye—he has considered the position. And taking for himself the ear of the President, what does he offer? The gleanings of three years' insistent and childlike spiritual adventuring, which involves him in considerations of the nature of God and the Devil, magic, violence, cancer, and excrement. What impudence!

To judge from past responses, however, what most of Mailer's confreres are apt to find being violated here is not their sense of the sanctity of John F. Kennedy (though now, of course, that too) but rather their traditional commitment to what should be the sanctity of *Norman Mailer*. Those liberties of his that have always been most violently objected to are not the liberties taken at the expense of public propriety and responsibility but the ones that threaten certain hard-earned pieties of the literary community itself. The truth is that a writing man may with impunity act out just about anything in relation to the society out there—complacency, cynicism, destructiveness, even criminality—anything, that is, except a simple desire to be implicated in its power.

The trouble with Norman Mailer as a literary figure, then, is that he is always, in the radical sense of the word, so unruly. No sooner is he settled among us at peace, holding our major concessions to his talent and achievement and promise, than he is off again, setting up the next test of his personal strength—and of our willingness to venture. For where he goes he must take everyone, must have confirmation, assent, bigger and newer concessions. When he should be gratified, he turns out to be restless; when he is engaged in what would go down as interesting play, he turns out to be in dead earnest, demanding of us an answering dead earnestness. When he should, above all, be consolidating his position as a Leading American Novelist, he announces that he is running for President, or mayor of New York, or whatever. He is, in short, an altogether untrustworthy citizen of the Republic of Letters.

One always speaks of him this way, as a figure, a citizen, instead of merely as a writer; it is really impossible to separate the two. Nor does Mailer himself do so. He gives over his personal gestures and his prose equally to the judgment of the age. For what he is seeking at every moment is the *effect*, the visible effect of his power to create new possibilities, to work what he has called "a revolution in the consciousness of my time." Therefore everything about him is made to matter: not only his books and pieces and poems, but his discoveries of mood as well; or that he beat William Buckley in debate and the New York *Times* failed to record his victory; or that he had divined a victory for Patterson in the sixth round, who never even made it through the first; or that he had on a certain occasion not been smoking; or that, to take the matter about as far inside as it can go, some of the body cells had probably expired as a result of a given spiritual onslaught. Now it would not be polite to ignore the fact that such pressure on the material of experience can also be called by a simple, ugly, clinical term. But clinical terms are not so much beside the point as beneath it. For the real point is not that Mailer defines a world over which his being is sovereign, but rather that he risks finding all the dimensions of the real world in himself. He is to be the social microcosm —and thus our voluntary scapegoat for weaknesses and corruptions and inadequacies. This is not a modest or endearing ambition. Its stakes are murderously high. But on the other hand, were Mailer to win, he would win all.

It is important to remember about Norman Mailer that though his gestures can be foolish—in the sense of being wasteful, disruptive, misplaced—they are almost never without the grace of consciousness. (As it often works out, he comes under indictment for just those aspects of his behavior and attitudes that he himself finds it necessary, for the sake of what he would assert, to expose. I am thus-and-such a kind of fool, he says, and those who cannot really bear his disorderliness tend to accept at face value this offering of his self-irony.) The closest he has ever come to being utterly graceless is in his piece on Jackie Kennedy. He tells us that after the appearance of his essay on the convention that nominated her husband, she sent him a letter clearly full of praise. In his answer to her he announced that he was contemplating a work on the Marquis de Sade and later tried to explain this egregious blunder on grounds of inaccurate sociology. But when a gentleman tries to interest a distant, beautiful, and famous lady in *his* interest in the Marquis de Sade, he is obviously making love to her. And in Mailer's case the love he was making—just like the whole misbegotten impression he presented of the lady in the first place—was merely the expansion of some feeling of pleasure with himself. It was unintelligent of him not to know that; he deserved her silence.

But such lapses are rare. Considering the particular fates chosen for tempting by this man, and the number of temptations offered them, it seems something of a miracle of the spirit that they are so rare. He manages, for instance, to swagger through his introductions, propose solutions to the problems of juvenile delinquency and capital punishment, discuss his hatred of masturbation, analyze the cause of cancer, or even mount a poetic attack on the book reviewers of *Time*—all without making himself look the least bit prettier. He distances himself from nothing, and he withholds nothing. In the shattering account of his almost diabolically perfect louse-up at the famous Liston press conference, one comes upon the denouement—Mailer, a parched beggar, finally wringing one moist "I like this guy" from the world champ—knowing that no matter what his pose of the moment, he will never allow one to be deceived in him. Whether or not he is making a revolution in the general consciousness, he has, perhaps alone in this country, succeeded in investing public unruliness with a serious style. At the very least, then, he may effect a permanent improvement in the manners of radicalism.

The seriousness with which he faces up to his personal demands on this society—and with which he is therefore able to count their cost to the soul—is not merely a matter of bravery (though it is a measure of the corruption of thought and feeling just how brave a man has to be to get down to things so self-evidently simple as wanting to be a member of a world championship). Partly Mailer's daring has to do with something not, I think, sufficiently taken into account about him, and for which *The Presidential Papers* brings massive evidence. And that is how *American* he is. By "American" I do not mean anything literary-metaphysical. I mean quite simply that he owns America. He unquestioningly and unambiguously belongs here; and the whole country gives itself up to him in a range of natural assumption and reference that seems, in its ease and artlessness, quite unavailable to the rest of the special community he inhabits. The America of the essay on Kennedy is not a thought-out or striven-for place but an experienced one, geographically, socially, and culturally. It is a country which by virtue of its solidity, rather than its abstractness, lends itself to subtle analysis— and by the same token, to real subversion. Probably a lot of this has to do with the fact that Mailer as a very young man experienced an enormous American-style success, virtual movie stardom. But whatever the reason, one thing is clear: he has not the slightest doubt, and therefore needs not the slightest justification, of his right to be important. He calls himself an existentialist, but he is no snob of existences. If he is alienated (sanctified condition), it is an alienation from within, the kind one suffers in relation to one's family rather than to one's neighbors. The difficulty, of course, is that his own family has the power to make even the soberest and most mature of men misbehave. But on the other side, no one can have more power than he to hit them where they live.

This freedom to take for granted the terms of his own culture without flinching has made of Mailer a very earnest man. He forever takes one by surprise with his earnestness. It is a quality not much associated with sophistication or subtlety: passion, yes, and even a capacity for murderous reduction—but not the kind of dogged, megalomaniacal earnestness that was meant earlier by the word "childlike." In this book, for example, the Devil, plastic, and cancer, his three main symbols for the totalitarianism he maintains is threatening to swallow up man's being, are not interesting or illuminating metaphors for evil; they are the actual, material conditions of evil. The God described by Mailer as dependent for his continuing sovereignty on the strategic successes of his human troops is the living God in Mailer's firmament. The waste that results from people's inability to make heroic acceptances and undergo heroic assimilations is—their excrement. At least half of *The Presidential Papers* is taken up directly, and the rest indirectly, with relating these conditions to a varying group of subjects (one should really say objects): from Fidel to birth control to Hasidism; sometimes with blinding brilliance; sometimes with great wit and spirit; sometimes with the kind of clumsiness that comes with bearing down too hard on one's words and being too solemn in one's soul. Only a very reckless man would be in such a hurry to convert his images into new categories of thought. And only a very generous one would leave it so obvious where these categories do and do not work.

I think it is safe to assert that Mailer will not, at least in his own terms, win all. No one less than a major philosopher could succeed in synthesizing what are so far only the bits and pieces of the revolution he means to achieve. And Mailer is no philosopher: his "philosophy" is poetry, requiring always his discrete and precise perceptions of the moment to persuade us. Partly from intellectual brashness and partly from a novelist's habit of thought, he is in the end not sufficiently respectful toward the history of man's difficulties with the problems raised in this book. When he writes discursively of the possibility that there are extranatural connections between natural phenomena, for instance, he manages only to convince us of how sincerely he believes in them. But when he works his willingness to consider the power of magic against something he has actually seen or known—when, in short, he acts the observer he supremely is—he is able to provide all the evidence needed for the truth and rightness of his own sense of things. His *Commentary* column on dread and the absolutely breathtaking description of Patterson's defeat are examples of how Norman Mailer can illuminate those things on heaven and earth our philosophy has not lately bothered to dream of. The man in the state of existential dread and Floyd Patterson are not appropriate figures for a universal discourse, but they are, inescapably, one's fellow Americans. Whatever else Mailer may have failed to do, he has, by a grand fidelity to the character of his own perceptions, given these men's experience a necessary new dimension. If he has not earned the right to deal with the universe, natural or otherwise, no one is currently telling us more about the United States of America.

1964

4

Fitzgerald at the End

"Yes," objected Amory, "but isn't it lack of will-power to let my imagination shinny on the wrong side?"
—*This Side of Paradise*

In 1938, so the story is often told, when Walter Wanger assigned the young Budd Shulberg to collaborate with F. Scott Fitzgerald on a script for a movie about Dartmouth, Shulberg said, "Fitzgerald—I thought he was dead." So too, apparently, had the group of drama students who produced *The Diamond As Big As the Ritz* in a small room above the Pasadena Playhouse in 1939 and who were nonplussed and embarrassed to receive a backstage visit from Fitzgerald—in full evening dress—on opening night. It was not so much that Fitzgerald had disappeared—he was publishing a little in those days, though by his former standards very little; and, after all, *Tender Is the Night* had come out only in 1934. It was that by some kind of unspoken consensus Fitzgerald was labeled "finished" and put away. Perhaps at the time there was a deep public courtesy involved in thinking him dead, for his life, which neither he nor anyone else had ever succeeded in separating from his work, had become an ugly spectacle, marked by illness and Zelda's insanity and alcohol and failure. The man—like the age he had been saddled with representing, like the American dream itself—

had finally collapsed. He was violently and often viciously drunk much of the time. He was in debt, apparently unable to work. And in 1936, when to do such a thing was taken to be a clear sign of selling out, he went off to Hollywood to make some money and learn how to write successful movies. He himself had publicly announced his collapse in three articles in *Esquire* ("The Crack-Up," "Handle with Care," "Pasting It Together"). The articles were of course in their very nature a lie: true, they were the exploration of their author's feeling of personal ruin, his "spiritual bankruptcy," but they were also among the strongest and most trenchant products of a writer still capable of first-rate work.

When, in 1940, Fitzgerald did die, he left behind six chapters of a novel and voluminous notes for its completion. He left behind, too, a feeling, and one that has persisted through the last eighteen years of posthumous publication and reams of serious criticism and acclaim, that some special redress of a wrong is due him. Or if "redress" and "wrong" are too emphatic, that some kind of subtle imbalance in the world's view of Fitzgerald must be set right. At the end of his biography Arthur Mizener says, "Like Gatsby . . . Fitzgerald loved reputation, the public acknowledgment of genuine achievement, with the impersonal magnanimity of a Renaissance prince. He lived, finally, to give that chaos in his head shape in his books and to see the knowledge that he had done so reflected back to him from the world. He died believing he had failed. Now we know better, and it is one of the final ironies of Fitzgerald's career that he did not live to enjoy our knowledge." That "now we know better," written ten years after Fitzgerald's death and at the end of a painstaking biography, strikes the curious personal note of apology—not so much for Fitzgerald as *to* him—that sounds so often in the writing about him.

Now Sheilah Graham, who lived with Fitzgerald during his last four years, has, with the aid of Gerold Frank, written her autobiography, *Beloved Infidel,* and the section about their life together is also a moving personal defense of him.

Sheilah Graham was sent to Hollywood by the North American Newspaper Alliance to take over its syndicated movie gossip column. Before coming to America from London, she had held many posts in a rather stunning career of imposture and social climbing: born Lily Sheil in London's East End and raised in an orphanage, with no education, no experience and a bad accent, by her late twenties she had managed to marry respectably, to make something of a success on the musical comedy stage, to be presented at court, to crash the society of the English county aristocracy, and finally to get in some semiprofessional experience as a newspaper feature writer. *Beloved Infidel* is unfortunately one of those autobiographical memoirs written in collaboration with Gerold Frank, in which all the author's real feelings, ideas, and responses to what has happened in life are buried beneath the most irritating narrative style ever invented. Everything in the book is reduced to an event coming at Miss Graham from the outside; her own part in it gets squeezed into a few handy mass-magazine formulas ("This was wonderful. This was the answer to everything" or "Even now, I wonder, who looked after me?") so that the reader is left begging for a little relief from the specter of those wide-open baby-blue eyes. Nevertheless, merely from Sheilah Graham's story itself, and from the reconstruction all its flatly told facts makes inevitable, one can understand something of what must have been, what must be, the quality of this remarkable woman. There is, for instance, the fact that at each crucial moment of her life some man was waiting, and always just the man needed, to give her the protection and the training for the next audacious push of her ambition—the acme of which, I suppose, was reached in a proposal of marriage from the Marquess of Donegall, who has one of the oldest peerages in Britain. She was pretty; she was absolutely devoted to the climb; but these are somehow not enough to account for her astonishing career. Beyond them what she clearly had was grace, some Midas touch of the personality. However, what makes her most remarkable of all is that, with her gift of grace and given her lower-class romance about the rich and her totally expedient morality, she did not stop with the British aristocracy, the Marquess of Donegall, her fantasy of having children called the Earl of Belfast and the Lady Wendy of Chichester. She went on to an American newspaper career and to Fitzgerald. She never makes clear what prompted her to this last seemingly unaccountable step. She says she went to America looking for "love," but love is something no more easily to be found in New York than in London, and her street sense must have told her so even if her romantic literary ego no longer does. She describes a very unpretty scene between Randolph Churchill and Charlie Chaplin at a posh London restaurant in which Churchill was overbearing and arrogant and Chaplin was obsequious, and talks of her own shock at discovering that even genius must bow to the blood. Years earlier, as a hungry young girl strolling down Piccadilly night after night, money and titles had seemed the best the world could offer. But when she got access to them, she wanted something better, something by whose terms Charlie Chaplin did not have to be patronized nor she to be a liar. And when she met Fitzgerald in Hollywood, she was able to decide almost immediately that he was what she wanted. She had never known anyone like Fitzgerald—writers and literary intellectuals during her brief stay in New York had intimidated her—but her infallible instinct must have seized on what, even by the time she sat down to do this book, she could only express indirectly and cumulatively: that with Fitzgerald she had come to the *very* best.

Fitzgerald educated her. He would prepare detailed reading lists for her, discuss her assignments when she had read them; they listened to music, read criticism, and they called it the F. Scott Fitzgerald College of One. If there is something embarrassing and pathetic in the way she talks about her studies ("I thought, suddenly, I will not be in this position again. They discuss Franz Kafka and T. S. Eliot and Wallenstein and Richelieu and the Thirty Years' War and I sit on the outside, looking in.") and about the reading lists themselves, there is also something new and striking in such a picture of Fitzgerald: the man who with Edmund Wilson and other friends seemed humbly to accept his role as intellectual inferior, whose spelling was a public joke, had with delight and great energy taken on the role of "intellectual conscience" to someone else. And so much of what Miss Graham presents of Fitzgerald comes at us this way. She found him all by herself. She hadn't known who he was; she hadn't read his books. For her there were no staled or hackneyed public images, no old history, coming between them. This is why she can make us *see* the things his friends and Mr. Mizener could only refer to in writing about him: his wit, his charm, his astonishing profligacy of spirit, and his self-hatred. Even his drunks, which had until this book become distant and legendary—one of them already the subject of a famous novel and play—are made real; meaner, nastier, more shocking, perhaps, than it had become necessary to think—but for the first time the real behavior of a real man. The F. Scott Fitzgerald Miss Graham found because she looked for herself and because she had the proper need of him was a strong man. He educated her; he gave her values.

The final twist about the Fitzgerald we see through Sheilah Graham's eyes is that for her he had become the exponent of the values he embodied as a creative artist—he who had seemed so helpless to come to terms with them himself.

Perhaps nobody's values have been subjected to the kind of critical scrutiny Fitzgerald's have. Virtually everything he wrote raises in the minds of his readers the question of his own relation to the moral and spiritual emptiness of the ethos he so poignantly chronicles. Does he stand inside or outside the terms by which his characters judge the world and on account of which they are doomed? It would take only a small failure of imagination, only a minute but essential shutting off of sympathy, to find Fitzgerald's life doomed as are the lives of his characters, and for something like the same reason: not because he seemed so much to dignify their illusions but because the illusions he dignified were so cheap.

Like Sheilah Graham, Fitzgerald had done a great deal of traveling to get to the Hollywood where they met. If her journey can be described as one straight up, then his was one down through the bottom and out the other side. Both of them had displayed great courage, but hers, of the nervy kind, risked only not succeeding; he had risked failure. In order to be something it was impossible for him to be—what he called "an entire man in the Goethe-Byron-Shaw tradition, with an opulent American touch"—he had handicapped himself and his thick, easy, generous talent at every turn, and in the end probably only left one book and a few stories that will outlast the rapid social changes of the next few decades. The "entire man" he dreamed of was a man always to be remembered as much for what he was as for what he did, in whom it would be impossible to distinguish the boundary between personality and achievement, a "figure." But Fitzgerald was born into a world in which everyone *begins* as a figure. In St. Paul the confusion between personality and achievement, though on another level, comes easy. You do not attain it, you fall victim to it. In a place like the snowy, red-cheeked, robust, self-made world of "The Ice Palace" and "Winter Dreams," what you do is the public definition of what you are, the exclusive and exhaustive one. And the problem, if you do something so indefinable and subversive of order as write, is not to impose a public image but precisely to protect your private personality from the exactions of an image foisted on you, as it were, almost at birth. Under the circumstances, Fitzgerald did not have to become the embodiment of the Jazz Age or anything else—without some great effort he could not have avoided it. In seeking the old unity of life and art, what he achieved was an immensely fertile but almost fatally costly confusion of experience with the meaning of experience, of identification with empathy. He became someone for whom there was neither escape from innocence nor retreat from consciousness.

That he kept the cost from being fatal, that he made his self-conscious innocence work for him, is, after all, only an ambiguous victory. Nevertheless, it is a victory, and one to which we owe a unique, irreplaceable record of what Americans come from and what they must all get through in order to grow up. In some ways the purest product of Fitzgerald's special gift is *This Side of Paradise*. Certainly the book is a chaos, an adolescent riot of literary mismatched limbs, changing voice and sexual incompetence. Amory Blaine's predicament often seems like child's play, but Fitzgerald's keen inside sense of it, his respect for its urgency cuts through the triviality of its specific content and makes us see it for what it really is: an expression of the great American conflict between a meanness of culture and a grandeur of pretension—the struggle between the coarseness of attitude that gives Americans so much will to deal with the world and the faint, delicate image of beauty that is to be the object of that will.

This Side of Paradise lacks even the pretense of a plot. Fitzgerald does not know what must become of Amory and therefore cannot make what happens to him fit into some pattern of becoming. "I know myself—but that is all!" is Amory's last cry—and it is Fitzgerald's cry too. Nor does he really plot the later novels (of course, and always, excepting *Gatsby*). Anthony Patch and Dick Diver get older; their lives themselves have taken on more form, and therefore the books do. Fitzgerald is able to take these characters farther—he takes them, in fact, up to the point of dissolution. But he does not really either get beyond them in time and look back or outside them and look in. He is never re-creating life but only making a progress report on it.

With *Gatsby* something different happened. Gatsby is not a character in Fitzgerald's sense, not a life in the process of unfolding. Gatsby is an idea. In writing the book Fitzgerald was clearly seized by a vision, a pure distillation of his relation to something large and abstract—to America—and at the end of this vision there was Gatsby's corpse floating in the pool. The corpse, the abstraction, gave him the freedom he never sought or took elsewhere to direct all the movement that led to it.

Tender Is the Night, then, is Fitzgerald's last progress report on his odyssey into figuredom. The report is a bad one. Dick Diver is finished, and finished in a way seemingly prophetic for Fitzgerald: he is no longer useful to those it had become the meaning of his life to serve. The year *Tender Is the Night* came out Fitzgerald and Zelda published a little piece ("Auction—Model 1934") taking inventory of the acquisitions of their life together. They unpack their household goods and find themselves left with a heap of attic-bound junk, the bric-a-brac of former good times and enthusiasms and wastefulness. The article is written in a tone rather lyric and tender, but the inventory has the finality of a last counting. They end by saying: "We shall keep it all—the tangible remnant of the four hundred thousand we made from hard words and spent with easy ones these fifteen years. And the collection, after all, is just about as valuable now as the Polish and Peruvian bonds of our thriftier friends."

There is no human stance so attractive as the refusal to be thrifty. To the Midwestern boy Fitzgerald was for such a long time, using up with easy words what had been earned with hard ones became a point of self-respect. More than that, it must have seemed the only possibility for purging himself of the littleness, the spirit of husbandry, bred so inescapably in the struggle of his forebears to make some permanent mark on the wide, shifting middle reaches of a vast continent. Surely in his projected ideal triumvirate of the "entire man," it was the force of Byron that Fitzgerald felt most keenly. And like Byron, he was to write one book out of the wisdom that comes with knowing the self has given all it had to give and that therefore it need give nothing: *The Last Tycoon* is his *Don Juan*.

If the collection of stuff that in only a few years came to be relics of an ancient and dead past was no more worthless than the Polish and Peruvian bonds of the prudent, unlike the bonds it had to be paid for twice. It was yet to present Fitzgerald with a bill in the form of a terrible crisis of spirit. Fitzgerald was to be forty years old and totally unable to write—he who had sometimes knocked out stories in a matter of hours—before his romantic conscience could decide he had paid enough and was now permitted to muster the thrift to save himself. *The Last Tycoon* and the Pat Hobby stories, written during the time with Sheilah Graham, signal his capitulation—or, if you will, his advance—to a new role. He was now to be that most intensely partial, un-"entire" of men, an artist.

He was ashamed of the new demands he felt obliged to

make and spoke of them with heavy irony: "And if you were dying of starvation outside my window, I would go out quickly and give you the smile and the voice (if no longer the hand) and stick around till somebody raised a nickel to phone for the ambulance, that is if I thought there would be any copy in it for me. I have now at last become a writer only." To Sheilah Graham he spoke of his demands not at all. But though the best of the times they had together were often idyllic, often gay, though Fitzgerald was tender and infinitely sympathetic, what she says makes it clear that *happiness* for him then was work.

The Last Tycoon finished might have turned out to be his best novel or his worst, but it would have been a novel different in kind from all the others. The completed chapters and notes are written by a Fitzgerald who had finally settled for the wisdom that can come this side of paradise and for the comforts of the traditional relations between a novelist and his society: the one not taking meaning from, but giving meaning to, the other.

1959

5

Highbrowland

David Bazelon is a figure who in a quieter or more orderly century might be seen by its historians to have spanned ages. He came to New York in 1943, a bright young would-be writer, and headed for Greenwich Village, still in time to catch the last reverberations of the battle on the field of radicalism engaged by his literary elders. And he remained to reflect, to participate in, and finally to help direct the dizzying forced march on which World War II and its aftermath—down to this very day—set the American intellectual community. Through Marxist politics and *avant-garde* culture, through liberal politics and a concern for American mass culture, through philosophies for individual survival and psychologies for mass survival, and on up—or, if you will, back once more—to the proving ground of such primal questions as What is liberty? and What is justice? all in the space of less than twenty years.

Bazelon became one of those literary picaros whose careers, in the present age of nondeferred gratifications, seem unlikely to be much emulated. He has been a sometime writer of fiction and of poetry. He has been a far more regular writer of literary criticism and movie criticism, or, rather, that cross-fertilized breed of intellectual and literary endeavor that used just to be called criticism. He has been a lawyer and the student of a far from dismal science which yet dares to call itself economics, and of a kingly rather than queenly science which ought nevertheless to call itself sociology, being a study of the true relations of power. Thus he is a member of that rare species of writer—growing rarer with each new graduating class—whose talents have been subordinated to the need of their possessors to know and understand rather than the other way around.

In his lengthy autobiographical introduction to *Nothing But a Fine Tooth Comb,* a collection of his magazine pieces, Bazelon speaks of his fellow Chicagoan, the late Isaac Rosenfeld. One is caught up short by the reminder that in its literary aspect the world is, after all, a very small place. For resembling neither of his most immediate compatriots, neither Isaac Rosenfeld nor Saul Bellow, in any clearly discernible way as a writer, he yet has certain enduring—can they be Chicago-bred?—qualities in common with both. In addition to their almost infuriating precocity and their special gift for saying the most serious things by way of the snappiest wisecracks, the three of them were able to sustain intact a certain original boyish vulnerability to the flesh of a shapely idea. Moreover, the driving urge behind their work, different as this work has been in all other respects, is the same: somehow to close the gap between experience and the language of experience.

In Bazelon's work, this urge has found expression through the agency of an altogether idiosyncratic and unmistakable voice. One feels impelled to say "voice," instead of the more abstractable "style," because it is of the essence of Bazelon's writing that the language appears to come to the reader straight from the mind that has conceived it, without mediation and without too much display of a prior assumption of good posture. Of course, as anyone who has ever set pen to paper knows, such an appearance is almost totally deceitful; to be successfully tough-talking and direct and slapdash involves perhaps the most delicately balanced posture of all. Nevertheless, the attempt to come on in this way results, as I have said, in a written voice that can only and forever be David Bazelon's. How, then, to characterize it and, in so doing, something of the mind to whose necessity it answers? The voice is one far from quiet and yet precisely at its fullest volume, subject to the quickest and subtlest of modulations; very far from elegant and yet precisely at its most insistent, given to sudden flights of truly classy playfulness; the voice, in short, of a Jacob who cannot be at peace until some minimally honorable reparation has been made to his brother Esau.

The pieces collected in this book were written and published (a few were written and for one reason or another not published) over the course of many years. They are strung together with the kind of introductory comments so happily invented by Norman Mailer for his *Advertisements for Myself*—pitting the Man Today against the Author Then, with the whole constituting a kind of spiritual autobiography. In putting the material together, Bazelon sorted it, alas, according to theme rather than to simple chronology, an arrangement which only drives the reader to reorganize and cross-refer as he goes along.

But taken in proper historical order, *Nothing But a Fine Tooth Comb* serves as both a chastening and illuminating record—through the ideas overtly expressed as well as in the prose itself—of the collapse of a community. Bazelon introduces himself as a man who was once a son and is now a father. This theme, and it is a uniquely American one, obsesses him: Was he, in his own youthful ignorance of his father's life, sinner or sinned against? and now, in relation to his son, which of these roles again? In his own terms, this growing noncommunity gets to be coextensive with American society itself. Or rather, to put it more sympathetically to the argument of the Man Today, American social and cultural arrangements reflect a variety of strategies for creating some ersatz of the community men have always needed and might not anymore be permitted to experience. Now, there is a question as to whether Americans, as Americans, have ever enjoyed a community in this sense. If they have not, then to speak of what they *have* managed to create as a substitute, or ersatz, is unhelpful, to say the least. But such questions aside —and there are several raised in or by this book, all equally important and all equally unnerving to confront head on— David Bazelon the thinker and writer is a man forced to live in only a tiny company of fellows. When he first arrived in New York, in that intense interlude between sondom and fatherhood, there was a community to receive him. Such an experience is formative; it fixes one's expectations. To be sure, that community was small, perhaps personally scandalous, certainly intellectually litigious. But it was held together by a common definition of reality, a common ordination of virtues and values, and a common language. Its main source of news was *Partisan Review,* and among its Sunday supplements were Dwight Macdonald's *Politics* and Elliot Cohen's *Commentary.* Its name was Highbrowland.

Not much was properly understood about the place by those who lived elsewhere and were hostile. To the Stalinist Marranos keeping their rituals alive in cellars, it was a hated island of apostasy. To the philistines who were the innocent, or not so innocent, but in any case "objective," allies of these Stalinist Marranos, Bazelon's short-lived community was an ingathering of arrogant and intimidating boors: men who insistently violated the hypocrisy and mental prissiness by which the middlebrows kept themselves in cultural power and served, by pretending they had no relation with them, those in economic power. In a culture growing sick and sodden with pretended refinement and a self-imposed, mincing "seriousness," Highbrowland was virtually the last enclave of he-men.

Thus, to take a small but definitive example, when Bazelon, or the late Robert Warshow, or Manny Farber, or Pauline Kael spent their time devouring Hollywood movies, they were not rebelling against their radicalism or "buying American," as was so often charged by the professional prigs. They were asserting the demand of their spirits—exactly the same demand as that involved in their reading of Yeats or Dostoevsky or Henry James—for some vital connection between experience and profession, between who they really were and what they could claim to be of importance to them.

Perhaps the strain was too great. Perhaps it is too difficult to *be* a he-man in a culture which makes it so easy and so rewarding to give a merely made-up, stylized imitation of one. Perhaps again—to touch a fine Bazelon nerve—the highbrows were unwilling or somehow rendered incapable to take on the task of generation. It would take either volumes or one genius stroke of cultural history to tell how and why it happened; but whatever the explanation, the particular community of which I speak did not replenish itself and did not within itself resist the pressure to disintegrate. Year by year, its denizens deserted. In symposium after symposium, people said things of their past experience they knew not to be true. In review after review, critics praised works they knew to be bad. In article after article, writers offered a liturgical recitation of passions they knew themselves not to feel. All in the name of expressing a relation to America which denied the very virtues of mind and spirit that had once brought them all together—honesty, hardness of mind, fineness of sensibility, and the abjuration of cant. And in the expression of that false relation, the pretending not to know things they in fact knew, one by one they were gathered into the waiting arms of the enemy, the philistine middlebrow, freed now from his concealed devotions and no longer timid. These symposia contributions, reviews, and articles were no small acts; the willful violation of language is the destruction of community.

Small wonder, then, that in surveying his work, Bazelon finds one of its central themes to be the need for some workable substitute for what he once believed himself to possess. Very likely he imagines it is now *his* turn to become a Marrano, to husband the faith in secret where it will be out of danger. He is one of a tiny band of stragglers (as is, still the compatriot, Saul Bellow) and the winds are howling through the empty places. But let him take heart. Soon, very soon, will begin the trek of footsore refugees returning home, crying woe, and requiring the likes of Bazelon to administer relief.

1970

6

St. Paul and the
American Condition

Is there a place on earth about which I have been so in-
curious, and really know so little, as this one? I was born
here, grew up here, lived and went to school here until the
age of nineteen. I spoke, before the teasing of friends and the
erosion of time together erased most of the natural character
from my speech, in its flat, open-mouthed and tight-throated
accent. I perhaps thought its thoughts and assumed its assumptions; I perhaps judged with its judgments—although
that is difficult to know: for the very act of trying to bring
one's unthinking thoughts, assumptions, and judgments, even
of long ago, into consciousness alters and ironizes them. Let
us just say that although many people are surprised by the
fact now, when I first arrived a yearning young immigrant to
New York City, no one had the least difficulty in recognizing
me as an immigrant from the deep Middle West.

Some new acquaintances, as I remember, valued this in
me, finding the manners I did not then know I had to be
open, cordial, bouncy, after what they probably took to be
the fashion of the open prairie. Others did not value it and ill
concealed their answering winces at some or another mark of

a too-easy familiarity or over-hospitality on my part. In either case, the point is that I was almost a full-blown adult, as people nearing twenty seemed to be in those days, and the recency of my arrival from a home somewhere else—from this particular somewhere else—was not only a fact but a vital element in my relations with people.

Nor, though I am now most often, and in my opinion most accurately, taken for a real New Yorker, have my deepest connections with this home been severed. My mother and father remain here. So do my sister and her family and innumerable cousins, some of whom are my friends. I have come here almost once a year for more than twenty. Some of my visits, particularly when my children were infants, were quite extended.

Yet I drive through these streets now, as I was driven through them in childhood, without either knowing or deeply caring to know any of the sorts of things I have made it my business to find out about other places visited only for a weekend or sometimes just passed through. Being an unreconstructed amateur sociologist—which is to say, a twentieth-century American given to a certain degree of self-awareness—I find at the least stimulus of the new that my mind is filled with minute questions of power, of hierarchy, of relation, of history. Recently Walker Percy described the experience of being stuck one afternoon in Philadelphia and suddenly seized with puzzlement at the thought that so many people, tokened by the houses and offices and traffic all around him, should in of all places be living in Philadelphia. I responded to that passage, beneath the joke it was making, as probably only one of Mr. Percy's contemporary Americans could respond to it. For in this country we know that men do not volunteer for their fate, and yet—sense of order assaulted almost constantly by the spectacle of men, families, communities in motion, in transit—we feel a perpetual need to know and be able to name what has driven them.

In and about my hometown, however, I have felt no such need. I cannot, for instance, name its really powerful men. I know where once could be found its celebrated pockets of wealth, know this because they were incorporated into the local myths of my childhood—and where, having been so, they probably no longer represented the effective truth: Mr. James Jerome Hill, founder of the Great Northern Railway and, with it, of the fortune that was a cornerstone of civic pride, whose great Summit Avenue mansion had become a nunnery (or so we children told one another); the Weyerhaeusers, lumber giants, whose name and designation in the pantheon brought to childish imaginings associations with that other Giant Lumberman, Paul Bunyan. But the figures of whom we were encouraged to speak were these unseen, these historic ones, railroads, lumber, mining, whose names had receded to legend or graced the street signs, and whose money now floated above in the great abstract cloud bank of philanthropy: foundations and public good deeds.

But of the others, the living, all-too-unlegendary men whose decisions come to define the daily condition of the rest of us in this place, I know not even a title beyond "they." I sit having lunch in the Victorianate dining room of the Minnesota Club with an immensely busy stranger who offers me his time and attention out of some deep private obligation to kindness. This club is the precinct of power and the terminal station of arrival in St. Paul, Minnesota; I have never been here before. Emboldened by my identification with New York, and in the smarty, tough-guy posture of that identification, I put the question to my host bluntly: Who runs this town? For answer, he includes the roomful of our fellow diners within a single sweeping gesture of his hand. He rapidly identifies for me this bank, that bank, an insurance company or two, an industry whose name refers to a piece of heavy machinery I'm not sure I could recognize by sight. . . .

These men are clearly very clever, for one has to be clever to reach the point of pinning down the destiny of a busy and not unimportant city. They are also fools. For they have made plans—perhaps in this very room—torn up the entire downtown section of the city, crisscrossed it with superhighways, planted their specimens of this era's architecture in squared-off ranks among the bombed-out sites and asphalted-over parking lots; and each of these plans, superhighways, renewals, and glass-walled office buildings has been argued for and undertaken for the sake of some civic "need." They are fools because they do not seem to know that in all this exercise of the power to transform—cannot know it, or else they would have been forced to find one touch with which to vary the inexorable logic of their tearing and building—they have been herded into doing exactly the same thing that everyone in power in cities from the Atlantic coast to the Pacific is doing.

Other things I have no precise knowledge of regarding the place of my birth: the nature of its real political arrangements; its ethnic composition (its predominant religious affiliation is Catholic, which makes it extraordinary among Midwestern cities); the sexual mores of its regular middle class, professional middle class, or, for that matter, any other class; and above all, the criteria for its success or failure as a civic, and civil, organism.

I don't suppose many of us know such things about the hometowns departed in our youth. Maybe not even if we are impelled, as I am during this visit, to take to the library and seek out the available research. The city in which we spend childhood and adolescence and that in which we might seek to be knowing adults are two different places. The former is so local and particular, so bound up with the accidents of private condition—family custom, neighborhood custom, friendship—as to remain forever unreachable by those avenues of detachment and skepticism needed to bring us to the latter. A child's city is run by its celebrities, and the effective power over his life, as he sees it, rests exclusively in the hands of parents, teachers, public officials, and the social leaders among his contemporaries.

Within the past few years I have run into several people who also grew up in St. Paul but were not known to me here. It was they, I think, who taught me this lesson. One of them, for example, an important Negro leader, spent a good part of his childhood on a street and in a condition I had literally never seen; another, a Jew from Russia, grew up in the slum at the opposite end of town from the pleasant and tidy, though far from elegant, middle-class neighborhood in which

my family lived. We speak of St. Paul and we speak not
only of different worlds but of actually different cities: at a
time, mind you, when the place boasted a population of
around 200,000 and was completely circumnavigable by car
in less than an hour.

And if you are a girl, there is an extra reinforcement to
your child's passivity toward the definition of existence
handed you at birth. Little girls live from the very beginning
with the consciousness that childhood is transitory, that their
identities rest with the future and will be provided from the
outside. They do not poke about in the material world so
much, do not in my opinion suffer the anguish of their in-
completeness and powerlessness so much, do not later seem
to remember so much of being tried and tested and failing, as
little boys. For them childhood is less an apprenticeship than
a slow gathering of the arsenal with which to prove their
mettle against what the world, and fate, has in store for
them. In short, they are expecting to be and learning to fit
themselves to be somebody's wife. And a wife is a person
who has learned not to question the terms of existence but
rather how to seek to turn them to her advantage. So when
they are young, girls tend to be concerned mostly with the
selves they will be transporting to wherever it is life has it in
mind to take them, and very little with where they happen to
be now.

I had thought, in coming this time, to take the train. It
seemed such a profound and fitting thing to do. You travel
overnight to Chicago and spend the better part of a day
going north alongside the course of the Mississippi River.
The trip is not particularly scenic or impressive, as the river
itself is not at this point in its travels—having nothing, say,
of the sweep, or in Paul Goodman's marvelous term, the lord-
liness, of the Hudson, which flows by me almost beneath my
window every day. But what mighty thoughts I could have
induced myself to have in those hours!—thoughts of a place
called America and of my connection, as a former Mississippi
River dweller, to it. St. Paul only exists at all, of course,
courtesy of the Mississippi River; early in the nineteenth
century it was the northernmost navigable point at which to

set up an Army outpost to contain the Indians and a trading post to relieve them of their trappings. But even the dim historic titans of my childhood—railroads and lumber—were figures of that phase in the conquest of the continent that superseded the river. The settlers who followed on the heels of the Army left behind a painstaking chronicle of the day in each year when the ice was sufficiently melted for the first boat to get through; to judge from the journals and diaries they left behind, life was a sort of inevitable round of being wiped out by fire and renewed by water, fires in the winter and boats in the summer. And if St. Paul exists courtesy of the Mississippi, there is, too, I suppose, a level on which it is possible to say I exist courtesy of St. Paul. I have not, however, anywhere in my being experienced either of these propositions, and in my mind, only just now and only by an effort of will. For me the Mississippi was always as simply given, as accidental and merely decorative, as the giant fir tree that lived in our front yard. We crossed it to get to Minneapolis, our twin city; we parked our cars on its embankment to neck; we took an occasional moonlight excursion downstream 20 miles or so and back on an old-fashioned stern-wheeler; once on a dare, and with a feeling of terror so vivid I can still revive the ache in my lungs intact, I crossed it in a light canoe. But the original, primitive, nonaccidental lives of the river and of that girl whom I remember as myself did never genuinely intersect.

So I came by plane, arriving in the only St. Paul that truly belongs to me. The jet plane, and the vast hollow and hostile air terminal it has created—in my hometown as everywhere else—are of a technology more recent than my growing-up here, but the spirit and the tendency bespoken by them are not.

Yet it is not just the greedy indifference of childhood that keeps one from coming to grips with the nature of one's social existence here in St. Paul. Those who have remained here to participate in its adult world of getting, begetting, and spending—or even those who, like certain of my cousins, have come here from the little towns in the Dakotas, Minnesota, Wisconsin, whose true metropolis this has always been—seem as ungrounded as I both in history and in a theory to account for their present condition.

My mother, for instance, was born here and spent a large part of her girlhood in a tiny section of town adjacent to the downtown that must in those years have constituted for her, as Groveland Park did for me, a whole universe. By the time of my own girlhood this section was known as lowertown—a largely lifeless slum, then being allowed to crumble into the earth—and several years ago the whole thing was simply converted into an expressway facilitating approach to the State Capitol. I doubt, though, if I had been given enough of a feeling of stake in the place even to ask, that my mother could tell me who then owned the neighborhood and who, for what real motive, decreed its erasure.

She is as rooted in St. Paul as any Yankee Brahmin in Boston. True, the little graveyard we sometimes used to pass on our way to the lake, just twenty miles out of the city, where we spent our summers (and where my mother and father still do), holds no generation earlier than that of her parents; but, then, after all the city itself is not all that much older. It is maybe her very rootedness that has propelled her, so unself-conscious, so unresisting, along the course of upheaval after geographic upheaval that has brought her finally to a semiluxury apartment in what is, as closely as I can count, the sixth neighborhood away from that of her origin. For so much of America the name of the game was move west and don't look back. The city, too, played it, and so did she.

My researches produce the name of the first child born to the community of settlers that originally claimed this ground. The settlers were French, fur trappers they were, and fur traders, and the baby's name was Basil Gervais. The name jumps off the page at me. We pronounce it "Jarvis" —one of the dozens of lakes that skirt the city bears this name—but that is not why I am interested. This is the name, the marriage name, of the housemaid who looked after the household, and especially me, from the time I was six or seven until I turned thirteen. Those were Depression years, and we were not well-to-do, but everyone had housemaids then. They were farm girls whose fathers had been reduced to debt and penury, and they cleaned and cooked and sewed and nannied for five or six dollars a week and the chance to live with their feet on pavements. I was the youngest in the family, and, as was the tradition, Rose was particularly my property. She kept me in line and taught me about sex and told me her secrets, and when she converted to Catholicism in order to marry her fiancé of more than ten years' standing, it was I who drilled her in her catechism. Her husband-to-be was a wiped-out farmer who worked as a handyman on the grounds of a children's TB sanitorium out in the country. Every night after the dinner dishes were done, he would arrive in a beat-up Model T coupe, park along our back alleyway, and Rose would go out to sit there with him for hours and hours until long after I was asleep.

Years after she married and left us, the summer that I myself was preparing to leave, I ran into her holding by the hand a tiny, frail, brilliantly black-eyed little boy—was his name, too, Basil? She told me the Gervaises were farming again. Now I ask my father, I ask my host at lunch, I ask a cousin: "The small truck farmers around these parts . . . what are they doing? Do they make a living?" Nobody really knows. They all wonder, and quite rightly, why I am asking such an unlikely question.

No, they cannot tell me, my family and friends from my school years, "who runs this town" or "who makes a living." Nor could they tell me, if I were to throw off the easinesses of a Midwestern upbringing enough to wish to delve into the matter, what really happened to all of us when I was growing up—nor even what has happened since.

My hometown produced one writer, F. Scott Fitzgerald. What was best about Fitzgerald was the way he understood —as perhaps Middle Westerners preeminently are given the opportunity to understand—the crippling of the spirit that comes in a society incapable of making a clean breast of the order of its valuations. What was worst in him was the seepage from his own inability to make a clean breast of the order of *his* valuations and so to free himself from them. But they seem to care very little in St. Paul either for or about Fitzgerald. Certainly I do not remember his having been mentioned to us in school as a local boy who made good (although we knew the name of every movie star born in the state of Minnesota and of every major-league ballplayer who had ever played on one of its minor-league teams). He was not even denounced as a traitor to his home and people. I meet a young boy, son of an old friend, literarily inclined and well educated, a senior in Fitzgerald's old school, the St. Paul Academy. "Do they make a great fuss about Fitzgerald at SPA?" I ask him. "They never mention him" is the answer. I think St. Paulites pay no special attention to Fitzgerald not because they disapprove of him but because, since with the exception of a couple of stories the reference has not been made explicit, they have never understood or believed that he was writing about them.

Why should we all have cared to know so little? And how did we escape knowing more? Not because, in the fashionably republican claim, "average" people are largely indifferent to the affairs of the world around them. For if such claims are true, or even by a number of other criteria, the people of whom I am mostly speaking here, the people I know, are not "average." They are educated beyond the average, serious, philanthropic, and community-minded beyond the average (if there is one), and certainly live on an annual income and in a style far beyond what the Department of Labor anyway would deem to be the average. And anyone who has not seen the operations of an intense civic spirit among the serious middle class of a middle-sized city in the middle territory of these United States cannot even imagine what the words "civic spirit" mean.

Our serene innocence had rather to do with the way in which, if you live in St. Paul, you get conditioned to a sense of the inseparability of self and place. Another name for this sense, I suppose, is provincialism. But provincialism will not quite serve, either. The city has in its time been unmistakably racked by the general predicaments of nation and world;

and yet those of its inhabitants not immediately involved, and even some who have been, have felt no call to include the racking in their notion of its history.

One of the most dramatic examples of this had to do with Prohibition. Somewhere close to dead center of the route from Canada to Al Capone's Chicago, St. Paul was a busy relay station for traffic in bootleg whiskey, with all the riot, anxiety, and cynicism that went with it. A certain number of moderate fortunes were made, a certain number of impressive fortunes were initially bankrolled, in the driving of trucks to Chicago for Capone or someone ultimately connected to him. Throughout my childhood it was whispered of some people I knew that they had been in jail, and there were other whisperings too, disjointed, imprecise, of kidnappings, beatings, men being doused with alcohol and set on fire. They lived among us, the objects of these whisperings, and prospered—at least those I came to know, the ones who by definition lived, as they say, to tell the tale, did. But they and their presence were to teach us nothing about ourselves.

Then there were other kinds of stories, tales for children, about the desperadoes of the Depression who traveled the Midwest and spent time among us: Dillinger, Baby-Face Nelson, Pretty-Boy Floyd. St. Paul in the late twenties and early thirties might have been a television producer's dream. In the Snelling Cafe, where we sometimes went for hamburgers after the movies, someone had been gunned down in full daylight; they said if you knew where to look, you could still see the bullet scars in the wall. At some point the city also became a gangster's dream of haven, the police chief, whose name I cannot remember but whose underworld nickname was reported to be The Cardinal, offering the deal that one could live at peace with the authorities in St. Paul if the plying of one's somewhat troublesome trade were confined across the river in Minneapolis or elsewhere.

And still, childish romancing aside, crime had no part in the possibilities we represented to ourselves as those within the limits of our life in society. Neither crime nor violence— not to mention alcoholism, rape, incest, homosexuality—nor even, finally, tragedy, this last term being reserved in our common usage for handicapping illness or untimely death. All these evils, to be sure, existed (though of this, too, there were those who had their doubts) , but not, no never, here.

"Provincialism," as I said, is not really the word. "Provincialism" means the imposition of a limited experience on the definition of a larger. What was at work in us was something more intractable and madder. It was not experience we lacked, only the ability to admit that we had had it. Only that which we could allow ourselves to be could we allow our city to contain. We allowed ourselves to be the kind of Americans we believed in: we were friendly, we were decent, and above all, we were the masters of our will, victims in any misfortune of nothing but our own failure to order things better. We were certainly not free of sin, neither venial nor mortal—there were too many Catholics among us to believe that. But we were beyond question free of any taint of secret knowledge. Our city, then, was a friendly place, decent, and in control of itself. Nastiness, largely imported, might make an appearance here from time to time, but there was no deeper, subterranean reality flowing beneath the façade of our everyday language. And the Americans we believed in were the true, the only true, Americans. The troubles that others got themselves into were of their own alien making. They could not happen here. Even in the very midst of their happening here, we denied it.

Across the river, and in some places merely across the street, was Minneapolis: bigger, busier, more heavily industrialized, Protestant, given to the workings of grace and damnation. We went there for entertainment, grace and damnation being the source of art in America. Minneapolis had nightclubs, Italian restaurants, gay bars, a burlesque house, a low-down main street of movie theaters, penny arcades, and popcorn—and we did not. Minneapolis had an art museum, an orchestra, a great university, and though we were the capital, we did not. St. Paul went dark and quiet every night; Minneapolis did not. The two cities, as can be seen, were rivals, and naturally much sport, and not all of it good-natured either, was made of their rivalry. But I do not think that anyone on either side—except perhaps St. Paul's

small merchants left behind to do business in what even in
my childhood was a dying downtown, sacrificed to the conservative policies or maybe even certain ulterior designs of
St. Paul's investment money—felt any envy. To us the arts
and wiles, the leavening, of Minneapolis were an available
convenience; we were, and as I gather most St. Paulites still
are, content to let the Minneapolitans pay the everyday price
for them. "Let them have the culture," one of the town's
leading bankers is reported to have said as late in the era of
nationwide culture consciousness as last year, "as long as we
have a solid payroll."

Our refusal to incorporate the élan, together with the
turbulence, of the city next door into the realm of our defined possibilities grew a fortiori infinitely more intense when
it came to those other vast and distant cities, New York and
Chicago. If Chicago was at least a grand aberration from life
as we recognized it, in the sense that we could find some
common ground with its public manners and could hear no
very discernible difference in its accent, New York was quite
beyond the pale. My father had come to St. Paul from New
York as a very young man. I was taken there for the first time
when I was six to visit my grandparents in Brooklyn, and I
remember a moment in which, among a traffic of baby car-
riages, howling children, chattering women, bathed in an
overpowering mixture of bakery and delicatessen smells on
Bay Parkway, I experienced a first hazy resolve to live in this
place someday. But whether my resolve was forgotten,
buried, or whether it was precisely strengthened by such an
attitude, we were all given to the "knowledge" that New
Yorkers were a different breed of people from us and conse-
quently lived a very different life. They did not "entertain,"
for instance, did not involve themselves in community affairs,
were not friendly and helpful, and, most of all, went their
way open-eyed and passive in the presence of the unimaginable.

The point is not worth pressing very heavily. To live in
New York is to be told at least a dozen times a year and in a
dozen different contexts by people who live elsewhere—be it
Washington, Detroit, Dallas, or Los Angeles—that your atti-

tudes, concerns, and experiences have nothing to do with those of the rest of America. In St. Paul, this very standard idea was given only one added twist: the un-Americanism of New Yorkers was in some way their own fault. If by the very tolerant not to be censured, it was not to be pitied either. After all, no law kept them there in all that filth and difficulty. . . .

But denying the experience to awareness or not, my hometown has managed to ring every single one of the changes that American society has put to urban existence. On each succeeding visit, particularly within the past decade, I have found a city in exactly the same process of development as has overtaken every other in the land, even—dare I say it? —my own poor, beset and embattled New York.

One enters the city by means of an air terminal like every other; makes one's way on one of the nonstop parkways that have also in the end congested, and from the beginning defaced, every other; arrives in a new suburban neighborhood that, only because St. Paul happened to have the room for it, is inside the city but otherwise indistinguishable from every other; and listens to anxious talk of college admittances, black demonstrations in the high school, the replacement of slum neighborhoods with industrial parks, the lack of facilities for the aged. On my next visit, the pollution of the Mississippi will undoubtedly have been added to the list.

It does not, however, matter that a whole generation of my friends and contemporaries set up housekeeping in a concert of style and concern dictated to them from everywhere without their knowing it. Had they known, would they have had any alternative? It does not matter that in knocking the old city down and trying to put it together again, St. Paulites believed their decisions to be tailored to their preferences rather than cut so accurately from a national assembly-line pattern one could predict the results with one's eyes closed. It is being knocked down and put together pointlessly all the same.

America may have reached the point, St. Paul, I think, has

surely reached it, where knowledge of their share in a much
larger predicament would spare people nothing.

The first day I am here my sister drives me to the campus
of the university. We are on a not very serious sentimental
quest for the haunts of our student days. She is three years
older than I, so our years in the university overlapped for a
little. We plan to visit the house of the sorority we both once
belonged to, but it is vacation time, the sorority house is
closed up, and neither of us cares. We are both mothers of
teen-age girls, and touring the university, it is not the past
but only the future that really interests us. The university,
like everything in the world we share, has expanded almost
beyond recognition, and part of the expansion is a new, still
unfinished, and muddy campus on the west bank of the river.
This campus, I believe, houses the first two years of the lib-
eral-arts program. In any case, I do not have to be told anything about the West Bank, for as we drive along the streets
that border it—and they are deserted now—the whole story
tells itself. Here there are neither sorority houses nor dormi-
tories but apartment buildings, some very new, some very
old. There is a head shop, replete with tired psychedelic
posters, junk jewelry, and the dusty, inevitable lapel buttons;
a boutique whose display of wares in the window cannot be
sexually differentiated; a paperback bookstore.

What more is there to tell? It is here that international
youth culture has planted its flag of claim to Minnesota. One
extrapolates the rest: dropouts, shack-ups, marijuana, ampli-
fied guitars, interracial mating and sexual war, and all the
lares and penates of that new religion of love which is nothing but the infinite adumbration of narcissism. My sister is
upset by the place, and I am momentarily annoyed with her.
What is she so upset about? What are they all so upset
about? Did they think, did they actually believe, when they
first heard and read of these things and watched their advance guard on television capturing the exploitation market,
that they would be hazards only to the children of others?
But my annoyance passes as quickly as it is roused. She is a
child of my own mother, and mother to my niece; what intellectual formulation stands against that? I am no calmer, for

all my habit of analysis and setting of contexts, on my own territory. Besides, she is that kind of girl, she has never done a drop of harm to anyone but herself.

I am to hear talk of the West Bank, in one form or another, over and over again before I leave. They must decide, my old friends, even as I must decide—and not in the name of society, for that is easy, but in the name of the intimate responsibility they have assumed for their children—what they think about drugs, sex, race, even what they think about life.

I know now that because I am a New Yorker, my experience is the more truly, the more typically, American one. It is my America that is moving in on them. God is about to bless them with an opportunity, and may He also save them from it, but there is no turning back now.

1969

7

Growing Old in America

In every park in every city in the United States on almost
every day of the year small children and aging adults meet to
take the air. The adults sit quietly on the benches while the
little ones run around, swing from the fences, and make a
general commotion. The old returned to the haunts of the
very young, natural allies laid by together out of the way of
the bustling and "responsible" world—so it may seem to the
casual passerby. However, the feeling that actually domi-
nates the park is not one of alliance; it is one of hatred. And
what goes on between the two groups is not an idyllic confrontation but a war—no other word will serve. Perhaps back
home the two do maintain their traditional conspiratorial
connection, grandparents and grandchildren; but outside,
where they are equal claimants to the use of certain facilities
of idle time, the issue between them stands naked: some of
them are at the beginning of life and some of them each day
get nearer to its end. The young ones are totally absorbed in
their own demands for the attention of the world, and the old
ones, far from looking on this with that natural sense of the
seasons that a life properly lived should have given them, are

resentful and bitter and envious. It is easy, after Freud, to be tolerant, and even admiring, of the lack of sympathy in little children. But it is quite impossible to look without fear upon the simple malice that can play in the face of a white-haired old woman—who is probably herself a mother and a grandmother—as she watches an infant struggling to take his first steps. Where does such malice come from? What can it mean?

To be sure, not all, not even most, of the 17,500,000 people in America over the age of sixty-five are habitual park sitters. One out of five is still gainfully employed, full or part time; half are still married; 60 percent maintain homes of their own; roughly another 20 percent live with relatives. Thus, many of the aged in our society have resources that the malicious old woman on the park bench presumably lacks— something to do and somewhere to go. Yet the fact remains that even the most fortunate of the aged share to some extent —and *know they do*—in her predicament. Hers is merely the extreme form of a threatened general condition, for she teaches this lesson about old age in our society: that it is a bad time, one that is more likely to bring a bitter envy toward those who are still active or coming to be active than the traditionally promised rest and peace and ease.

Why this should be so is by no means obvious. That it is so, however, is abundantly obvious, if only from the intense preoccupation with the problems of the aged evident everywhere in our culture. Social scientists and medical researchers of all descriptions have collected themselves into an academic discipline called gerontology—the science of old age —and each year brings its lengthy and grave reports of their findings. A third of the voluntary social agencies in this country now have special programs for the aged; others have plans to create them. And federal and local government agencies are constantly engaged in a study of new ways to expand those facilities that serve the retired population.

Much of this preoccupation, of course, stems from the fact that there are more leisured elderly in our midst than ever before. Not only do more people live longer, but retirement, as measured against life expectancy, comes relatively early. This does not mean, as so many people think, that modern science—medicine, sanitation, etc.—has succeeded in pushing back the frontiers of death. Despite the propaganda of the various national foundations, which creates the impression that money given to combat their pet diseases is about to do battle with death itself, the outer limits of the length of human life have remained fairly constant. What *has* happened through modern science is that vastly greater numbers of people are surviving uneventfully what were once the perils of childhood, youth, and middle age: the diseases that nowadays kill most of us (atherosclerosis, cancer, kidney ailments) are diseases of the aging organism.

What has also happened through science, however, is that the elderly on the whole enjoy better health than they once did, and this has effected a radical change in the image of retirement. No longer represented by a stooped, feeble old retainer shuffling up to receive his gold watch for forty years of service and then returning home to wither away, the term "retirement" now brings to mind the picture of a sixty-five-year-old man who may or may not be perfectly vigorous, doing his job one day and the next being handed a pink slip: The American Labor Force No Longer Needs Your Services. In other words, the same modern technology that has brought about increased life expectancy has also necessitated earlier retirement. (Indeed, it seems likely that if technology were given its own rational way with the lag of custom, retirement would have been brought forward even further than it already has.)

No one, it might appear, could respond to these twin developments with anything but gratitude. People *want* to stay alive as long as possible and for as much of the time as possible in good physical condition. And it is equally natural for them to want to know that one day they will be freed from the necessity of work. We learn from the anthropologists that many primitive societies kill off their feeble old because they cannot afford to keep people who must eat without working. But primitive does not mean natural; and the outlook of anthropology in some ways dulls the imagination on this point: because a man reaching old age in a parricidal culture accepts the inevitability of the system, it cannot be that he faces with any less terror the knowledge that he must either work or die. Biologists tell us of the aging body that it seeks and needs a lessening of noise, a brightening of light, and ever-increasing quantities of rest. In short, to live long and to have time to waste are among the deepest of human aspirations.

Of those millions of Americans who would fall under the technical definition of being aged, then, a very large number would seem to have reached a state toward which men naturally yearn. No more than 3 percent are helpless enough to be shut away in custodial institutions; among the rest, there are many people so youthful, so vital, so healthy that experts involved in their problems are enjoined from using the word "aged" altogether and must refer to them in embarrassed terms like "senior citizens"—in their "golden age." Given all this, why is so much social concern being expressed over the predicament of the aged?

An important part of the answer, surely, is that the aged are undergoing in a special way an experience that promises to become nearly universal. This experience is called the problem of leisure, but in truth is the problem of supererogation. To put the case very simply, there are not enough jobs to go around, and there may be even fewer as automation proceeds on its inexorable course. The young are being kept out of the labor force for as long as it can be managed, and when they cannot be kept out any longer, the old must make room for them. Where often in small primitive societies manpower is so desperately needed that there can be no provision for those who do not supply it, in our situation hordes of people must regularly be put out to pasture.

It is generally assumed—probably even by the aged themselves—that the trouble lies here: in the humiliation, the sense of futility, that result from being shunted aside. Psychologists tell us that one of the main disabilities suffered in the life of retirement is a loss of self-esteem. Social workers center their programs for the aged on the question, "What can we do to give older people some greater sense of their continuing, valuable participation in the world around them?" Many medical researchers talk about helping even the ailing and disabled and institutionalized among the aged to cope far more adequately with their environment. All this makes sense, in its own terms; surely the feeling of being a valuable member of the world is a good, and a necessary, thing. In every instance, however, the terms of discussion themselves turn out to be circular and lead away from the primary question, the only question that can yield anything new either to the understanding or to the making of programs: why do those who are relieved—for whatever reason —of a tiresome burden feel themselves instead to be bereaved?

Let us take the matter of self-esteem. Certainly a man forced to retire when he is still able to perform his work easily and competently must feel himself to be the victim of an unmitigable injustice. Indeed, even a man who before retirement had begun to find his work enormously taxing, and might therefore look forward to retiring, must be left with the sense that his being forced to leave this work represents a personal failure. By one of those queer ironies of psychology, so long as retirement is a thing decreed from the outside, it will appear to operate as some kind of judgment. Nevertheless, it is difficult to believe that the unhappiness of the aged can be explained in such terms. For even granting that there is a loss of self-esteem involved in the loss of employment, we are still left wondering why the compensations of leisure and security (in those cases where economic need is not a factor) do not operate any more powerfully than it is assumed they do.

For women, to be sure, the situation is somewhat different. The terms of their "employment" are vaguer. When all her children have grown up and moved away, a woman still has her domestic empire—now considerably diminished, but perhaps in due proportion to her diminished physical power —to rule. Whatever difficulties an aging woman experiences, therefore, are generally thought to stem from the fact that her main function in life, to oversee the welfare of her children, has been taken from her.

In this connection sociologists and psychologists have spoken a good deal about the revolution in the institution of the family brought about by the urbanization of American life. That is to say, families now live together by and large in "conjugal" units, consisting only of a mother, a father, and their offspring, who in turn break away upon reaching maturity to form new conjugal units of their own. This means that with the marriage of her last child, a woman is "retired" no less forcibly than her husband is when he arrives at his sixty-fifth year. But here again, one wonders whether the relief every woman must feel at having this particular burden of responsibility lifted from her is not being scanted in discussions of her psychic problems. Moreover, it is extremely doubtful that the aging American woman of today has any cause to regret the passing of the old rural, clan-shaped, agglomerating family. She and her contemporaries established their own conjugal families not only, not even principally, in order to bring up children but out of a belief in their right to privacy, to freedom of decision, to independence of their parents and grandparents—in short, out of a sense (a modern, urban-bred sense, to be sure) of obligation to self. Why should they now feel differently? It can be seen that as people get older, and if circumstances permit, they more and more shape their style of life to fit comfortably around their predilections; this is what is called "getting set in one's ways." And a small, self-centered household is obviously the one to facilitate this process. Thus it seems unlikely that the aging parents of today, once themselves children who left the parental home, feel quite so deprived when *their* turn comes as popular legend and social work theory would have us think.*

---

* For those who have *always* lived alone, the problem is entirely different—probably, except for its aesthetics, very little affected by age. Where such people are concerned, self-involvement is not the earned privilege of time and nature but a spiritual disease having a very early onset. The World Health Organization estimates that somewhere between 10 and 20 percent of the world's aged population are "isolates," but it is difficult to know how many are the victims of plain injustice and how many represent the kind of human tragedy that social thought has always been powerless to deal with.

In line with the idea that the aged must be given something to do in order to prop up their failing self-esteem, the social workers and rehabilitators are attempting to create, out there in the pasture, what amounts to a virtual parody of the world of the very young. From one end of the country to the other, groups with titles like Golden Age clubs and Senior Citizens' classes have been established. A typical list of their activities includes such things as crafts, singing, dancing (even the twist), dramatics, picnics and fishing trips (in Chicago, there is an annual two-week senior citizens camp; in Menlo, California, there are five-day excursions to the national parks), hobby and antique shows, dressing dolls for the Salvation Army, collecting radios and magazines for state hospitals, repairing clothing for needy families, and stuffing envelopes for the League of Women Voters.

How the people who sponsor these programs can believe that the elderly men and women who participate in them will thereby overcome the loss of self-esteem involved in their feelings of uselessness is rather a mystery. Having somewhere to go and something—anything—to do is undoubtedly better than having nowhere to go and nothing to do. But it is not equivalent to having something useful and valuable to do, and it is from the conviction that one's activities have value that self-esteem arises. When the young are herded together for similar activities, the idea is that they can afford to wait, and in the meantime they need to be kept off the streets. To the aged, however, despite the fact that they have countless unfilled hours from day to day, time is the commodity above all others that is in short supply: what else does getting old mean? And by social work's own avowed understanding of the matter, society must find the way to keep them *on* the streets, not off.

In short, so much discussion of the problems to be faced in retirement revolves around what look like sensible ideas on how to "prepare" people for leisure, how to provide them with "real" interests, how to get them to use their "resources," and so forth, that everyone tends to lose sight of the fact that idle time is not the same thing as free time. Time can only be free when its possessor is using it to do what *he* wants to do and respects doing.

People in the Golden Age clubs may dance and may sing— they are asked to do so even from their wheelchairs in the nursing homes—but this is not the makings of a new life in retirement; it is a pasteboard version of the old. The aging may out of desperation accept it, but can anyone expect them to be "fulfilled" in doing so?

In this connection it is baffling how little of the professional, or merely the interested, talk ever gets around to the mention of money. Naturally, everyone knows that money has more than anything else come to be regarded as the measure of a successful life, and therefore of a man's sense of his own worth; this much everyone does say—and piously deplores. The money that is not talked about, as though it were impolite to mention it, is another kind of money: the money that buys things.

There is a whole body of American folklore dedicated to the question of what money can and cannot buy. In its application to old age, the folk wisdom for some reason seems to concentrate on the "isn't everything" aspect—maybe because rich and poor alike get wrinkled (though in the case of women, even this is not necessarily true), or maybe because the sentimentality that is the usual response to death reflects backward on the old age that foreshadows it. But if money, as they say, cannot buy health, it can buy the most comfortable alternative to it: the retirement cottage in Florida or New Mexico, the services necessary to carry on a relatively normal life without strain. If it cannot buy happiness, it can, for most men, help provide the means of expressing strength of spirit—whether this be the regular pursuit of a hobby, the exercise of power over others, or worthwhile civic activity. It can most of all, despite our pieties, buy the elementary kind of respect that is extended to people who do not have to depend on others.

Money is something not very many of the aged have very much of. It is hard to be precise about this because the collectors of data must depend on individual reporting, but what figures there are indicate that as of January, 1960, nearly 60 percent of those over sixty-five had a cash income of less than $1,000 per year per individual; around 25 percent had between $1,000 and $2,000; the rest had over $2,000, but of these only 4 percent had more than $5,000.

In their eagerness to avoid confronting the bearing of such figures—even allowing for inaccuracies—on the question of leisure as we know it, sociologists have engaged in some curious studies and made some curious findings. One such study that comes to mind is an investigation of the relation between the preferred uses of leisure and class attitudes.* Seventy-five percent of the former managers interviewed, and only 55 percent of the former manual workers also interviewed, said they were getting as much fun out of life as they used to. On the other hand, 41 percent of the manual workers, as against only 25 percent of the managers, felt that they would be interested in joining a Golden Age club. Now, what sociologists mean by class attitude may indeed greatly influence certain choices of leisure—for example, the kind of thing a man prefers to spectate, whether ball games or symphony concerts, or even (though all this is far more taken for granted than it has a right to be) whether or not he is apt to spend time reading books and newspapers. But when it comes to "getting fun out of life," to the large, over-all choices about how to fill up and shape one's declining years, there is something almost comic about the sociologists' inability to come right out and say that the amount of money a man has to live on will, more than anything else, determine his sense of the possibilities that exist. (A researcher somewhere has even made the startling discovery that there is a significant correlation between level of income and the use of travel as a leisure activity.)

In any case, an income of one or two thousand dollars leaves a man very little alternative but to fall into the benign hands of gerontology—if, indeed, it can even carry him that far out into the world. I do not mean to imply that the un-

* As reported by Max Kaplan in his chapter in *Handbook of Social Gerontology* (University of Chicago Press, 1960).

happiness of the aged is yet another of those social problems that leads on a straight road back to the question of the inequitable distribution of wealth in this country; primarily it is not. But for that tiny percentage who manage to make a wide enough detour, there are many, and very real, compensations.

Just about everyone takes a significant cut in income upon retiring, a point which goes beyond the merely socio-economic and becomes a paradigm of life itself. The way things stand now, a man must in the course of his working life earn both his current keep and his future (or his widow's) support in idleness. The prolongation of life means that he must either earn more—financially, spiritually, emotionally —or there will be less to go around in the late years. Therefore the leisure we speak of these days is a condition that would not traditionally have gone by that name. Traditionally leisure was the result of an unearned abundance, or at least a quickly and easily earned one. Retirement, at its very best, is a geometrically diminishing payoff for a life of hard work and careful attention to the rules.

And here we come to the heart of the problem—for all of us, but the aged particularly, in whom it stands most brutally exposed. Not a sudden inactivity, which might be pleasant; not the absence of familial or community concerns, which might be a welcome relief; not even the approach of death, which can only mean what men make it mean: it is the rules by which Western urban men have been taught to live that lie at the base of a bitter or empty old age. The faces of resentment that we see beneath the whitening hair are the faces of people who have been "had"—and for whom it is too late to do anything about it now. They have been had in several ways. They have worked hard and worried much, as they have been told they must do, only to find that all the work and worry was for the sake of those who come after, and who must anyway themselves go through the same round of work and worry, eternally. They have saved their money, only to find it serving as a crutch against debility, or at the most as a weapon against the disregard of the struggling young. They have sacrificed great quantities of their human substance, their longings, itches, and imaginings, to the working and the saving—only to find that the spirit is a substance which turns rancid in storage.

Our "senior citizens" are people who were once taught that by denying themselves what D. H. Lawrence called the "good, warm life" they would be earning some great reward at the end—and who are living long enough to watch all the possibilities run out. The cry of the woman on the park bench, and of all her sisters and brothers, rich or poor, loved or unloved, would be, if she could make it: "But I never lived, and now I'm never going to."

The system of rules that sets up its steady tattoo in the nervous system, "Save, defer, lay by, put off," is a system that was devised when life was brutish and short. The reward it promised was heaven. Put to the test in our time, when there is so much space between the cessation of toil and the end of life, the system reveals its great empty gaps. Old age is a period in which it must become increasingly difficult to deceive oneself. Many of the aged may still believe in the heaven they have been striving to earn; but, as their troubles tell us, they can no longer find this belief a sufficient preparation for solitude and death. That, as the poets and philosophers have always known, can only come from the collection of all those present moments that might one day become real and self-defining remembrances.

1963